FIT Food

FIT Food

Eating Well for Life

ELLEN HAAS

With the editorial team of FoodFit.com

Foreword by George L. Blackburn, M.D., Ph.D., Harvard Medical School

healthylivingbooks
New York • London

A HEALTHY LIVING BOOK
Published by Hatherleigh Press
5-22 46th Avenue, Suite 200
Long Island City, NY 11101
Visit our Web site:
www.healthylivingbooks.com

Library of Congress Cataloging-in-Publication Data

Haas, Ellen.
Fit food eating well for life / Ellen Haas, with the editorial team of FoodFit.com.
p. cm.
ISBN 1-57826-146-5
1. Nutrition. I. Title.
RA784.H315 2004
613.2--dc22
2004025567

This book is for educational purposes and is not intended as a substitute for medical advice. All matters regarding your health require medical supervision. Please consult your health care providers for individual health and medical advice. Neither Hatherleigh Press nor the author shall have any responsibility for adverse effects arising directly or indirectly as a result of the information provided in this book.

Cover designed by Calvin Lyte and Deborah Miller
Interior designed by Deborah Miller and Calvin Lyte

10 9 8 7 6 5 4 3 2 1
Printed in Canada

Acknowledgements

With exceptional talent, a strong commitment to promoting the health of consumers, and an exuberant passion for good food and active living, the FoodFit team has consistently created outstanding content, making our website, FoodFit.com, the leading online resource for delicious recipes and healthy living solutions. This creative energy and celebration of food is reflected in the book because of the individual contributions of our incredible staff. I am sincerely grateful for the contributions of the following dedicated and capable people whose work has enriched this book:

First, a big thank you goes to the FoodFit editorial team of Pat Kelly, Angela Moore, and Leila Corcoran, who brought the concept of *Fit Food* to a wonderful reality. They carefully organized and presented the wealth of information about each of the foods so that all the chapters are reader-friendly, nutritionally accurate, and written with grace and style.

I am so grateful to Bonnie Moore, our FoodFit Executive Chef, for her enormous contributions and hard work to make our original FoodFit recipes both delicious and healthy. Her exquisite taste and culinary skill is seen in the book's collection of about 200 healthy, easy, and mouth-watering recipes that she and our award-winning chefs developed. Bonnie's commitment to good health and good taste is unsurpassed and her passion for cooking with the seasons is felt throughout the book.

A word of gratitude goes also to the 32 nationally recognized chefs who are a part of FoodFit's Chef's Network and have recipes in this book. These outstanding and committed chefs include: Jody Adams, John Ash, Lidia Bastianich, Jeff Buben, Kathy Cary, Ann Cashion, Ann Cooper, Roberto Donna, Tom Douglas, Todd English, Gale Gand, Joyce Goldstein, Susan Goss, Andy Husbands, Kate Jansen, Michael Lomonaco, Brian McBride, Mary Sue Milliken and Susan Feniger, Nora Pouillon, Ann Quatrano, Steven Raichlen, Michael Romano, Anne Rosenzweig, Jimmy Schmidt, Annie Somerville, Susan Spicer, Allen Susser, Rick Tramonto, Norman Van Aken, Alice Waters, and Bill Wavrin.

The nutrition elements of *Fit Food* are essential and required the skill and experience of our team nutritionists. Thank you especially to Susan Oliviera who provided careful analysis, JoAnn Hattner who reviewed the manuscript for accuracy and clarity, and to Ann Coulston and Christine Palumbo for their continuing advice and input.

The staff of FoodFit deserves special recognition for their excellent work and steadfast commitment, including Al Tanenbaum, Lynn Pina, Brian White, and Garth Rademaker.

Also, thank you to our intern Sun Cho for coordinating the chefs' entries and many other tasks.

The FoodFit Advisory Board plays a central role in guiding FoodFit's content direction and provides the standards, principles, and support for all that we do. A special thank you to Advisory Board member George L. Blackburn, M.D., Ph.D. for his insightful foreword. We are grateful for the long-standing involvement of the entire Board including: John Ash, Nancy Clark, Ann Coulston, Susan Feniger, Ray Goldberg, Joyce Goldstein, Sandy Gooch, James Hill, Sol Katz, Susan Lord, Nicholas Mezitis, Mary Sue Milliken, Patrick O'Connell, Nora Pouillon, Michael Romano, George Strait, and Alice Waters.

I am thankful to everyone at Hatherleigh Press for their encouragement and editorial support and to Lori Baird who initiated this project. My agent, Timothy Seldes, deserves our appreciation for his ongoing advice and his enthusiasm about this book and the work of FoodFit.

Contents

Foreword

Good eating adds an extra 25 years to your life. Experts at the American Cancer Society estimate that each year approximately one-third of America's 500,000 cancer deaths are due to this nation's unhealthy eating habits. In fact, a mountain of medical research—done in the top research institutions in the country by leading nutrition researchers—bears witness to the simple message: Eating the right way can help keep you healthy. And if you are sick, eating the right way can very often help you heal.

Healthy foods such as fruits, vegetables, whole grains, poultry, and fish are typically classified as part of the "prudent diet." Hundreds of studies indicate that diets rich in these foods can decrease the risk of cancer, cardiovascular disease, diabetes, stroke, high blood pressure, and many other diseases in both men and women. So, what exactly is the right way to get the healthy food you need?

The FoodFit.com website is a guide to smart eating and good energy. Many years have gone into developing straightforward solutions that enable you to prepare your meals in a simple, economical, and fun way. In particular, FoodFit has developed luxurious recipes and healthy menus containing fruits and vegetables, which are key to preventing the diseases mentioned above. FoodFit shows you how to enjoy these delicious foods and menus while also helping you to lose weight, look younger, and feel more energized. None of this is difficult.

Ellen Haas has had a lifelong mission to promote healthy food and nutrition. By founding FoodFit, she has integrated the joy of cooking into a nationally recognized source of healthy eating, cooking, and fitness information. FoodFit knows that taste is king and pleasure is queen when it comes to food selection. In our busy, modern lives, the art of cooking has been lost. FoodFit has easy, fun solutions for purchasing healthy foods and cooking healthy meals.

As a member of the FoodFit Advisory Board, I have been part of the site's growth to reach millions of consumers, and I helped develop the FoodFit Plan, a healthy weight-loss program. I get such satisfaction in seeing the results of my involvement with FoodFit benefit my family, now involving four generations. I am amazed to see my three-year-old and six-month-old grandchildren enjoy broccoli as a preferred food. The family gathers around plant-based meals of three vegetables, not counting a glorious mixed green salad and fruit dessert. I know that leaving my family with the FoodFit philosophy will be one of the most valuable legacies for generations to follow.

FoodFit is ready for these new generations. It provides simple concepts that are the keys to good health, including a customized diet plan combined with a state-of-the-art approach to fitness. You can continue to use these simple keys to make healthy food choices for you and your family for the rest of your life. When you move from the basic rules of good health and start considering specific foods, you will see some of the extra benefits FoodFit offers. FoodFit works closely with you to discover the best-tasting and healthiest foods for your individual needs. There are tantalizing recipes created by the finest chefs to help you with this mission.

At long last, there is an innovative approach to healthy eating. Choosing the right foods will improve your health, reduce your disease risk, and raise the quality and quantity of your life. This book is for readers who are serious about achieving a long life without disease by embracing good-tasting, healthy, fit food.

George L. Blackburn, M.D., Ph.D.
S. Daniel Abraham Chair in Nutrition Medicine
Harvard Medical School

Introduction

Ever since we launched FoodFit.com in January 2000, the celebration of good food has been a central focus of the dynamic content we offer millions of consumers every day, and for good reason. The connection between the food we eat and how healthy we are is remarkably strong and well-documented scientifically. Together with active living, healthy eating and healthy cooking are the cornerstones of wellness and well-being. *Fit Food* was conceived as an easy-to-use guide to help you eat deliciously and make the best choices to optimize your health—for life.

Over the years, I have worked in many ways to promote the health of consumers and encourage a lifestyle that values good food and good energy. I began my career as a consumer advocate in the 1970s when my daughter, Lisa, and son, Jason, were just entering elementary school. As president of Consumer Federation of America and head of Public Voice for Food and Health Policy, I fought for better food policies such as nutrition labeling on all food products, improving seafood safety, and reforming the school lunch program.

This record of advocacy and education led to my appointment by President Bill Clinton to be the top federal nutrition official as Under Secretary of Agriculture for Food, Nutrition and Consumer Services. From 1993 to 1997, I worked to improve the nutritional standards for the National School Lunch Program. Unbelievably, these were the first nutrition revisions in 50 years to school lunches, which are eaten by more than 26 million American children each day. A key part of the changes was a public education campaign called Team Nutrition that encouraged our nation's schoolchildren to make healthier food choices. At the Department of Agriculture, my responsibilities extended from the food programs to overseeing the development of the 1995 Dietary Guidelines and Food Guide Pyramid, the foundation of U.S. nutrition policy and the basis for teaching what makes a healthy diet.

Launching FoodFit was a natural extension of my long career dedicated to consumer advocacy. Through our healthy eating, healthy cooking, and fitness areas, we provide trusted and credible food and nutrition information so that you can take action to achieve a life of health. Seasonal guides to fruits and vegetables and other food guides provide solutions for healthy living along with a suite of interactive tools and more than 2,000 recipes. With FoodFit's expert Board of Advisors, our Chef's Network, and our extraordinary, experienced team of nutrition, food, and fitness professionals, we bring a healthy lifestyle within your reach.

Fit Food captures the essence of the valuable information found on FoodFit.com. Starting with the basics of nutrition and health, this book takes you beyond the science to focus on the everyday foods that contribute to your health, and it showcases these foods in recipes that are simple to make and delicious to enjoy. This linking of food, taste, and health makes *Fit Food* so unique—and so useful. There are hundreds of books with just nutrition facts and cookbooks that include only recipes, but *Fit Food* brings it all together for you.

Our focus is on the 21 Fit Foods—all nutrition stars—that contribute to a healthy, disease-fighting diet. This book is organized so that each Fit Food has its own chapter to help you easily identify these special ingredients and the other members of their families in the market. Just as your local grocery store is arranged in different departments to make shopping easy, we have grouped the Fit Foods by type to make finding them simple and enjoyable. The 21 Fit Foods appear in the following sections:

- Vegetables
- Fruit
- Grains, Beans, Nuts & Seeds
- Poultry, Fish, Meat & Dairy

Within each food chapter, there is practical information on Nutrition and Health, What to Look For, Easy Storage and Preparation, and Best Uses. Each chapter also includes an impressive collection of related recipes that maximize both taste and nutritional value.

These 200 original, mouth-watering recipes were created and tested by FoodFit Executive Chef Bonnie Moore and 32 of the award-winning chefs in our Chef's Network. With her passion for fresh, seasonal ingredients, Bonnie Moore has been FoodFit's executive chef from the beginning. She is the former sous chef at the five-star, five-diamond Inn at Little Washington. There she established relationships with area farmers so that the Inn could use the freshest local produce. Today she is the president of Women Chefs and Restaurateurs. Along with the 100 members of our Chef's Network, she creates recipes that reflect a commitment to good food, good health, and great taste.

To help you get started, here are a few of the FoodFit team's suggestions for bringing the Fit Foods into your kitchen and reaping their amazing benefits.

COOK WITH THE SEASONS AND ALWAYS USE YOUR SENSES

Using fresh, seasonal ingredients makes successful cooking a breeze. And when fruits and vegetables are in abundance, they are also more economical. Food that is picked or harvested at the peak of the season is simply the best and easiest way to cook with full flavor. Also, be sure to use all your senses. Taste, touch, see, feel, and smell as you cook. You will find it really makes a difference.

HEAD TO YOUR LOCAL FARMER'S MARKET OR GROW YOUR OWN FOODS AT HOME

The popularity of farmer's markets has soared all over the country because they offer seasonal produce grown by local farmers at reasonable prices. (Many markets now also have cheese, breads, and meats.) If you have a green thumb, planting your own garden brings the freshest of tastes to your table as well. There's nothing better than taking a bite of a tomato you have grown yourself.

GO ORGANIC FOR QUALITY AND PURITY

Seek out organic products whenever you can and look for the seal showing they have been grown to meet the USDA organic standards. Organic foods are a great choice for both health and taste reasons. Choosing organic products helps support small farms and reduces your risk of ingesting contaminated and pesticide-exposed foods. Plus, many people feel that organic foods offer more flavor.

USE THE RECIPES AS A GUIDE AND DON'T BE AFRAID TO EXPERIMENT

Get creative and remember that cooking is a personal experience. Explore all the possibilities. For instance, feel free to substitute halibut with another white fish from the market such as grouper or cod, or use apples instead of pears in a dessert recipe if your children prefer them. Try new foods often to widen and please your palate.

The message of *Fit Food* is a simple one: It's easy to discover the enjoyment of eating a variety of foods that are packed with the nutrients you need to be healthy, and to find the pleasure that comes from bringing these healthy meals to your table. My wish for you is that this book makes eating well central to your life and that you enjoy many memorable meals together with your family and friends. Let the Fit Foods be your springboard to good health for a lifetime.

Ellen Haas
Founder and CEO
FoodFit.com

PART I

Fit Foods

for a Healthy Lifestyle

Chapter 1: Eating Well for Health

What we eat fuels our bodies, shapes our health, and is central to our well-being. Every year, scientists learn more about the strong relationship between food and health. Three of the four leading causes of death are diet-related, and healthy eating can also help prevent the onset of chronic diseases like diabetes, heart disease, and osteoporosis. As a nation, we have become more weight-conscious than ever in the face of epidemic obesity. Luckily, eating right has never been easier to do or more delicious for your taste buds—when you know how. The Fit Foods—everyday foods like blueberries or turkey or yogurt—are your ingredients for wellness, deliciously. They are wonderfully good for you and wonderfully tasty. Together, the 21 Fit Foods reinforce each other's health benefits and supply your body with the nourishment it needs for a long and healthy life.

FoodFit.com was created in the year 2000 to promote good food, active living, and weight loss, and to offer consumers solutions to enhance their health and well-being. Our guiding principle is Good Food and Good Energy for Life. With our advisory board of top-notch nutritionists, medical professionals, fitness experts, and chefs, FoodFit.com quickly became a nationally recognized source of up-to-date information on nutrition, cooking, and exercise. "FoodFit provides the most accessible, usable messages about food and health on the Internet," says U.S. Food and Drug Administration Acting Commissioner Lester Crawford, one of FoodFit's original advisory board members. This book grows from the wealth of information on the site.

The Fit Foods are based on the Dietary Guidelines for Americans, key health recommendations crafted by the U.S. Departments of Agriculture and Health and Human Services, with guidance from a committee of the nation's leading scientists. The guidelines are the cornerstone of federal nutrition policies, and allow policy makers and educators to speak with one voice about nutrition and health issues. The 21 Fit Foods ensure that your diet is well-balanced and varied so that your body gets all the nutrients it needs for good health.

The dietary guidelines are updated every five years to reflect the latest scientific and medical knowledge. The most recent advice is that Americans need to improve the quality of their diets, exercise regularly, and keep calories under control. That means choosing nutritious, minimally processed, low-calorie Fit Foods like fruits, vegetables, whole grains, lean meat, and non-fat or low-fat milk. Poor diet and obesity are the leading contributors to chronic diseases. Today, two-thirds of Americans are overweight and nearly one-third are obese. By comparison, 20 years ago less than half of Americans had a weight problem. Obesity may soon overtake smoking as the leading preventable cause of death in the United States.

The 2005 dietary guidelines urge Americans to eat more fruits and vegetables and at least 3 1-ounce servings of whole grains each day to promote good health. It's important to eat a rainbow of fruits and vegetables—from sun-kissed citrus fruits to rosy berries to dark green, leafy vegetables—in order to get all the vitamins, minerals, fiber, and important health-promoting antioxidants they have to offer. The dietary guidelines emphasize eating a variety of foods in general. Variety and balance foster good health. The Fit Foods mirror this philosophy.

Many of the Fit Foods are fruits and vegetables, reflecting their nutritional richness. This book overflows with fruit and vegetable recipes that are flavorful, healthful, and a cinch to prepare, to help you incorporate more of these foods into your diet. We'll show you how to include vitamin-rich citrus juices in your salad dressings, add berries to main course dishes for a burst of flavor, bake veggies with herbs and olive oil, and make a tasty salad with vitamin-B-rich brown rice.

The appealing recipes, understandable nutrition facts, and other helpful information in this book are your road map to a new, more healthful diet for you and for your family. The sooner you get started, the better. It's never too late or too early to start investing in your health; eating right is important for all ages. The marked rise in obesity in America has not been limited to adults. Today, it is estimated that 9 million American school-aged children are obese. Children's eating habits are set by the time they are 12, so making a nutritional impression at the start has long-term effects. Research shows that people who ate fruits and vegetables and drank milk when they were young are more likely to do so as adults. Also, children will try new foods more often if they see their parents eating them.

As George L. Blackburn, M.D., Ph.D., the associate director for nutrition at the Harvard Medical School and a member of FoodFit's advisory board says, "We need to understand that food is not the problem, but the solution."

Each chapter highlights one Fit Food and offers information about other healthful options in the same food group. For example, broccoli is featured but you will also learn about other good-for-you members of the disease-fighting cruciferous vegetable family. We'll tell you how to shop for the freshest ingredients, how best to store foods at home, how to pair foods for maximum flavor, and how to cook with the seasons.

There are 200 scrumptious recipes in the book, as well as dozens of chef tips, created by FoodFit Executive Chef Bonnie Moore and members of our chef's network, a group of more than 100 acclaimed chefs from around the country who share FoodFit's mission to promote healthy eating. Each recipe is based on nutritional standards and scaled to a healthy portion size. They all reflect a commitment to using seasonal, fresh ingredients. The result is superb-tasting food. Your family can connect with nature by celebrating spring with an asparagus dish or marking the end of summer with juicy, red tomatoes. Visits to the farmer's market are a fun-filled experience. Whenever possible, fresh is best, but you can substitute frozen and canned fruits and vegetables. Or, choose wholesome convenience foods such as Healthy Choice® frozen entrees.

The Fit Foods aid in reaching a healthy weight, which is central to wellness. The recipes in this book meet the criteria of the FoodFit Plan, a healthy lifestyle program for lasting weight loss created by FoodFit in partnership with the University of California Davis Medical Center. Based on the latest scientific recommendations published by the National Academy of Sciences, the Plan provides personalized diets with menu plans and chef-created recipes, as well as fitness recommendations. It includes FoodFit's customized tools, recipes, tips, and guides, all of which help members lose or maintain weight while eating great-tasting meals. (For more information, see Appendix B.)

This book is a springboard to a better lifestyle that will minimize your risk of disease and maximize your health. With each bite, you will be doing your body good, protecting it, nourishing it, and energizing it.

TEN STRATEGIES FOR HEALTHY LIVING

FoodFit's mission is to promote and enhance the health of consumers. Our website is a highly regarded source of the latest nutrition information. Here are our top ten recommendations for enhancing your overall health and well-being.

Be mindful of portion size. How much you eat can matter as much as what you eat. Learn the ideal serving sizes for the foods you consume. Paying attention to portions can be your best ally in controlling calories to reach and maintain a healthy weight for life.

Eat plenty of fruits and vegetables. These foods are packed with vitamins, minerals, fiber, and important health-promoting antioxidants and reduce your risk of heart disease and other illnesses. Enjoy a wide selection, from potassium-rich avocados and bananas to lycopene-rich tomatoes. The 2005 guidelines recommend consuming 2 cups of fruit and 2 1/2 cups of vegetables each day.

Eat plenty of fiber. Fiber, a complex carbohydrate found in fruits, vegetables, beans, and whole grains, is incredibly healthful. High-fiber foods are rich in nutrients, help prevent heart disease and other chronic illnesses, and affect how your body digests food in ways that can lead to weight loss.

Limit your intake of refined carbohydrates. The carbohydrates in processed foods and drinks made with white sugar, corn syrup, and white flour are packed with calories and bereft of nutrients. Opt for the good-for-you carbohydrates in fruits, vegetables, and whole grains.

Choose protein foods wisely. Most Americans get plenty of protein in their diets. Focus on eating moderate amounts of fresh, lean red meats, fish, and poultry.

Choose fats wisely. High levels of fat are linked to an increased risk of heart disease and certain cancers. Set a cap of no more than 30 percent of calories from fat in your diet. Try to limit your saturated fat intake to below 10 percent of calories and replace it with unsaturated fats such as nuts, olives, and avocados, along with canola and olive oils. Unsaturated fats protect against heart disease and can help lower cholesterol. Avoid

PORTION SIZES MADE EASY

How much you eat can matter just as much as what you eat. Most of us do not have a clue about serving sizes. These rules of thumb make it easy to remember what constitutes a portion.

- *1 serving of pasta: 1 cup, cooked*
- *1 serving of meat or fish: the size of a deck of cards or your palm*
- *1 piece of fruit: a medium-size apple*
- *1 serving of juice: 3/4 cup*
- *1 serving of vegetables: 1/2 cup*

artery-clogging trans fatty acids (also sometimes called trans fats) which are found in processed and fried foods. The 2005 dietary guidelines advise keeping trans fat intake as low as possible.

Limit your sodium intake. High levels of sodium go hand in hand with an increased risk of high blood pressure. Many processed foods tend to be high in sodium. The 2005 guidelines suggest that people consume fewer than 2,300 milligrams of sodium each day or the equivalent of a teaspoon of salt. Herbs are a good substitute for salt to enhance the flavor of food.

Get plenty of calcium. This mighty mineral is essential for building and maintaining healthy bones and teeth. Rich sources of calcium include low-fat or non-fat milk and yogurt; dark green, leafy green vegetables like broccoli and kale; fortified fruit juices; cereals and breads.

Exercise regularly. Experts say 30 to 90 minutes of physical activity most days of the week is the gold standard for health. Regular exercise reduces your risk of heart disease, diabetes, and other chronic illnesses. It's important for the muscles, bones, and joints. It's also helpful for your mental health.

Enjoy a balanced, varied diet. Including a wide array of foods in your diet is key for good health, since no single food can supply all the nutrients your body needs. The Fit Foods are a basket of complementary choices for well-rounded eating.

Chapter 2: Nutrition Basics

Healthy eating depends on getting a variety of nutrients. The nutrients in food work alone and in concert to give our bodies energy and maintain our health. There are 2 kinds of nutrients—macronutrients, which the body requires in large amounts, and micronutrients, which the body needs in tiny amounts. In addition, there are health-enhancing compounds in foods that offer untold benefits. In this chapter, we walk you through the nutrition basics so you learn about the nutrients your body needs for optimal health.

THE MIGHTY MACRONUTRIENTS

There are three basic macronutrients: fats, carbohydrates, and protein. They provide the fuel your body needs to function day to day. Choosing the right types and levels of macronutrients is paramount to keeping your body working at its best. The National Academy of Sciences (NAS) recommends that adults get 45 to 65 percent of calories from carbohydrates, 20 to 35 percent of calories from fats, and 10 to 35 of percent of calories from protein.

Fats

Fats are vital for proper growth and development. They help the body to absorb fat soluable vitamin E, A, and D. And because they are dense in calories—nine calories per each gram of fat, compared to four calories per each gram of protein or carbohydrate—relatively small amounts of fats make the body feel full.

Fats that are part of a healthy diet include the monounsaturated and polyunsaturated fats found in olive oil, canola oil, avocados, and nuts, as well as fatty fish such as salmon, which is rich in omega-3 fatty acids. Omega-3s are a type of fat that has been shown to greatly enhance heart health. So strong is the link that for the first time ever the 2005 dietary guidelines recommend eating omega–3-rich fish twice a week. The American Heart Association does the same. However, women who are pregnant or may become pregnent, women who are nursing, and small children are advised to avoid eating fish with high mercury content. (For additional information, see Chapter 21.)

Limit your consumption of saturated fat, including fatty cuts of red meat, butter, and ice cream. Diets high in these fats increase cholesterol and are associated with greater risk of obesity and heart disease. Ann Coulston, M.S., R.D., the past president of the American Dietetic Association and a member of the FoodFit's advisory board, offers a simple way to choose fats wisely. "If you can't keep track of which foods have which fats," she says, "remember this rule: Animal fats are higher in saturated fat, and plant fats are generally higher in unsaturated fats."

Likewise, limit your intake of artery-clogging trans fatty acids or trans fats. These fats are formed when vegetable oils are heated in a process called hydrogenation, which turns the oils into a more solid form in order to preserve flavor and increase shelf life. Hydrogenated oils are found in many processed and fried foods as well as margarine. The 2005 dietary guidelines advise keeping trans fat intake as low as possible.

Carbohydrates

Carbohydrates are the body's main source of energy. Recently, they have been branded a culprit in the nation's obesity epidemic. Like fats, not all carbs are equal. They fall into 2 broad categories: simple and complex.

Simple carbs include sweets, added sugars, corn syrup, and many white foods like rice, potatoes, certain pastas, and white bread. It is wise to limit these types of carbohydrates because they are high in calories, can increase blood sugar, and contain little nutritional value. Studies suggest a link between drinking sweetened beverages and weight gain. What's more, research shows that people who consume foods and beverages that are high in added sugars tend to consume more calories while getting fewer nutrients.

In contrast, the complex carbs in fruit, vegetables, brown rice, and whole-grain breads travel much more slowly through the body and provide much-needed fiber, as well as beneficial vitamins and minerals. Whole grains alone, such as corn, oats, wheat, and rice, are important sources of 14 nutrients. These foods are low in calories, protect against chronic diseases, and are a crucial part of a nutritious, healthy diet.

Protein

The body relies on protein, which is mainly composed of amino acids, for proper muscle, organ, hormone, and enzyme functioning. Your body produces 13 of the 22 amino acids it needs, but must rely on food sources for the remaining 9, called essential amino acids. Animal foods such as eggs, poultry, meat, fish, and dairy contain all of the essential amino acids and are known as complete proteins. Plant foods such as beans, rice, peanut butter, and whole-wheat bread are missing some essential amino acids but can become complete when eaten in combination.

Select lower-fat cuts of meat, remove the skin on poultry, and trim the fat from meats to avoid unhealthy saturated fats. Try to make beans a regular part of your diet.

MEET THE MICRONUTRIENTS

Micronutrients are vitamins and minerals, which your body requires for normal growth, function, and health. They are called micronutrients because you only need them in small amounts. Fruits, vegetables, and whole grains are great sources for micronutrients.

Vitamins

The 13 known vitamins provide a huge range of health benefits from helping you see in the dark, to preventing birth defects to fighting heart disease. Vitamins are either water-soluble or fat-soluble. The water-soluble vitamins are vitamin C, biotin, and the 7 B vitamins. These dissolve in water and aren't stored in your body in any significant amounts. The fat-soluble vitamins are A, D, E, and K. Any surplus of these vitamins not used by your body right away is stored in your body fat and liver.

Minerals

Minerals are essential to maintaining strong bones and teeth and otherwise help your body grow and stay healthy. Minerals are divided into two categories. The major minerals, which earn their name because your body needs them in relatively large amounts, are calcium, chloride, magnesium, phosphorus, potassium, sodium, and sulfur.

The trace minerals, needed only in scant amounts, are chromium, copper, fluoride, iodine, iron, manganese, molybdenum, selenium, and zinc.

HEALTH-ENHANCING COMPOUNDS

Fiber, antioxidants, and phytochemicals are wholesome substances found in fruits, vegetables, grains, and beans. They provide a range of benefits from offering protection against such illnesses as heart disease and being highly nutritious to helping you shed unwanted pounds. Scientists have

Water

Like the macronutrients and micronutrients, water is essential to life. In fact, it makes up 75 percent of your total body weight. In addition to regulating body temperature, water serves to transport nutrients to the cells and remove toxic substances and wastes. It provides moisture for the respiratory system and is essential for digestion. It also helps take the edge off your appetite.

For a long time, the common advice was to drink eight glasses of water each day, but now experts simply recommend consuming water when you are thirsty. Food usually provides one-fifth of our water needs. Foods high in water content include soups, fruits, and vegetables. Make sure to drink enough water every day, especially when temperatures are high or when you are active.

only just begun to fathom the depth of their health-promoting attributes, but it is crystal clear that they are a part of a healthy diet.

Antioxidants

Antioxidants are vitamins, minerals, and enzymes that help to protect the body against the harmful effects of unstable oxygen molecules called free radicals, which are created as part of normal cell function but may contribute to cancer and heart disease. Antioxidants act as scavengers and clean up the cell damage. Scientists are only beginning to understand their myriad of health benefits.

Some antioxidants occur naturally in your body, others are found in food. Foods high in antioxidants are vitamin- and mineral-rich fruits and vegetables, such as blueberries, oranges, spinach, and Brussels sprouts.

Fiber

Fiber, an undigestable complex carbohydrate found in plants, is a functional powerhouse with specific health benefits. Fiber slows the absorption of food and makes you feel full or satisfied. Eating a diet rich in fiber may reduce your risk of heart disease, diabetes, and other chronic illnesses, help lower your cholesterol levels, and assist in weight loss. It is also thought to protect against cancers.

The National Academy of Sciences recommends that women eat 25 grams of fiber each day, and that men under 50 eat 38 grams of fiber each day. For men and women over 50 years old, a slightly lower intake is suggested.

Every gram of fiber in the diet increases bulk. Whole-grain breads, brown rice, carrots, celery, and the skins of fruits and vegetables all help prevent constipation.

Phytochemicals

Phytochemicals, which means plant chemicals, is the blanket term for an array of substances that occur naturally in fruits, vegetables, grains, and beans. Scientists believe that they offer protection against many illnesses, including cancer and heart disease. Phytochemicals are responsible for the coloring and flavor of fruits and vegetables—like the ruby red in grapefruits and the pungent taste of onions. Foods rich in phytochemicals include tomatoes, broccoli, greens, soy, onions, and citrus fruits.

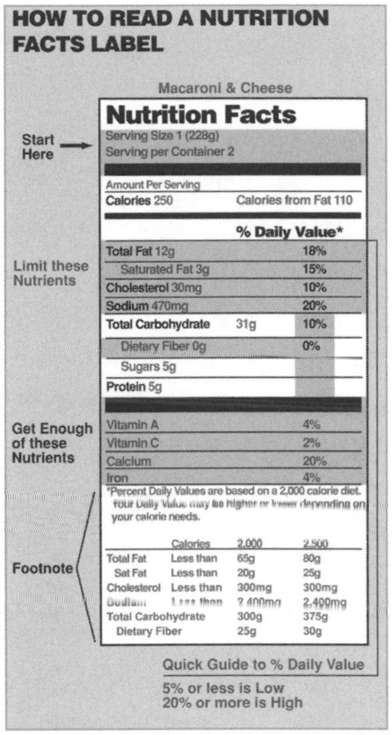

Nutrition Facts Label

The quickest way to find out whether your favorite packaged food or beverage fits into a healthy diet is to check out the Nutrition Facts label. Calories, fat, carbohydrates, and other helpful nutrition information are spelled out on the label, along with important information about serving sizes. The current label is shown above. By 2006, trans fat information will be listed under saturated fat. The FDA is also considering revisions to the label to put more emphasis on calories.

PART II

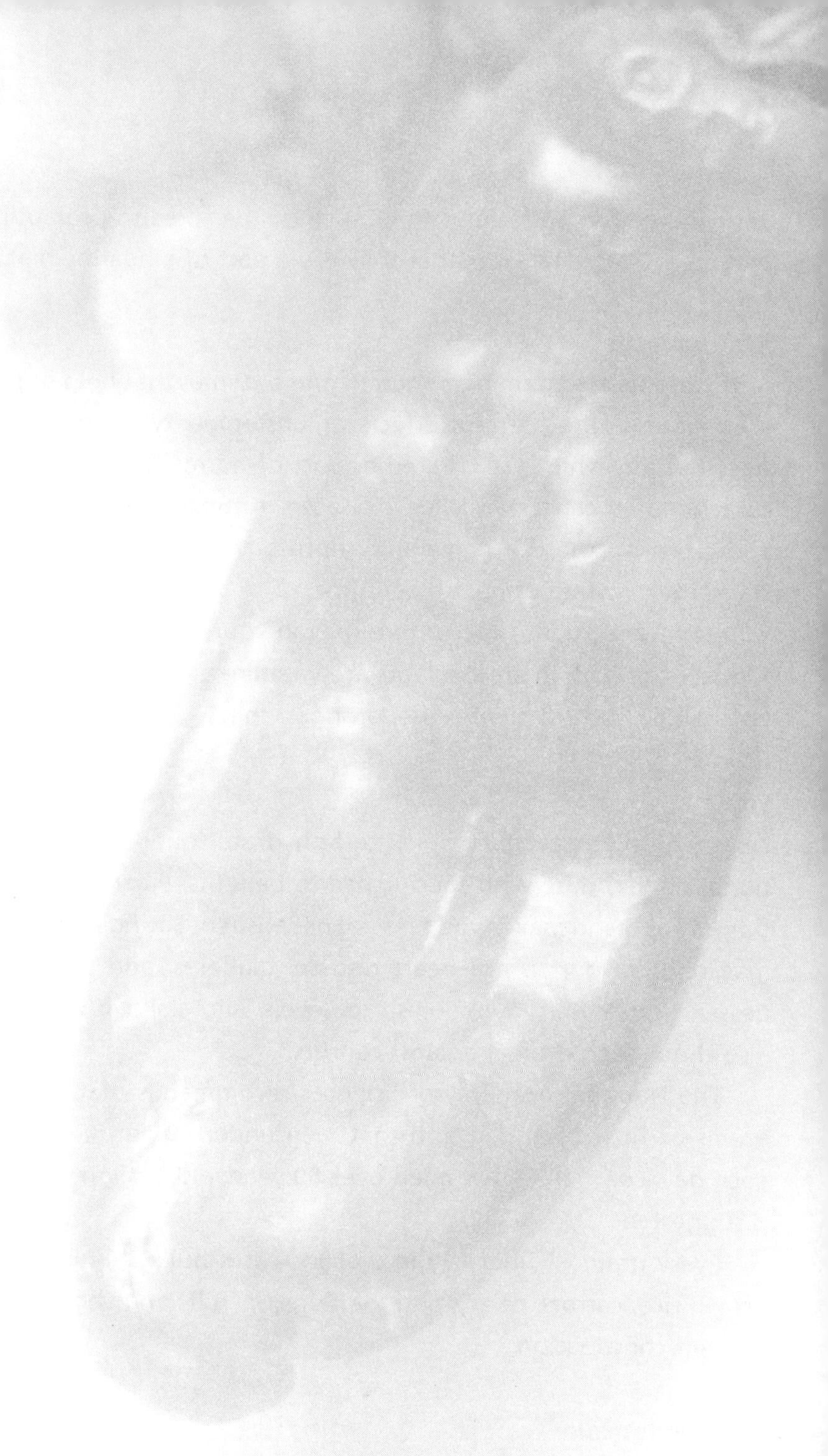

Vegetables

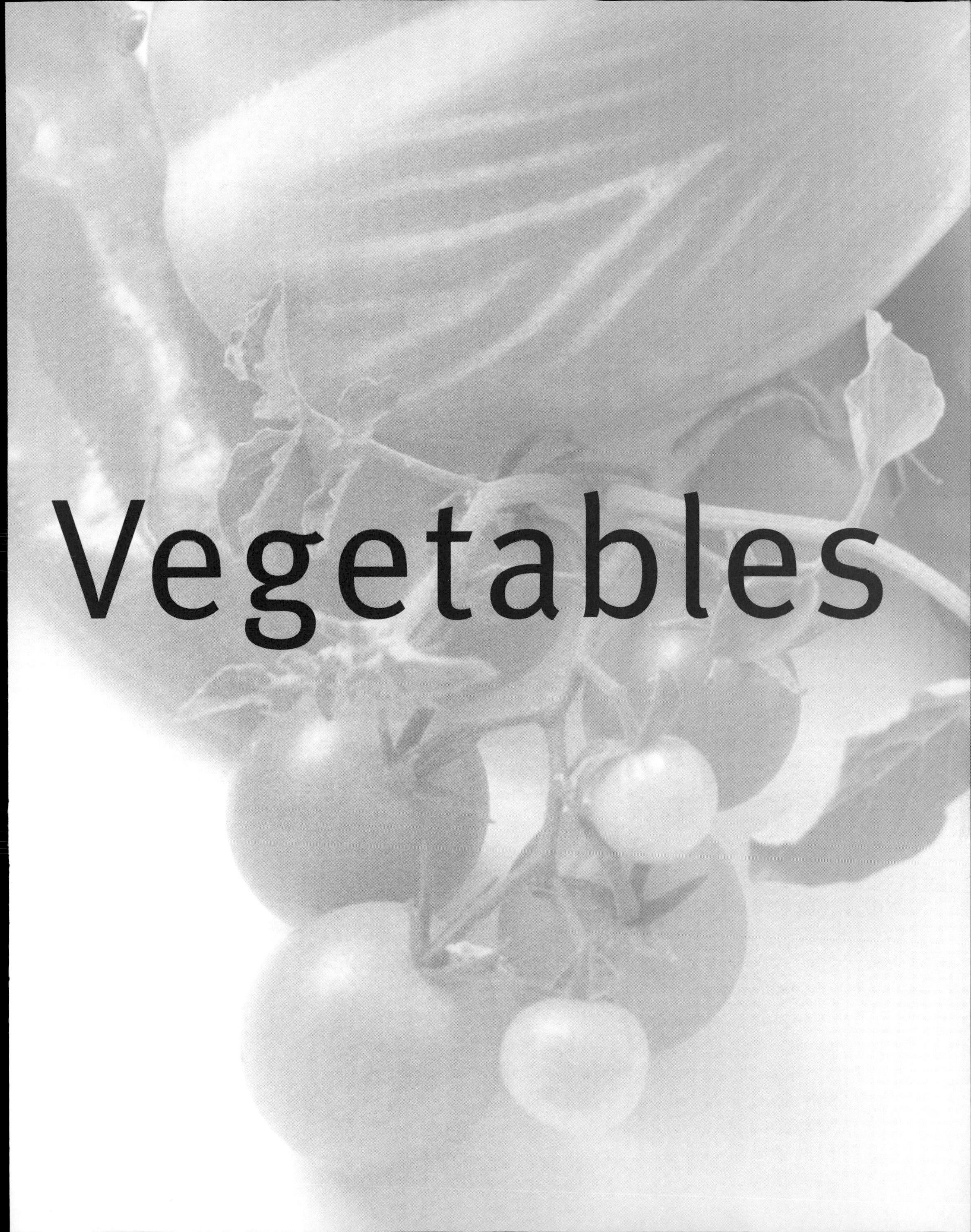

Chapter 3: Broccoli, Cauliflower, and Cabbages

RECIPES IN THIS CHAPTER:

- Curried Cauliflower Soup with Parsley Cream
- Marinated Coleslaw
- Broccoli Sauté with Garlic and Olive Oil
- Roasted Broccolini with Balsamic Vinegar
- Chestnuts, Brussels Sprouts, and Parsnips
- Farfalle Pasta Salad with Broccoli, Grape Tomatoes, and Yellow Peppers
- Shrimp Stir-Fry with Chinese Cabbage, Carrots, and Broccoli
- Chicken and Broccoli Casserole

Broccoli, the most popular member of the cruciferous or cabbage family, comes from the Mediterranean, where it has been a favorite on the menu since Roman times. Broccoli is incredibly healthful. It tastes delicious on its own and pairs well with other foods in a range of dishes from soups to pastas.

In markets today, you'll find several varieties of broccoli to choose from. The most common has the standard green head, but there's also a purple-headed broccoli that turns green upon cooking, the smaller broccolini (which is sort of a broccoli/asparagus cross) with thin, longer stems, Chinese broccoli with longer leaves, thinner stems, and a fewer bud clusters that are pale in hue, and the original Roman broccoli called romanesco, which is a bright chartreuse color and has spiral, pointed florets.

The cruciferous or cabbage clan got its name because the plants have four flowers that form the shape of a cross. Other members of this illustrious family include **cabbage**, **cauliflower**, and **Brussels sprouts**.

NUTRITION AND HEALTH

Broccoli and other cabbages are extremely nutritious foods—they are fat-free, low in calories, and packed with vitamins, minerals, and important cancer-fighting phytochemicals.

The members of the cruciferous family are rich in vitamin C. There is more vitamin C in a cup of cooked broccoli than in a navel orange. Vitamin C contributes to good health in a variety of ways: It heals wounds, strengthens blood vessels, and builds connective tissues, to name a few. Broccoli is also full of the important B vitamin, folate. It contains iron and calcium, as well as other B vitamins, vitamin A, and potassium.

Brussels sprouts offer folate and potassium, while cauliflower is rich in folate. The members of the cruciferous clan are all high in fiber.

WHAT TO LOOK FOR

At the market, select broccoli with a deep green color and tightly closed buds. Avoid vegetables that have yellowed.

Choose firm, bright green Brussels sprouts. Smaller is better—little sprouts are more tender than big ones.

Buy tight, firm, heavy heads of cabbage with no broken or bruised leaves.

Look for firm, white or cream-colored heads of cauliflower that are free of bruises or brown spots. The leaves should be bright green and crisp.

EASY STORAGE AND PREPARATION

Broccoli will keep for about four days in the refrigerator. Store it in a plastic bag. To use, rinse and remove the outer leaves and tough stems. Cut tender stems and florets into even-sized pieces.

Most cruciferous vegetables will keep for about the same length of time, but don't store Brussels sprouts longer than three days, or they will develop a strong flavor. Before you cook Brussels sprouts, cut an X in the base of the sprout so that it cooks at the same pace as the leaves.

BEST USES

- Cruciferous vegetables can all be served boiled, sautéed, steamed, or stir-fried.
- Broccoli and cauliflower are great served raw in salads or with dip; just cut them up into bite-size pieces.
- Broccoli and cauliflower make a good addition to casseroles.
- Because broccoli has a mildly assertive taste, it partners well with pungent flavors such as garlic, anchovies, capers, olives, and hot pepper. Lemon juice, cheese, parsley, and dill also liven up broccoli.
- Cauliflower and cabbage complement a variety of flavors, including garlic, lemon, curry, and cheese.

Surprise yourself with how easy it is to incorporate cruciferous vegetables into your everyday diet. These recipes showcase cabbage, cauliflower, broccoli, and more in dishes ranging from a simple sauté to a savory casserole. You'll find yourself eating more healthy veggies than you ever imagined.

ABOUT HERBS AND SPICES

Dill is an herb with feathery leaves and a delicate, tangy taste. Look for fresh and dried leaves and seeds. Dill flatters broccoli, green beans, cucumbers, tomatoes, potatoes, and fish. It's best to add fresh dill just before serving because cooking diminishes the flavor. Dill seeds are good in bread, braised cabbage, meat stews, and for pickling.

Curried Cauliflower Soup with Parsley Cream

ingredients

1/2 tablespoon olive oil
1/2 cup finely chopped celery
1 large onion, chopped
1/2 teaspoon curry powder
salt to taste
freshly ground black or white pepper
1 small russet potato
1 bay leaf
about 1 quart low-sodium chicken broth or vegetable broth
5 cups cauliflower florets
1/4 cup chopped, fresh parsley
3 tablespoons non-fat sour cream

nutrition facts

Serving Size about 1 1/2 cups

AMOUNT PER SERVING
Calories **92**
Total Fat **2 g**
Saturated Fat **1 g**
Cholesterol **3 mg**
Sodium **216 mg**
Total Carbohydrate **15 g**
Dietary Fiber **4 g**
Protein **5 g**
Percent Calories from Fat **21%**
Percent Calories from Protein **21%**
Percent Calories from Carbohydrate **58%**

Prep Time: **20 minutes**
Cooking Time: **40 minutes**
Serves **6**

cooking instructions

1. Heat the olive oil in a saucepan over low-medium heat. Add the celery, onion, and curry powder, season lightly with salt and pepper, and cook for 10 minutes.

2. Peel and slice the potato and add it to the pot. Add the bay leaf and broth and bring to a boil quickly over high heat.

3. Lower the heat and simmer until the vegetables are completely tender, about 15 minutes.

4. Add the cauliflower and simmer until just tender, about 5 to 7 minutes.

5. In a separate bowl, blend the parsley and sour cream together and set aside.

6. Remove the bay leaf and puree the soup in a blender. Strain and adjust the salt and pepper.

7. Serve the soup in bowls with a dollop of parsley cream.

Marinated Coleslaw

ingredients

1 head of cabbage, finely shredded

1 large onion, finely sliced

1 cup white wine vinegar

1/4 cup canola oil

3/4 cup sugar

2 teaspoons salt

1 tablespoon dry mustard

1 tablespoon celery seeds

2 cups low-sodium chicken broth

nutrition facts

Serving Size about 1/2 cup

AMOUNT PER SERVING

Calories	**130**
Total Fat	**5 g**
Saturated Fat	**0 g**
Cholesterol	**1 mg**
Sodium	**433 mg**
Total Carbohydrate	**19 g**
Dietary Fiber	**2 g**
Protein	**2 g**
Percent Calories from Fat	**36%**
Percent Calories from Protein	**6%**
Percent Calories from Carbohydrate	**58%**

Prep Time:
20 minutes
Plus Marinating Time

Cooking Time:
2 minutes

Serves **6**

cooking instructions

1. Layer the cabbage with the onion slices in a non-reactive container by placing one-third of the cabbage in the container, then half of the onions, another third of the cabbage, the remaining onions and finally the remaining cabbage.

2. Bring the remaining ingredients to a boil and pour them over the cabbage mixture. Do not mix. Marinate for 6 to 8 hours or overnight in the refrigerator.

3. Toss the marinated cabbage mixture as if it were a salad. Serve chilled.

Broccoli Sauté with Garlic and Olive Oil

ingredients

1 tablespoon olive oil
1 teaspoon crushed garlic
4 cups broccoli florets
salt to taste
freshly ground black pepper

nutrition facts

Serving Size about 1 cup

AMOUNT PER SERVING
Calories **36**
Total Fat **1 g**
Saturated Fat **0 g**
Cholesterol **0 mg**
Sodium 97 mg
Total Carbohydrate **5 g**
Dietary Fiber **3 g**
Total Carbohydrate **5 g**
Protein 3 g
Percent Calories from Fat **30%**
Percent Calories from Protein **25%**
Percent Calories from Carbohydrate **46%**

Prep Time:
5 minutes
Cooking Time:
5 minutes
Serves **4**

cooking instructions

1. Heat the olive oil in a 10" skillet over medium-low heat.

2. Add the garlic and cook for 1 minute.

3. Add the broccoli, salt, and pepper, and toss with the olive oil and garlic until the broccoli turns bright green and becomes tender. Remove from the skillet and serve.

Roasted Broccolini with Balsamic Vinegar

ingredients

2 bunches (about 8 ounces each) broccolini
1 tablespoon olive oil
kosher salt to taste
1 tablespoon balsamic vinegar

nutrition facts
Serving Size about 2 spears

AMOUNT PER SERVING	
Calories	**53**
Total Fat	**2 g**
Saturated Fat	**0 g**
Protein	**3 g**
Sodium	**101 mg**
Total Carbohydrate	**6 g**
Dietary Fiber	**1 g**
Percent Calories from Fat	**38%**
Percent Calories from Protein	**20%**
Percent Calories from Carbohydrate	**42%**

Prep Time: **5 minutes**
Cooking Time: **10 minutes**
Serves **6**

cooking instructions

1. Preheat the oven to 450°F.

2. Trim the stem ends of the broccolini and spread the spears on a baking sheet. Brush them with olive oil (especially the flowering part) and sprinkle with salt.

3. Roast the broccolini on the top rack of the oven until the stems become tender when pierced with a knife, about 10 minutes.

4. Toss the broccolini with the balsamic vinegar and serve.

Chestnuts, Brussels Sprouts, and Parsnips

Recipe by FoodFit Chef Ann Cashion, Cashion's Eat Place, Washington, D.C.

ingredients

1/2 pound chestnuts
4 cups chicken stock or water
1 small carrot
1 stalk celery
3 sprigs fresh thyme
salt to taste
freshly ground black pepper
1/2 pound Brussels sprouts
1 pound parsnips
3 tablespoons olive oil
Italian parsley, for garnish

nutrition facts
Serving Size about 3/4 cup

AMOUNT PER SERVING
Calories **208**
Total Fat **8 g**
Saturated Fat **1 g**
Cholesterol **0 mg**
Sodium **112 mg**
Total Carbohydrate **34 g**
Dietary Fiber **8 g**
Protein **3 g**
Percent Calories from Fat **32%**
Percent Calories from Protein **5%**
Percent Calories from Carbohydrate **63%**

Prep Time: **15 minutes**
Cooking Time: **40 minutes**
Serves **6**

cooking instructions

1. To prepare the chestnuts: score the hulls with a small, sharp knife and put them in a saucepan with cold water. Bring the water to a boil. Remove from the heat. Remove the chestnuts from the water a few at a time. They should peel easily. The fresher they are, the more easily they peel.

2. Cover the peeled chestnuts with chicken stock or water. Add the carrot, celery stalk, and thyme. Salt lightly and add a grinding of pepper. Bring to a simmer. Cook until the chestnuts are no longer raw but not soft or crumbling, about 15 to 20 minutes.

3. To prepare the Brussels sprouts: Bring a saucepan of water to a boil. Salt the water generously. (This will keep the Brussels sprouts green and bring out their flavor.) Trim the stem end of the Brussels sprouts. Add them to the boiling water and blanch until still slightly crisp, about 8 to 10 minutes. Drain. Refresh by running under cold water.

4. To prepare the parsnips: Peel the parsnips, cut them in half across the middle. Cut the fatter half of the parsnip into quarters lengthwise. Cut the thin part in half lengthwise. With a small knife, remove the core from each piece. You are trying to produce 3 to 4" lengths of parsnip of roughly the same width.

5. To finish the dish, heat the olive oil over medium heat. Add the parsnips, season with salt and pepper. Sauté the parsnips over medium heat, tossing occasionally, until they begin to color slightly, about 8 to 10 minutes.

6. Add the Brussels sprouts and the chestnuts. They will heat through while the parsnips finish cooking. Chestnuts may also pick up some color during this process. Remove from the heat when the parsnips are tender with streaks of golden brown. Adjust the seasoning, and serve immediately sprinkled with Italian parsley.

Farfalle Pasta Salad with Broccoli, Grape Tomatoes, and Yellow Pepper

ingredients

1 package (16 ounces) farfalle pasta (bow-tie pasta)

2 cups broccoli florets

1/2 cup Roasted Garlic Vinaigrette (page 62), or use a reduced-fat bottled vinaigrette

1 cup grape tomatoes, sliced in half

1 cup chopped yellow bell pepper

1/2 cup chopped scallions

2 tablespoons chopped, fresh basil

2 tablespoons chopped, fresh Italian parsley

salt to taste

freshly ground black pepper

4 cups arugula

1/2 cup goat cheese

nutrition facts

Serving Size about 1 1/2 cups of pasta

AMOUNT PER SERVING
Calories **229**
Total Fat **9 g**
Saturated Fat **2 g**
Cholesterol **3 mg**
Sodium **144 mg**
Total Carbohydrate **45 g**
Dietary Fiber **3 g**
Protein **10 g**
Percent Calories from Fat **28%**
Percent Calories from Protein **13%**
Percent Calories from Carbohydrate **62%**

Prep Time: **15 minutes**

Cooking Time: **12 minutes**

Serves **6**

cooking instructions

1. Bring a large pot of salted water to a boil over high heat. Add the farfalle and cook until it is al dente, about 12 to 14 minutes. Drain well.

2. In another small pot, bring 2 inches of water to a boil, insert a steamer basket with the broccoli florets and steam for 2 minutes (or until the broccoli turns bright green) once the water comes to a boil. Then remove from the heat and run the broccoli under cold water to stop the cooking process.

3. Place the farfalle in a large bowl and toss with the Roasted Garlic Vinaigrette. Add the broccoli florets, grape tomatoes, yellow pepper, scallions, and herbs and gently stir to combine. Season to taste with salt and pepper.

4. Serve the farfalle pasta salad on a bed of arugula (4 cups) and sprinkle with 1/2 cup of fresh goat cheese. Serve at room temperature.

Shrimp Stir-Fry with Bok Choy, Carrots, and Broccoli

ingredients

1 tablespoon peanut oil or vegetable oil
1 teaspoon chopped garlic
1 tablespoon chopped ginger
1 cup thinly sliced bok choy (Chinese cabbage)
1 cup thinly sliced carrots
1 cup broccoli florets, cut into small pieces
1 pound shrimp, peeled and deveined
freshly ground black pepper
1/4 cup low-sodium soy sauce

nutrition facts
Serving Size about 1 cup

AMOUNT PER SERVING
Calories **182**
Total Fat **6 g**
Saturated Fat **1 g**
Cholesterol **172 mg**
Sodium **719 mg**
Total Carbohydrate **7 g**
Dietary Fiber **2 g**
Protein **25 g**
Percent Calories from Fat **28%**
Percent Calories from Protein **56%**
Percent Calories from Carbohydrate **17%**

Prep Time: **15 minutes**
Cooking Time: **10 minutes**
Serves **2**

cooking instructions

1. Heat the oil in a skillet or wok large enough to accommodate all the ingredients over medium-high heat.

2. Add the garlic and ginger and stir quickly for 30 seconds.

3. Raise the heat to high. Add the bok choy, then the carrots, then the broccoli, then the shrimp, stirring quickly after each addition.

4. Season with pepper.

5. Add the soy sauce and cook until the shrimp are fully cooked and opaque, about 2 minutes.

Chicken and Broccoli Casserole

ingredients

2 cups low-sodium chicken broth
1 cup dry white wine
salt to taste
1 pound boneless, skinless chicken breasts
3 cups broccoli florets
2 tablespoons olive oil
2/3 cup flour
1/2 cup grated Gruyere cheese
1/4 cup freshly grated Parmesan cheese
1/2 teaspoon ground nutmeg
freshly ground black pepper
1/2 pound yolk-free egg noodles

nutrition facts

Serving Size about 2 cups

AMOUNT PER SERVING
Calories **429**
Total Fat **12 g**
Saturated Fat **4 g**
Cholesterol **59 mg**
Sodium **186 mg**
Total Carbohydrate **40 g**
Dietary Fiber **4 g**
Protein **32 g**
Percent Calories from Fat **28%**
Percent Calories from Protein **32%**
Percent Calories from Carbohydrate **40%**

Prep Time: **15 minutes**
Cooking Time: **25 minutes**
Serves **6**

cooking instructions

1. Preheat the oven to 350°F.
2. In a large saucepan, heat the chicken broth, white wine, and a generous pinch of salt over medium heat. Add the chicken breasts and poach them over low heat for 10 minutes or until the chicken breasts are cooked through. Remove the chicken from the liquid and set aside. When the chicken is cool enough to handle, cut it into strips.
3. Bring the poaching liquid to a boil, add the broccoli florets, and cook for 2 minutes. Remove the broccoli and set aside. Reserve the cooking liquid.
4. In a separate saucepan, heat the olive oil over medium heat. Whisk in the flour and cook for 3 minutes. Whisk in the cooking liquid and simmer for 5 minutes. Stir in the cheeses. Add the nutmeg and season with salt and pepper.
5. Meanwhile, cook the noodles in a large pot of salted water until they are al dente; drain, and put them in a large casserole dish.
6. Add the chicken and broccoli to the casserole dish and pour in the sauce. Bake the casserole in the oven for 20 minutes. Let the casserole stand at room temperature for 5 minutes before serving.

Chapter 4: Spinach and Leafy, Green Vegetables

RECIPES IN THIS CHAPTER:

Spinach is a wonderfully versatile and nutritious leafy, green vegetable. Very popular in French and Italian cuisines, this delectable green is now becoming more popular in the United States as Americans get more creative in cooking it.

We can thank the Spaniards for bringing spinach, originally from the Middle East, to America. Spinach has been commonly available in the United States since the early 19th century, usually served cooked. Southerners have been enjoying leafy greens like spinach for years, which quickly became an important part of the southern dinner table.

Spring, summer, and fall are all seasons for greens—**mustard greens**, **arugula**, **Swiss chard**, **bok choy**, **mache**, **watercress**, **kale**, and others join year-round stand-bys like **spinach** and **lettuce** in the market.

NUTRITION AND HEALTH

Spinach and other leafy greens are, like most vegetables, fat-free and extremely low in calories. Spinach has an equal ratio of carbohydrates to protein; there are two grams of each in two cups of raw spinach.

Spinach is a standout when it comes to vitamin A. Vitamin A plays an important role in vision, bone growth, and maintaining your immune system. Spinach also supplies vitamins B2 and B6, folate, magnesium, and protein.

Kale and arugula have the rare distinction among vegetables of being calcium-rich. Swiss chard offers vitamins E and K. In addition, greens are packed with vitamin C, fiber, and disease-fighting beta-carotene.

WHAT TO LOOK FOR

Pick greens that have a rich color and a vibrant look. Fresh spinach, for example, should have firm, crisp, deep green leaves. When selecting fresh greens, watch for blemishes, insect damage, or wilting. The stems should be crisp, not limp. Yellowing, limpness, and spotting are signs that the greens are old and may taste sour when cooked.

Bok choy should have dark green, glossy leaves and bright white stalks. Avoid heads with brown spots on the leaves. This discoloration often means that it was stored at too low a temperature and results in flavor loss.

Swiss chard should have bright-colored, crisp, tender leaves that are not overgrown. Swiss chard is available year round, but tends to be tough and woody in hot summers.

EASY STORAGE AND PREPARATION

To store greens, refrigerate them in plastic bags. (Try adding a paper towel to the bag to absorb excess moisture.) Greens will keep in the refrigerator for just a few days. When you're ready to use them, tear off any central ribs that are large and tough.

Wash greens well in several changes of water to remove sand. Let them soak for a few minutes while the dirt settles to the bottom and then lift the greens out of the soaking water. Repeat as necessary.

BEST USES

- You can use spinach and other greens raw or cooked. Young, small greens are great raw in a salad or on a sandwich. Use small, raw spinach leaves in salads with mushrooms, red onion, and a sprinkle of chopped, cooked egg.
- Medium-size greens should be cooked lightly, such as sautéeing or stir frying. You can also steam greens using only the water that clings to the leaves after washing. Season with shallots, nutmeg, salt, and pepper.
- Fully mature greens can be stewed to soften their texture and mellow their flavor.
- Spinach can be added to soups and casseroles, and adds color (and nutrients) to omelettes.
- Vinegar pairs well with chard, kale, collards, and many other greens.

Leafy, green vegetables are in peak season from summer through fall, but some varieties of fresh spinach and lettuce are available year-round. The following recipes offer many ways of preparing spinach and other delectable greens throughout the seasons, from a hearty lasagna to a light chicken entrée.

ABOUT HERBS AND SPICES

Mint is an herb with spicy-sweet leaves. There are 30 different varieties, but the most popular are peppermint and spearmint. Look for fresh leaves and crumbled dried leaves. Mint is a delicious addition to desserts, fruit salads, lamb, and vegetable dishes. It's also great in iced tea and jellies, and dried mint is often used in Middle Eastern dishes, especially for cheese pastry fillings, yogurt dressings and for stuffing tomatoes and bell peppers.

Chickpea and Spinach Soup with Shrimp, Almonds, and Garlic

Recipe by FoodFit Chef Joyce Goldstein, cookbook author

ingredients

1 1/4 cups chickpeas, (garbanzo beans), rinsed and soaked overnight in cold water and refrigerated (or 3 cups canned beans, drained and rinsed)

1 ham hock, optional

2 tablespoons olive oil

2 onions (about 2 1/2 cups), coarsely chopped

1 clove garlic, finely minced

1 small russet potato, peeled and sliced, about 2/3 to 1 cup

5 cups chicken stock (or more if needed)

1 teaspoon salt

1/4 teaspoon freshly ground black pepper

2 tablespoons butter or oil

6 cups spinach, washed and cut into thin strips

6 tablespoons sliced almonds, coarsely chopped and toasted

1 teaspoon finely minced garlic

18 (or more, if serving as an entrée) medium-size cooked shrimp, shelled and deveined

nutrition facts

Serving Size about 1 bowl

AMOUNT PER SERVING

Calories **254**

Total Fat **11 g**

Saturated Fat **1 g**

Cholesterol **122 mg**

Sodium **754 mg**

Total Carbohydrate **20 g**

Dietary Fiber **5 g**

Protein **19 g**

Percent Calories from Fat **41%**

Percent Calories from Protein **29%**

Percent Calories from Carbohydrate **31%**

Prep Time: **14 minutes**

Cooking Time: **40 minutes**

Plus Time to Prepare Beans

Serves **8**

cooking instructions

1. If cooking the beans, drain the soaked chickpeas, rinse well, and put into a medium saucepan. Cover with fresh cold water, add the optional ham hock. Bring to a boil and reduce heat. Simmer, covered, for about an hour or until tender. Drain the cooked chickpeas and set aside. Discard the ham hock.

2. Heat 1 tablespoon olive oil in a large saucepan over moderate heat. Add the chopped onions and cook for about 10 to 15 minutes or until translucent. Add the garlic and stir for a minute or two. Then add the sliced potato, half the chickpeas, and the chicken stock and bring to a boil. Simmer and cook until the potato and beans are falling apart, about 20 minutes. Puree the soup in a blender. Season with salt and pepper. Just before serving, bring the soup to a simmer. It will have thickened, so thin it with more stock or water. In a very large sauté pan, heat 2 teaspoons of oil and sauté the spinach. Add the pureed soup. Stir in the remaining cooked chickpeas.

3. In a small sauté pan, over a medium heat, warm 1 teaspoon of oil. Sauté the almonds with the minced garlic in the oil. Cook a few minutes and add these to the soup. Finally, chop the cooked shrimp, add it to the soup, and warm through. Adjust seasoning. Serve at once.

Fall Spinach Salad with Pears and Pecans

ingredients

12 cups spinach leaves, washed and drained

1 recipe Sherry Vinaigrette (see page 27), or use a reduced-fat bottled vinaigrette

2 Bosc pears

1/2 cup dried cranberries

1 tablespoon pecans, chopped and toasted

nutrition facts
Serving Size about 2 cups

AMOUNT PER SERVING
Calories **152**
Total Fat **6 g**
Saturated Fat **1 g**
Cholesterol **0 mg**
Sodium **111 mg**
Total Carbohydrate **25 g**
Dietary Fiber **4 g**
Protein **2 g**
Percent Calories from Fat **34%**
Percent Calories from Protein **6%**
Percent Calories from Carbohydrate **60%**

Prep Time:
15 minutes

Serves **6**

instructions

1. Place the spinach in a large salad bowl.

2. Core and slice the pears and toss them with the spinach and vinaigrette. Sprinkle with the dried cranberries and toasted pecans.

Sautéed Kale with Garlic, Onions, and Lemon

ingredients

1 tablespoon olive oil
1/4 cup diced onion
1 teaspoon minced garlic
4 cups kale, washed
salt to taste
freshly ground black pepper
juice of 1 lemon

Prep Time:
5 minutes

Cooking Time:
5 minutes

Serves 4

nutrition facts

Serving Size about 1 cup

AMOUNT PER SERVING
Calories **71**
Total Fat **4 g**
Saturated Fat **1 g**
Cholesterol **0 mg**
Sodium **111 mg**
Total Carbohydrate **8 g**
Dietary Fiber **2 g**
Protein **2 g**
Percent Calories from Fat **46%**
Percent Calories from Protein **12%**
Percent Calories from Carbohydrate **42%**

cooking instructions

1. Heat the olive oil in a 10" skillet over medium-low heat.

2. Add the onion and cook until tender but not brown, about 2 minutes. Add the garlic and cook for 1 minute more.

3. Add the kale, salt, and pepper, and toss with the olive oil and garlic until the kale begins to wilt, about 2 minutes. Remove from the skillet, squeeze the lemon juice over the mixture, toss lightly, and serve.

Grilled Chicken Spinach Salad with Oranges, Walnuts, and Sherry Vinaigrette

ingredients

FOR THE SHERRY VINAIGRETTE:

1 tablespoon finely chopped shallots
3 tablespoons sherry vinegar
1 tablespoon honey
1 teaspoon Dijon mustard
2 tablespoons olive oil
salt to taste
freshly ground black pepper

FOR THE GRILLED CHICKEN:

4 skinless, boneless chicken breasts
1 tablespoon olive oil

FOR THE SPINACH SALAD:

2 oranges, peeled and sectioned
1/2 cup thinly sliced red onion
8 cups baby spinach leaves, washed and drained
1/4 cup walnuts, chopped and toasted

nutrition facts

Serving Size about 1 chicken breast with salad

AMOUNT PER SERVING
Calories **465**
Total Fat **17 g**
Saturated Fat **3 g**
Cholesterol **136 mg**
Sodium **380 mg**
Total Carbohydrate **21 g**
Dietary Fiber **6 g**
Protein **58 g**
Percent Calories from Fat **33%**
Percent Calories from Protein **49%**
Percent Calories from Carbohydrate **18%**

Prep Time: **20 minutes**
Cooking Time: **15 minutes**
Serves **4**

cooking instructions

For the sherry vinaigrette:

1. Place the shallots, vinegar, honey, and mustard in a small mixing bowl and whisk to combine. Continue whisking and slowly add the olive oil. Season to taste with salt and pepper. (This can be made in advance and stored in the refrigerator for up to 3 days.)

For the grilled chicken:

1. Preheat the grill to medium-high.

2. Brush the chicken breasts with olive oil and season with salt and pepper.

3. Grill the chicken on both sides until it is cooked through, about 6 minutes per side. (The chicken can be grilled in advance and stored in the refrigerator for up to 3 days.)

For the spinach salad:

1. Slice the grilled chicken breasts into strips and place them in a mixing bowl. Add the orange sections, red onion, and half of the sherry vinaigrette. Toss together.

2. Place the spinach in a separate salad bowl and toss it with the remaining vinaigrette. Arrange the chicken, orange, and onion mixture on top. Garnish with the walnuts.

Grilled Salmon and Fresh Spinach Wraps

ingredients

FOR THE GRILLED SALMON:

4 salmon fillets, about 4 ounces each
2 teaspoons olive oil
salt to taste
freshly ground black pepper

FOR THE WRAPS:

1/2 cup fat-free, whipped cream cheese
2 tablespoons minced, sweet onion
4 large flour tortillas
4 large spinach leaves, shredded

nutrition facts
Serving Size about 1 wrap

AMOUNT PER SERVING
Calories **342**
Total Fat **10 g**
Saturated Fat **2 g**
Cholesterol **61 mg**
Sodium **474 mg**
Total Carbohydrate **30 g**
Dietary Fiber **2 g**
Protein **31 g**
Percent Calories from Fat **27%**
Percent Calories from Protein **37%**
Percent Calories from Carbohydrate **35%**

Prep Time: **20 minutes**
Cooking Time: **15 minutes**
Serves **4**

cooking instructions

For the grilled salmon:

1. Preheat the grill to medium-high.

2. Brush the salmon fillets with olive oil and then season with salt and pepper. Cook them on the grill, about 3 to 4 minutes per side, depending on their thickness. Transfer the fillets to a cutting board to let cool and then cut into small pieces.

For the wraps:

1. In a small mixing bowl, combine the cream cheese and onion. Add salt and pepper to taste.

2. Lay out the tortillas on a work surface. Divide the cream cheese mixture among the tortillas, spreading it out in the middle of each tortilla. Divide the salmon among the tortillas, top with shredded spinach. Tightly roll the tortilla in a cylinder ending with the seam side down.

3. Slice the wraps on the diagonal and serve.

Spinach and Mushroom Lasagna

ingredients

1 pound lasagna noodles
4 teaspoons olive oil
1 pound white mushrooms, sliced
salt to taste
freshly ground black pepper
1/4 teaspoon dried oregano
4 cloves garlic, minced
4 bunches fresh spinach, washed and stems removed
2 cups low-fat ricotta cheese
pinch of nutmeg
2 cups Quick Tomato Sauce (see page 52), or use a basic jarred or canned sauce
1 cup shredded low-fat mozzarella cheese
1/2 cup bread crumbs

nutrition facts
Serving Size 1 piece

AMOUNT PER SERVING
Calories **354**
Total Fat **6 g**
Saturated Fat **2 g**
Cholesterol **8 mg**
Sodium **432 mg**
Total Carbohydrate **52 g**
Dietary Fiber **6 g**
Protein **21 g**
Percent Calories from Fat **16%**
Percent Calories from Protein **24%**
Percent Calories from Carbohydrate **60%**

Prep Time: **25 minutes**
Cooking Time: **50 minutes**
Serves **8**

cooking instructions

1. Bring a large pot of well salted water to a boil and prepare a large bowl of ice water. Add the lasagna noodles to the boiling water and cook until they are just al dente. Drain and plunge the noodles into the ice water to cool them quickly. Drain again and lay the noodles out on paper towels.

2. Heat 2 teaspoons of olive oil in a nonstick pan over medium-high heat. Add the mushrooms, season with salt, pepper, and oregano and cook for two minutes. Add half of the garlic and cook until the mushrooms are browned on the edges. Set the mushrooms aside in a strainer to allow the excess liquid to drain.

3. Wipe the inside of the pan with a paper towel and heat the remaining olive oil in it over medium-high heat. Add the remaining garlic, season with salt and pepper, and cook for 30 seconds. (It's easier to distribute the salt and pepper in the oil before adding the spinach.) Add the spinach (with the water that clings to it) and cook until it is just wilted. Set the spinach in a strainer to allow the excess liquid to drain.

4. Preheat the oven to 325°F.

5. In a medium bowl, season the ricotta cheese with salt, pepper, and nutmeg.

6. Cover the bottom of a large baking dish that is at least 2 inches deep with a thin coat of tomato sauce. Line the dish with a single layer of lasagna noodles. Spread 1/3 of the ricotta mixture over the noodles and sprinkle with some of the mozzarella cheese. Spread all of the mushrooms over the cheese and sprinkle with a few tablespoons of bread crumbs. Repeat with another layer of noodles, cheese, the spinach mixture, and bread crumbs. Continue with another layer of noodles, the remaining ricotta, a sprinkling of mozzarella, and the remaining tomato sauce. Finish with a final layer of noodles sprinkled with the remaining mozzarella and bread crumbs.

7. Cover with foil and bake for 35 minutes. Remove the foil and continue to bake until the top is golden brown, about 5 minutes more. Let stand for at least 15 minutes before cutting into squares and serving.

Orecchiette with Ricotta and Spinach

ingredients

1/2 pound orecchiette pasta
1 tablespoon extra virgin olive oil
1 clove garlic, minced
2 cups spinach leaves, washed
salt to taste
freshly ground black pepper
pinch of nutmeg
1/2 cup part-skim ricotta cheese

nutrition facts

Serving Size about 2 cups

AMOUNT PER SERVING
Calories **282**
Total Fat **7 g**
Saturated Fat **2 g**
Cholesterol **13 mg**
Sodium **281 mg**
Total Carbohydrate **45 g**
Dietary Fiber **3 g**
Protein **13 g**
Percent Calories from Fat **20%**
Percent Calories from Protein **18%**
Percent Calories from Carbohydrate **62%**

Prep Time: **10 minutes**
Cooking Time: **15 minutes**
Serves **2**

cooking instructions

1. Bring a large pot of salted water to a boil. Drop the pasta in it and cook for 12 to 14 minutes, until al dente.

2. Meanwhile, heat the olive oil in a large skillet over medium heat. Add the garlic and stir for 30 seconds. Add the spinach, salt, pepper, and nutmeg, and cook for 1 to 2 minutes, just until the spinach begins to wilt. Remove from the heat, and place the spinach mixture in a large bowl with the ricotta cheese.

3. Drain the pasta; immediately toss it with the spinach and ricotta, and serve at once.

Fettuccine with Swiss Chard, Garlic, and Parmesan Cheese

ingredients

3/4 pound fettuccine
2 pounds Swiss chard, washed and drained
1 tablespoon olive oil
1 large onion, chopped
salt to taste
freshly ground black pepper
2 cloves garlic, finely minced
pinch of nutmeg
2 tablespoons low-fat sour cream
1/4 cup Parmesan cheese

nutrition facts
Serving Size about 1 1/2 cups

AMOUNT PER SERVING
Calories **356**
Total Fat **8 g**
Saturated Fat **2 g**
Cholesterol **7 mg**
Sodium **710 mg**
Total Carbohydrate **59 g**
Dietary Fiber **6 g**
Protein **16 g**
Percent Calories from Fat **20%**
Percent Calories from Protein **17%**
Percent Calories from Carbohydrate **63%**

Prep Time:
15 minutes

Cooking Time:
15 minutes

Serves 4

cooking instructions

1. Bring a large pot of salted water to a boil. Add the fettuccine and cook about 12 minutes until al dente. Drain.

2. Meanwhile, cut the Swiss chard into 1/4-inch-wide pieces.

3. Heat the olive oil in a large sauté pan over medium-high heat. Add the onions, salt, and pepper and cook until the onions start to soften, about 5 minutes. Add the garlic and cook 1 minute more.

4. Add the chard and nutmeg to the skillet and cook for 5 minutes more. Stir in the low-fat sour cream and remove from heat.

5. Toss the fettuccine with the Swiss chard mixture.

6. Divide the fettuccine among 4 warmed serving plates and sprinkle with Parmesan cheese. Serve immediately.

Sweet and Sour Rockfish with Bok Choy

ingredients

1/2 cup sugar
1/2 cup rice vinegar
1/4 cup tomato juice
4 rockfish fillets, about 4 to 6 ounces each
salt to taste
freshly ground black pepper
1 teaspoon vegetable oil
1 cup low-sodium chicken broth
1 head bok choy, washed and cut into 1-inch lengths

nutrition facts

Serving Size 1 fillet

AMOUNT PER SERVING

Calories **289**
Total Fat **3 g**
Saturated Fat **1 g**
Cholesterol **67 mg**
Sodium **215 mg**
Total Carbohydrate **27 g**
Dietary Fiber **1 g**
Protein **38 g**
Percent Calories from Fat **10%**
Percent Calories from Protein **53%**
Percent Calories from Carbohydrate **37%**

Prep Time:
15 minutes

Cooking Time:
20 minutes

Serves **4**

cooking instructions

1. To make the sweet and sour sauce, combine the sugar and vinegar in a small saucepan and cook over medium heat until the mixture becomes syrupy, about 3 to 5 minutes. Remove from heat, slowly whisk in the tomato juice and set aside.

2. Season the rockfish fillets with salt and pepper. Heat the oil in a nonstick pan over high heat. Add the fillets and sauté until they are cooked through, about 2 to 3 minutes on each side.

3. Remove the pan from the heat and transfer the fillets to a platter. Add the chicken broth to the same pan and bring it to a boil. Add the bok choy, season with salt and pepper and cook until it is just tender, about 6 minutes.

4. Serve the fish on a bed of bok choy drizzled with sweet and sour sauce.

Spa-Style Chicken with Sun-Dried Tomatoes and Watercress

ingredients

1 tablespoon olive oil
2 tablespoons finely chopped shallots
1 cup white wine
2 tablespoons fresh lemon juice
2 tablespoons chopped fresh tarragon
1/2 cup sun-dried tomatoes, rehydrated
4 boneless, skinless chicken breasts, about 4 to 6 ounces each
salt to taste
freshly ground black pepper
1 1/2 cups water or more to cook the chicken
1 bunch watercress, washed and large stems removed

nutrition facts

Serving Size about 1 breast with watercress and sun-dried tomatoes

AMOUNT PER SERVING
Calories **290**
Total Fat **7 g**
Saturated Fat **1 g**
Cholesterol **73 mg**
Sodium **167 mg**
Total Carbohydrate **14 g**
Dietary Fiber **3 g**
Protein **31 g**
Percent Calories from Fat **26%**
Percent Calories from Protein **51%**
Percent Calories from Carbohydrate **23%**

Prep Time: **15 minutes**
Cooking Time: **25 minutes**
Serves 4

cooking instructions

1. Heat the olive oil in a large soup pot over medium heat. Add the shallots and cook for 3 minutes.
2. Increase the heat to high, add the wine, lemon juice, tarragon, and sun-dried tomatoes. Simmer for 1 minute.
3. Season the chicken breasts with salt and pepper and add them to the pan with enough water to cover them. Bring the liquid to a boil and adjust the heat so that the mixture simmers. Cook for 10 to 12 minutes, until the chicken is just cooked through.
4. Remove the chicken from the pan and set aside. Continue to simmer the cooking liquid until it has reduced by half.
5. Divide the watercress among 4 plates. Place the chicken on top of the watercress, garnish with sun-dried tomatoes, and drizzle the hot cooking liquid over the chicken. Serve immediately.

Chapter 5: Asparagus and Flowering Green and Yellow Vegetables

RECIPES IN THIS CHAPTER:

- Cold Zucchini Soup with Cinnamon, Cumin, and Buttermilk
- Asparagus Soup with Lemon Cream
- Roasted Asparagus Salad
- Green Beans with Lemon-Garlic Dressing
- Summer Squash Sauté
- Summer Beans with Cherry Tomatoes and Tarragon
- Fusilli with Summer Squash, Zucchini, and Sugar Snap Peas
- Penne with Asparagus and Red Peppers
- Chicken and Asparagus with Creamy Dijon Sauce
- Lamb and Artichoke Stew with Lentils

Quick, easy, tasty, and nutritious, asparagus is one of the joys of spring. This incredible vegetable has been wowing eaters through the ages, and is piled high in markets throughout the year.

Originally from Mesopotamia, asparagus was a favorite dish in Greek and Roman times. Roman emperors went so far as to keep special "asparagus fleets" to ferry choice stalks to their tables. A popular expression for quick action was "faster than cooking asparagus." Centuries later, famed King Louis XIV of France had his gardeners grow asparagus in greenhouses so he could dine on it year-round.

Flowering and green vegetables of all kinds have long been popular and include such favorites as **green** and **yellow beans**, **artichokes**, **snow peas**, **sugar snap peas**, **English peas**, **cucumber**, **okra**, and such summer **squashes**, as **zucchini**. English peas or green peas are the old-fashioned peas we all know from childhood. Sugar snap peas are a cross between English peas and snow peas. Green beans are also known as string beans, but the stringy part has been bred out of most varieties. These green delights abound in the market and are simple to prepare.

NUTRITION AND HEALTH

Asparagus and other flowering vegetables are a good source of fiber, which helps lower cholesterol and aids digestion. They join most other vegetables in being virtually fat-free and low in calories.

Asparagus is a great source of folate which helps prevent birth defects and may protect against cancer. Asparagus is also a source of vitamin C and iron.

Green peas are an excellent source of vitamin C, folate, and iron. Zucchini contains vitamin C, while cucumbers' high water content helps you stay hydrated during warm summer months. Artichokes are an excellent source of fiber and a good source of vitamin C, magnesium, folate, potassium, and iron.

WHAT TO LOOK FOR

When buying asparagus, choose firm, smooth stalks that have tight buds at the top and have no wrinkles. If the buds are drooping and open, the asparagus is past its prime. Likewise, the stalks should be straight and fresh-looking, not yellowed, shriveled, or woody.

Also avoid wrinkles when picking peas. Look for bright green pods filled with peas but not bulging. If the peas are too large, they are old and will taste starchy.

Look for beans that have a bright color without brown or soft spots, and avoid any that appear limp. Large pods may be tough or bitter.

Zucchini and yellow squashes should be fewer than 8 inches long, and have thin, glossy skin.

Select artichokes that feel heavy for their size and have tightly closed buds. Leaves should be soft green or purple. Avoid artichokes that are wilting, opening, or drying.

EASY STORAGE AND PREPARATION

Flowering and green vegetables should all be stored in the refrigerator for no more than a couple of days.

Don't leave asparagus tied in a bundle. It causes the stalks to sweat and the resulting moisture may mean they spoil faster. Instead, trim the stem ends and stand the spears in water like a bouquet of flowers.

Pull off any strings along a bean pod's seams before cooking. Beans may be left whole, cut lengthwise in thin slivers, or cut crosswise on the diagonal.

To prepare peas, just remove them from the inedible pod and rinse. Cook in boiling, salted water for 3 to 5 minutes. The pods of snow and snap peas, however, are edible.

Artichokes should be stored, stem-end down, in water; trim the stem first. They'll keep in the refrigerator for a few days. When ready to cook, trim the stem end and the first few bottom leaves of the artichoke. Cut off

ABOUT HERBS AND SPICES

Chives are green herbs that resemble grass and have a mild onion flavor. Look for fresh shoots or dried or frozen. Chives are delightful in soups and sauces, fish and egg dishes, and on baked potatoes. Long cooking diminishes their flavor, so it's best to add chives to a dish at the last minute. Fresh chives are often used as a garnish.

Tarragon is an herb with a licorice-like flavor and long, thin leaves. Look for fresh whole leaves or dried whole and crumbled leaves. Used often in French cooking, it's also a lively addition to salads, vinaigrettes, chicken, fish, shellfish, veal, vegetable, and egg dishes. Tarragon's flavor, although subtle, diffuses quickly through dishes and should be used sparingly.

the top inch of the head to remove the thorny tips of the uppermost leaves. After each cut, rub with lemon to prevent discoloration.

BEST USES

- Asparagus is simple and speedy to cook. It's delicious steamed, broiled, grilled, or roasted. Serve hot, drizzled with olive oil, lemon juice, salt, and pepper.
- Asparagus is also delicious served cold. To prepare, plunge cooked asparagus into ice water to chill thoroughly and serve with a vinaigrette.
- Carrots, pearl onions, and mushrooms pair perfectly with peas. Fresh dill and mint bring out the best flavor in fresh peas.
- Cooked green beans come to life when tossed with balsamic vinegar and fresh mint.
- Zucchini can be baked whole or halved, drizzled with olive oil, salt, and pepper, at 350°F, for 20 to 25 minutes. Fresh basil makes a good accompaniment.

Asparagus and other flowering vegetables are incredibly versatile. They can be served warm or cold and work well in side dishes, soups, salads, or entrées. Enjoy fresh asparagus and artichokes during the spring, and zucchini and beans during the summer for a bright flash of health-giving green in your meals.

Cold Zucchini Soup with Cinnamon, Cumin, and Buttermilk

Recipe by FoodFit Chef John Ash, Fetzer Vineyards, Napa Valley, CA

ingredients

1 pound zucchini, trimmed
2 1/2 cups vegetable or chicken broth
1 tablespoon olive oil
1 cup chopped onion
1/2 teaspoon seeded and minced serrano chili pepper
1/2 teaspoon fennel seeds
1/2 teaspoon ground cinnamon
1 teaspoon ground cumin
1 1/2 cups buttermilk
sea salt to taste
freshly ground pepper to taste
Garnish: chopped, fresh cilantro or mint
lime or lemon wedges

nutrition facts
Serving Size 1 cup

AMOUNT PER SERVING
Calories **129**
Total Fat **5 g**
Saturated Fat **1 g**
Cholesterol **5 mg**
Sodium **659 mg**
Total Carbohydrate **13 g**
Dietary Fiber **2 g**
Protein **7 g**
Percent Calories from Fat **37%**
Percent Calories from Protein **23%**
Percent Calories from Carbohydrate **40%**

Prep Time:
10 minutes
Cooking Time:
5 minutes
Serves **4**

cooking instructions

1. Chop the zucchini in large chunks.
2. Add the broth to a soup pot, bring it to a boil, and add the zucchini.
3. Reduce the heat and simmer, covered, for 4 to 5 minutes, or until the zucchini is barely tender and still bright green. Remove from heat and cool.
4. Meanwhile, heat the oil in a small, nonstick frying pan. Add the onion, chili pepper, fennel, cinnamon, and cumin, and sauté until the onion is soft, but not brown, and the spices are fragrant.
5. Put both the zucchini and spice mixture into a food processor and pulse until well chopped but still retaining some texture. Pour into a bowl, stir in the buttermilk, and season to taste with salt and pepper.
6. Chill for at least 2 hours. Serve garnished with a sprinkling of cilantro or mint and a few added drops of lemon or lime juice to taste.

Asparagus Soup with Lemon Cream

ingredients

1/2 tablespoon olive oil
1/4 cup finely chopped celery
1 large onion, chopped
salt to taste
freshly ground black pepper
1 small russet potato, peeled and sliced
1 bay leaf
1/4 teaspoon dried thyme
about 1 quart low-sodium chicken or vegetable broth
1 pound (about 5 cups) asparagus stalks, chopped
juice of 1/2 lemon
3 tablespoons nonfat sour cream

nutrition facts
Serving Size about 1 1/2 cups

AMOUNT PER SERVING
Calories **87**
Total Fat **2 g**
Saturated Fat **1 g**
Cholesterol **3 mg**
Sodium **187 mg**
Total Carbohydrate **14 g**
Dietary Fiber **3 g**
Protein **5 g**
Percent Calories from Fat **22%**
Percent Calories from Protein **22%**
Percent Calories from Carbohydrate **56%**

Prep Time: **20 minutes**
Cooking Time: **40 minutes**
Serves **6**

cooking instructions

1. Heat the olive oil in a saucepan over medium-low heat. Add the celery and onion, season lightly with salt and pepper, and cook for 10 minutes.

2. Add the potato slices to the pot. Add the bay leaf, thyme, and broth and bring to a boil quickly over high heat.

3. Lower the heat and simmer until the vegetables are completely tender, about 15 minutes.

4. Add the asparagus and simmer until just tender, about 5 to 7 minutes.

5. In a small bowl, blend the lemon juice and sour cream together and set aside.

6. Remove the bay leaf and puree the soup in a blender. Strain and adjust the salt and pepper to taste.

7. Ladle the soup in bowls and garnish with a dollop of lemon sour cream. Serve immediately.

Roasted Asparagus Salad

ingredients

1 1/2 pounds fresh asparagus
1 tablespoon olive oil
salt to taste
freshly ground black pepper
2 tablespoons white wine vinegar

nutrition facts
Serving Size about 6 spears of asparagus

AMOUNT PER SERVING
Calories **46**
Total Fat **2 g**
Saturated Fat **0 g**
Cholesterol **0 mg**
Sodium **151 mg**
Total Carbohydrate **5 g**
Dietary Fiber **2 g**
Protein **3 g**
Percent Calories from Fat **42%**
Percent Calories from Protein **19%**
Percent Calories from Carbohydrate **39%**

Prep Time:
5 minutes
Cooking Time:
10 minutes
Serves **6**

cooking instructions

1. Preheat the oven to 350°F.
2. Prepare the asparagus by cutting off the last inch or so of the woody stalk.
3. Place the asparagus stalks on a baking sheet. Brush them with the olive oil and sprinkle with salt and pepper to taste.
4. Roast in the oven for 10 minutes, until the stalks begin to get tender on the outside. (Thin asparagus spears will take less time than thick spears.)
5. Toss with the vinegar and serve.

Green Beans with Lemon-Garlic Dressing

ingredients

1 pound green beans, trimmed
salt to taste
1/4 cup fat-free mayonnaise
1 teaspoon Dijon mustard
juice of 1 lemon
2 (to taste) cloves garlic, peeled
1/2 teaspoon anchovy paste (optional)
pinch cayenne pepper
freshly ground black pepper

nutrition facts
Serving Size about 1/2 cup

AMOUNT PER SERVING
Calories **50**
Total Fat **0 g**
Saturated Fat **0 g**
Cholesterol **0 mg**
Sodium **144 mg**
Total Carbohydrate **11 g**
Dietary Fiber **3 g**
Protein **2 g**
Percent Calories from Fat **4%**
Percent Calories from Protein **13%**
Percent Calories from Carbohydrate **83%**

Prep Time:
5 minutes
Cooking Time:
5 minutes
Serves **4**

cooking instructions

1. Blanch the beans in a large pot of boiling, salted water until they are crisp-tender, about 3 to 4 minutes.

2. Drain the beans and immediately plunge them into a bowl of ice water to cool them quickly. Drain again. This may be done in advance and beans stored in the refrigerator for 2 to 3 days.

3. Combine the mayonnaise, mustard, lemon juice, garlic, anchovy paste (if desired), cayenne pepper, and plenty of black pepper in a blender or small food processor and puree. This may be done in advance and mixture stored in the refrigerator for 2 to 3 days.

4. Toss the beans with the mayonnaise mixture and serve.

Summer Squash Sauté

ingredients

1 pound summer squash (zucchini, yellow crookneck, and baby pattypan)
2 teaspoons extra virgin olive oil
salt to taste
freshly ground black pepper
1 tablespoon fresh lemon juice
1/4 cup basil leaves, thinly sliced

nutrition facts

Serving Size about 1 cup

AMOUNT PER SERVING

Calories **34**
Total Fat **1 g**
Saturated Fat **0 g**
Cholesterol **0 mg**
Sodium **149 mg**
Total Carbohydrate **5 g**
Dietary Fiber **2 g**
Protein **1 g**
Percent Calories from Fat **32%**
Percent Calories from Protein **14%**
Percent Calories from Carbohydrate **54%**

Prep Time: **10 minutes**
Cooking Time: **10 minutes**
Serves **4**

cooking instructions

1. Trim the ends of the squash. Cut zucchini and yellow squash in half lengthwise and then slice into half-moons about 1/8" thick. Cut pattypan squash in half or in quarters.
2. Heat the oil in a large nonstick skillet over medium-high heat.
3. Add the squash and season with a little salt and pepper. Cook, stirring occasionally until the squash is slightly tender and barely golden brown, about 5 to 7 minutes. Remove from the heat and add the lemon juice.
4. Sprinkle with the basil leaves and adjust the seasoning to taste.

Roasted Pepper

ingredients

1 whole red, yellow, or green pepper

Prep Time: **5 minutes**
Cooking Time: **8 minutes**
Makes 1 roasted pepper

cooking instructions

1. Slice the pepper in half lengthwise and remove the seeds.
2. Place the 2 halves on a cookie sheet and press down so they lie flat with the skin side up.
3. Place the pepper under a hot broiler until the skin is evenly blistered, about 5 to 8 minutes.
4. Carefully remove the pepper from the cookie sheet and place in a bowl.
5. Cover tightly with plastic wrap and let sit for 5 minutes.
6. Uncover and peel off the skin.

nutrition facts

Serving Size 1 pepper

AMOUNT PER SERVING

Calories **44**
Total Fat **0 g**
Saturated Fat **0 g**
Cholesterol **0 mg**
Sodium **3 mg**
Total Carbohydrate **11 g**
Dietary Fiber **3 g**
Protein **1 g**
Percent Calories from Fat **6%**
Percent Calories from Protein **11%**
Percent Calories from Carbohydrate **83%**

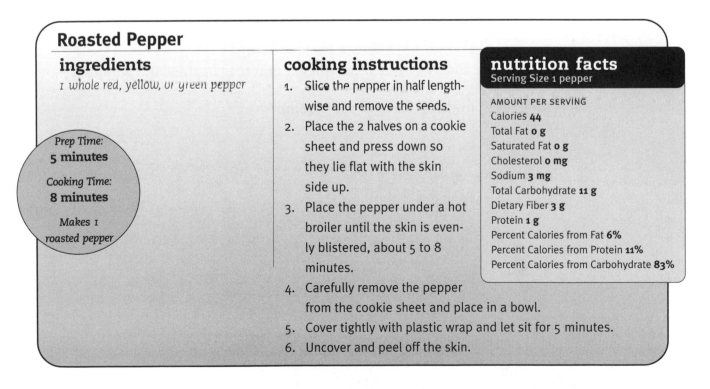

Summer Beans with Cherry Tomatoes and Tarragon

Recipe by FoodFit Chef Annie Somerville, *Greens Restaurant, San Francisco, CA*

ingredients

2 shallots, thinly sliced

2 tablespoons Champagne vinegar or white wine vinegar

salt to taste

1 pound fresh beans (any kind, or a combination of green and yellow types)

3 tablespoons extra virgin olive oil

1 tablespoon fresh, coarsely chopped tarragon

freshly ground black pepper

2 tablespoons sherry vinegar or red wine vinegar

1 cup halved cherry tomatoes

nutrition facts

Serving Size about 1 cup

AMOUNT PER SERVING

Calories **95**

Total Fat **7 g**

Saturated Fat **1 g**

Cholesterol **0 mg**

Sodium **173 mg**

Total Carbohydrate **8 g**

Dietary Fiber **3 g**

Protein **2 g**

Percent Calories from Fat **61%**

Percent Calories from Protein **7%**

Percent Calories from Carbohydrate **32%**

Prep Time: **10 minutes**

Cooking Time: **6 minutes**

Serves **6**

cooking instructions

1. In a medium-size bowl, toss the shallots with the Champagne or white wine vinegar to draw out their pink color.

2. Bring a medium-size pot of salted water to a boil. Drop in the beans and cook until just tender, 1 to 2 minutes for small young beans and up to 6 minutes for larger beans. Drain.

3. Immediately toss the hot beans with the olive oil, shallot and vinegar mixture, tarragon, 1/2 teaspoon salt, and pepper to taste. The beans will soak up the flavors as they cool to room temperature.

4. Just before serving, add the sherry or red wine vinegar and toss in the cherry tomatoes.

5. Adjust the salt and pepper to taste. Serve at room temperature.

Fusilli with Summer Squash, Zucchini, and Sugar Snap Peas

ingredients

1 pound fusilli (corkscrew-shaped pasta) or rotini

1 cup low-sodium chicken broth

1/2 pound summer squash, seeded and julienned

1/2 pound zucchini, seeded and julienned

1/4 pound sugar snap peas

1/2 teaspoon olive oil

1/2 cup freshly grated Parmesan cheese

1/4 cup fresh basil leaves, thinly sliced

salt to taste

freshly ground black pepper

nutrition facts

Serving Size about 1 1/2 cups pasta and vegetables

AMOUNT PER SERVING

Calories **430**

Total Fat **8 g**

Saturated Fat **3 g**

Cholesterol **94 mg**

Sodium **588 mg**

Total Carbohydrate **70 g**

Dietary Fiber **7 g**

Protein **21 g**

Percent Calories from Fat **16%**

Percent Calories from Protein **19%**

Percent Calories from Carbohydrate **65%**

Prep Time: **15 minutes**

Cooking Time: **15 minutes**

Serves **4**

cooking instructions

1. Bring a large pot of salted water to a boil. Add the fusilli and cook until al dente, about 7 to 9 minutes. Drain and set aside.

2. Meanwhile, bring the chicken broth to a boil in a skillet large enough to hold all the vegetables. Add the vegetables to the chicken broth, cover, and steam for about 3 to 4 minutes.

3. When the vegetables are just tender, add the cooked penne and the olive oil and toss until it is heated through.

4. Divide the pasta and vegetables evenly among 4 warmed plates or bowls. Sprinkle with Parmesan cheese and basil.

5. Adjust the salt and pepper to taste. Serve immediately.

Penne with Asparagus and Red Peppers

Recipe by FoodFit Chef Michael Romano, *Union Square Cafe, New York, NY*

ingredients

12 ounces penne pasta (ziti and rigatoni also work well)

4 tablespoons unsalted butter

1 pound asparagus, ends snapped off and stalks cut into 2" pieces

2 roasted yellow bell peppers, peeled and diced (see Roasted Pepper, page 41)

2 roasted red bell peppers, peeled and diced (see Roasted Pepper, page 41)

1 teaspoon minced garlic

1 1/2 cups low-sodium chicken broth

1 1/2 tablespoons minced, fresh thyme

2/3 cup grated Parmesan cheese

salt to taste

freshly ground black pepper

nutrition facts

Serving Size about 1 cup of pasta with vegetables

AMOUNT PER SERVING

Calories **546**
Total Fat **18 g**
Saturated Fat **11 g**
Cholesterol **44 mg**
Sodium **709 mg**
Total Carbohydrate **75 g**
Dietary Fiber **6 g**
Protein **21 g**
Percent Calories from Fat **30%**
Percent Calories from Protein **16%**
Percent Calories from Carbohydrate **54%**

Prep Time: **20 minutes**

Cooking Time: **15 minutes**

Serves **4**

cooking instructions

1. Bring a large pot of salted water to a boil. Add the pasta and cook until just before it becomes al dente. Drain and set aside.

2. Meanwhile, melt 2 tablespoons of butter in a 10" skillet over medium heat. Add the asparagus and cook, stirring occasionally, until tender and lightly browned, about 5 to 7 minutes. Add the peppers and garlic, and cook 1 minute more. Add the broth, bring to a boil, and lower the heat to medium.

3. Add the penne and thyme. Stir to combine the ingredients and simmer until the pasta is warmed through, about 5 to 7 minutes. Stir in half of the cheese and the remaining 2 tablespoons of butter. Adjust the salt and pepper to taste.

4. Transfer to warmed bowls, sprinkle with the remaining cheese, and serve.

Chicken and Asparagus with Creamy Dijon Sauce

ingredients

1 pound asparagus, cut into 2-inch lengths
1 tablespoon olive oil
1 pound chicken cutlets
salt to taste
freshly ground black pepper
1 small onion, finely diced
2 cloves garlic, finely minced
1/2 cup dry white wine
1 cup low-sodium chicken broth
2 tablespoons Dijon mustard
1/2 cup low-fat sour cream
2 tablespoons chopped, fresh tarragon

nutrition facts

Serving Size 4 ounces of chicken with asparagus and sauce

AMOUNT PER SERVING
Calories **273**
Total Fat **8 g**
Saturated Fat **1 g**
Cholesterol **67 mg**
Sodium **569 mg**
Total Carbohydrate **14 g**
Dietary Fiber **3 g**
Protein **32 g**
Percent Calories from Fat **28%**
Percent Calories from Protein **50%**
Percent Calories from Carbohydrate **22%**

Prep Time:
15 minutes
Cooking Time:
15 minutes
Serves **4**

cooking instructions

1. Place the asparagus in a microwave-safe bowl with a splash of water and cover it loosely with plastic wrap. Microwave the asparagus on high until it is just tender, about 2 to 3 minutes. Drain and set aside.

2. Heat the olive oil in a large sauté pan over medium-high heat. Season the chicken cutlets with salt and pepper and add them to the pan in a single layer. Sauté the chicken on both sides until golden brown, about 2 minutes per side. Transfer the chicken to a platter, and cover to keep warm.

3. Lower the heat to medium and add the onion to the sauté pan. Cook until the onion is soft and translucent, about 5 minutes. Add the garlic and cook for 1 minute more.

4. Add the wine to the pan and cook until it is almost completely evaporated. Add the chicken broth and cook until it is reduced by half. Whisk in the mustard, sour cream, and half of the tarragon and stir until the sauce is smooth and creamy.

5. Add the chicken and asparagus to the sauce to heat them for a minute or two longer. Transfer the chicken and asparagus to a platter, sprinkle with the remaining tarragon and serve.

Lamb and Artichoke Stew with Lentils

ingredients

6 to 8 small artichokes
2 tablespoons olive oil
1 cup chopped onions
1 1/2 pounds lean lamb stew meat, cubed
salt to taste
freshly ground black pepper
1 cup red wine
1 bay leaf
1 sprig fresh thyme
1 cup low-sodium beef broth
1 cup canned diced tomatoes
2 cups cooked lentils

nutrition facts
Serving Size about 1 1/2 cups

AMOUNT PER SERVING
Calories **588**
Total Fat **7 g**
Saturated Fat **4 g**
Cholesterol **115 mg**
Sodium **803 mg**
Total Carbohydrate **49 g**
Dietary Fiber **19 g**
Protein **54 g**
Percent Calories from Fat **25%**
Percent Calories from Protein **35%**
Percent Calories from Carbohydrate **32%**

Prep Time: **10 minutes**
Cooking Time: **1 hour**
Serves **4**

cooking instructions

1. Slice about 1/2" from the artichoke tops and trim the stems. Trim any hard, spiky points with scissors.
2. Heat the olive oil over medium heat in a stew pot.
3. Add the onions and cook, stirring occasionally, until they turn translucent, about 5 minutes.
4. Turn the heat to medium-high. Season the lamb well with salt and pepper and add it to the pot. Sear the lamb cubes well on all sides.
5. Add the red wine, bay leaf, and thyme. Turn the heat to low, cover the pot, and cook for 25 minutes.
6. Add the artichokes, broth, and tomatoes. Cover and cook for 10 to 15 minutes.
7. Add the cooked lentils and continue cooking for 15 minutes.

Chapter 6: Tomatoes, Peppers, and Eggplants

RECIPES IN THIS CHAPTER:

- Tomato Bruschetta
- Red Pepper Dip with Pine Nuts
- Tuscan Tomato and Bread Salad
- Sautéed Bell Peppers with Garlic and Basil
- Tomato and Summer Squash Gratin
- Toasted-Rolled Veggie Quesadillas
- Vegetarian Risotto with Three Bell Peppers
- Sautéed Sea Bass with Tomato and Mushroom Ragout

Conquistadors brought tomatoes, native to the lower Andes, to Europe where botanists rightly pegged them as a member of the deadly nightshade family, but wrongly branded them as poisonous. Today, Americans eat more tomatoes than almost any other food except potatoes and lettuce. A tomato is a fruit, not a vegetable, and was named a vegetable only for trade purposes.

With diverse flavors and whimsical names such as Lemon Boy, Golden Jubilee, Brandywine, Purple Cherokee, Sweet One Hundreds, Currant, and, of course, the hefty Beefsteaks, tomatoes are a popular feature at every farmer's market.

Tasty alternatives or complements to tomatoes are peppers and eggplants. In markets, peppers glisten like red, yellow, green, purple, brown, and variegated jewels. Mild-flavored peppers include **wax peppers**, **bell peppers**, **cubanelle peppers**, **pimientos**, and **gypsy peppers**. Similarly, there are many different varieties of **eggplants**, **Japanese** and **Italian** being the most common. Eggplants are available in the market year-round, but the peak season is August and September.

NUTRITION AND HEALTH

Low in calories and virtually fat-free, tomatoes are rich in vitamin C and also offer potassium, fiber, and some B vitamins. Plus, tomatoes are full of lycopene, a potent antioxidant. Tomato sauces, soups, and juices can contain five times more lycopene than raw tomatoes, and it is easier for your body to absorb the lycopene from cooked tomatoes. Lycopene is fat-soluble, so cook your tomatoes with a little fat, like olive oil, to boost absorption.

Similarly, peppers are an excellent source of vitamin C, although green peppers contain less than half the vitamin C found in the orange, red, and yellow varieties. Peppers are also a plentiful source of vitamin B6. Red peppers contain beta-carotene and beta crypotaxanthin, carotenoids thought to be associated with a reduced risk of cancer and heart disease.

Eggplants are not as nutrient dense as other vegetables, but they do offer fiber and potassium. Plus, they are practically calorie-free—a half cup of cooked eggplant has about 19 calories!

WHAT TO LOOK FOR

For the best tomatoes, follow your nose. Tomatoes that smell good will taste good. Look for rich-colored tomatoes that are firm but not rock-hard. Avoid tomatoes with any blemishes, wrinkles, or cuts. Color and shape vary according to variety.

Peppers come in many sweet and hot varieties. The latter are better known as chiles. While sweet peppers are at the market year-round, they are at their peak in the late summer and fall. The color of peppers should be uniform, glossy, and deep. Peppers should be well-shaped and firm and have thick walls with no soft spots.

Pick eggplants that are smooth, firm, and glossy, with a fresh-looking green cap at the stem end. The eggplant should feel heavy for its size. Avoid those that have blemishes or soft spots. Italian eggplants look like the deep purple, oblong variety common in the United States, only smaller. Japanese eggplants can be purple, white, or green, are long and skinny, and have thinner skins.

EASY STORAGE AND PREPARATION

Store your tomatoes in a cool place, preferably not the refrigerator, because the cold saps the flavor and makes them taste mealy. It's best to use ripe tomatoes in a day or two. You can keep a bowl of washed and dried cherry and grape tomatoes on the table in reach for easy, nutritious snacking. If fresh tomatoes are not available, substitute tomato products such as canned whole tomatoes, tomato paste, and sun-dried tomatoes.

Peppers will keep refrigerated for three days or longer. It's best to use eggplant right away. If you have to store an eggplant for a few days, place it in a paper bag, rather than a plastic one, which makes it

ABOUT HERBS AND SPICES

Basil is an herb with a generally sweet flavor and smell. There are many varieties which all taste different. These include purple opal basil, curly leaf basil, and lemon basil. Dried basil does not have the same flavor as fresh. Look for fresh leaves, dried or crushed. Basil is marvelous in Mediterranean-style dishes such as tomato and pesto sauces, soups and salads, or with chicken or fish.

Marjoram is an herb that has a taste similar to oregano but it's slightly milder and sweeter. Look for fresh leaves, whole dried leaves and crumbled dried leaves. Marjoram is a versatile herb that can be used in fish, meat, and poultry dishes. Fresh chopped marjoram can be added to salads. It's very delicate, so add fresh marjoram at the end of cooking.

spoil faster. Store in the refrigerator. After a few days, eggplants become unpleasantly bitter. The skin of an eggplant is edible and a good source of nutrients, but it may be peeled if you prefer.

BEST USES

- Tomatoes are wonderful in salads or pasta dishes, but they also make delectable soups and are a staple in stews.
- Tomatoes taste great with cheese, especially Parmesan, mozzarella, and feta. Basil, chives, tarragon, parsley, and thyme are ideal for tomato dishes.
- Sautéed sweet peppers can be served as a vegetable side dish, a topping for sautéed chicken or cooked fish, or added to a stew for a flavor nuance.
- Larger bell peppers or pimientos can be hollowed out and stuffed, nature's perfect container for seasoned rice, with or without meat.
- Eggplant is one of the few vegetables you can't enjoy raw. However, it makes a great entrée or a delicious addition to a stew.

Tomatoes, peppers, and eggplants are bountiful at the farmer's market during late summer and early fall. You can also try your hand at growing tomatoes and peppers, as they tend to flourish in home gardens. Show off your harvest of vitamin-packed veggies with these flavorful recipes for ragout, risotto, and more.

Tomato Bruschetta

ingredients

1/4 cup seeded and diced tomatoes
1 teaspoon fresh, chopped basil
salt to taste
freshly ground black pepper
2 tablespoons extra virgin olive oil
12 French bread slices
2 cloves garlic

nutrition facts

Serving Size about 1 slice of bruschetta

AMOUNT PER SERVING
Calories **79**
Total Fat **3 g**
Saturated Fat **0 g**
Cholesterol **0 mg**
Sodium **169 mg**
Total Carbohydrate **11 g**
Dietary Fiber **0 g**
Protein **2 g**
Percent Calories from Fat **31%**
Percent Calories from Protein **12%**
Percent Calories from Carbohydrate **57%**

Prep Time: **10 minutes**
Cooking Time: **5 minutes**
Serves 12

cooking instructions

1. In a mixing bowl, combine the tomatoes, basil, salt, pepper, and 1 tablespoon olive oil and set aside.

2. Toast the bread on both sides in a toaster oven, under the broiler, or on the grill.

3. While the toasted slices are still warm, rub them with garlic and drizzle them with the remaining olive oil on one side.

4. Put a dollop of the tomato mixture on each slice of bruschetta and serve.

Roasted Plum Tomatoes

ingredients

8 Roma tomatoes (plum tomatoes), cored
1 tablespoon olive oil
salt to taste
freshly ground black pepper
1 clove garlic, minced (optional)

cooking instructions

1. Preheat the oven to 400°F.
2. In a large mixing bowl, gently toss the whole tomatoes with the olive oil, salt, pepper, and garlic (if desired).
3. Spread out the tomatoes in a shallow baking dish in a single layer.
4. Roast the tomatoes for 30 to 40 minutes, or to desired doneness. Use a spatula to remove the tomatoes from the baking dish and serve warm or at room temperature.

nutrition facts

Serving Size about 2 tomatoes

AMOUNT PER SERVING
Calories **104**
Total Fat **5 g**
Saturated Fat **1 g**
Cholesterol **0 mg**
Sodium **112 mg**
Total Carbohydrate **16 g**
Dietary Fiber **4 g**
Protein **3 g**
Percent Calories from Fat **34%**
Percent Calories from Protein **10%**
Percent Calories from Carbohydrate **55%**

Prep Time: **5 minutes**
Cooking Time: **40 minutes**
Serves **5**

Red Pepper Dip with Pine Nuts

ingredients

2 cups plain low-fat yogurt
1 teaspoon olive oil
1 cup minced onion
1 clove garlic, minced
1 12-ounce jar roasted red peppers, drained, or 5 red Roasted Peppers (see page 41)
1/4 cup toasted pine nuts
salt to taste
freshly ground black pepper

nutrition facts

Serving Size about 3 tablespoons

AMOUNT PER SERVING
Calories **100**
Total Fat **3 g**
Saturated Fat **1 g**
Cholesterol **5 mg**
Sodium **252 mg**
Total Carbohydrate **12 g**
Dietary Fiber **1 g**
Protein **5 g**
Percent Calories from Fat **32%**
Percent Calories from Protein **19%**
Percent Calories from Carbohydrate **48%**

Prep Time:
10 minutes
Plus Draining Time

Cooking Time:
5 minutes

Serves **8**

cooking instructions

1. Place a strainer over a deep bowl. Add the yogurt to the strainer, cover, and refrigerate overnight. The yogurt will drain and thicken overnight. Discard the liquid. (This can be done in advance and stored for up to 1 week in the refrigerator.)

2. Heat the oil in a skillet over medium heat, add the onion, and cook until translucent, about 3 minutes. Add the garlic and cook 1 minute more.

3. In a food processor, puree the onion mixture with the red peppers and all but 1 tablespoon of the pine nuts. Stir the red pepper mixture into the strained yogurt. Season to taste with salt and pepper. Chill for at least one hour. (This can be made in advance and stored in the refrigerator for up to 3 days.)

4. Garnish with the remaining pine nuts. Serve with fresh vegetables and pita wedges.

Tuscan Tomato and Bread Salad

ingredients

2 large heirloom tomatoes, cored and cut into 1", bite-size pieces

1 small, 2-day-old baguette, cut into 1", bite-size pieces

3 tablespoons chopped fresh basil leaves

1 tablespoon balsamic vinegar

salt to taste

freshly ground black pepper

1 teaspoon finest-quality extra virgin olive oil

nutrition facts
Serving Size about 1 cup

AMOUNT PER SERVING

Calories **62**
Total Fat **2 g**
Saturated Fat **0 g**
Cholesterol **0 mg**
Sodium **58 mg**
Total Carbohydrate **10 g**
Dietary Fiber **1 g**
Protein **1 g**
Percent Calories from Fat **31%**
Percent Calories from Protein **8%**
Percent Calories from Carbohydrate **61%**

Prep Time: **10 minutes**

Serves **4**

instructions

1. In a large bowl, gently mix the tomatoes, baguette, basil, balsamic vinegar, salt, and pepper together. Cover and let stand for 15 minutes at room temperature.
2. Before serving, toss the salad once more and drizzle the olive oil over it.

Quick Tomato Sauce

ingredients

1 16-ounce can Italian plum tomatoes

2 cloves garlic

1 tablespoon dried oregano

1/2 cup fresh basil leaves

coarse salt

freshly ground black pepper

1 tablespoon extra virgin olive oil

cooking instructions

1. Combine all the ingredients in a blender or a food processor and puree. Taste and adjust with salt and pepper.

nutrition facts
Serving Size about 1/3 cup

AMOUNT PER SERVING

Calories **40**
Total Fat **3 g**
Saturated Fat **1 g**
Cholesterol **0 mg**
Sodium **105 mg**
Total Carbohydrate **4 g**
Dietary Fiber **1 g**
Protein **1 g**
Percent Calories from Fat **52%**
Percent Calories from Protein **9%**
Percent Calories from Carbohydrate **39%**

Prep Time: **5 minutes**

Serves **6**

Recipe by FoodFit Chefs Mary Sue Milliken and Susan Feniger, Border Grill, Santa Monica, CA

Sautéed Bell Peppers with Garlic and Basil

ingredients

1 tablespoon olive oil

1 teaspoon crushed garlic

3 large bell peppers (1 green, 1 red, and 1 yellow), seeds removed and sliced into thin strips

salt to taste

freshly ground black pepper

2 tablespoons freshly chopped basil

nutrition facts

Serving Size about 1 cup

AMOUNT PER SERVING

Calories **63**
Total Fat **4 g**
Saturated Fat **0 g**
Cholesterol **0 mg**
Sodium **84 mg**
Total Carbohydrate **8 g**
Dietary Fiber **2 g**
Protein **1 g**
Percent Calories from Fat **48%**
Percent Calories from Protein **7%**
Percent Calories from Carbohydrate **46%**

Prep Time: **5 minutes**

Cooking Time: **5 minutes**

Serves **4**

cooking instructions

1. Heat the olive oil in a 10" skillet over medium-low heat.
2. Add the garlic and cook for 1 minute.
3. Add the bell pepper strips, salt, pepper, and basil and sauté with the olive oil and garlic until the peppers become tender, about 4 to 5 minutes. Remove from the skillet and serve.

Tomato Vinaigrette

ingredients

1 16-ounce can diced tomatoes

3 tablespoons balsamic vinegar

1 teaspoon Dijon mustard

juice of 1 lemon

3 tablespoons chopped, fresh basil or dill

1 1/2 tablespoons extra virgin olive oil

salt to taste

freshly ground black pepper

cooking instructions

1. Place the tomatoes, vinegar, and salt in a saucepan. Bring to a boil and reduce the mixture to a thick consistency, cooking for about 5 minutes. Remove from the heat, place the mixture in a stainless steel or Pyrex bowl, and cool over ice.
2. Mix the mustard and lemon juice in a food processor. With the machine running, add the basil or dill and olive oil. Add the cooled tomato mixture and puree until smooth. Season with salt and pepper.
3. The vinaigrette can be stored in the refrigerator for 1 week.

nutrition facts

Serving Size about 2 tablespoons

AMOUNT PER SERVING

Calories **27**
Total Fat **2 g**
Saturated Fat **0 g**
Cholesterol **0 mg**
Sodium **153 mg**
Total Carbohydrate **3 g**
Dietary Fiber **1 g**
Protein **1 g**
Percent Calories from Fat **47%**
Percent Calories from Protein **7%**
Percent Calories from Carbohydrate **46%**

Prep Time: **5 minutes**

Cooking Time: **5 minutes**

Makes **1 cup**

Tomato and Summer Squash Gratin

ingredients

2 medium summer squash, cut in half lengthwise and sliced
1/4 cup chopped fresh oregano or parsley
salt to taste
freshly ground black pepper
2 large ripe tomatoes, cored and sliced
1/2 cup plain bread crumbs
1/4 cup freshly grated Parmesan cheese
2 cloves minced garlic
2 teaspoons olive oil

nutrition facts
Serving Size about 1/2 cup

AMOUNT PER SERVING
Calories **105**
Total Fat **4 g**
Saturated Fat **1 g**
Cholesterol **3 mg**
Sodium **160 mg**
Total Carbohydrate **15 g**
Dietary Fiber **3 g**
Protein **5 g**
Percent Calories from Fat **31%**
Percent Calories from Protein **18%**
Percent Calories from Carbohydrate **52%**

Prep Time: **10 minutes**
Cooking Time: **45 minutes**
Serves **6**

cooking instructions

1. Preheat the oven to 375°F.

2. In a large mixing bowl, toss the summer squash with half of the oregano or parsley and season generously with salt and pepper. Transfer the seasoned squash to a large baking dish and cover with the sliced tomatoes.

3. In a small bowl, combine the bread crumbs, the remaining oregano, Parmesan cheese, garlic, salt and pepper. Sprinkle the bread crumb mixture over the tomatoes and drizzle with olive oil. (This can be prepared in advance and stored in the refrigerator for up to 1 day.)

4. Bake until golden brown and bubbly around the edges of the dish, about 45 minutes. Let stand for 5 minutes before serving.

Toasted-Rolled Veggie Quesadillas

Recipe by FoodFit Chef Jody Adams, Rialto, Boston, MA

ingredients

2 tablespoons olive oil

2 green peppers, seeds removed and thinly sliced

4 scallions, thinly sliced

salt to taste

freshly ground black pepper

1 cup grated Monterey Jack cheese

1 cup cooked corn kernels

2 tablespoons freshly squeezed lime juice

6 whole-wheat flour tortillas

1/4 cup (or more to taste) prepared salsa, drained of excess liquid

nutrition facts

Serving Size about 1 quesadilla

AMOUNT PER SERVING

Calories **302**

Total Fat **13 g**

Saturated Fat **4 g**

Cholesterol **17 mg**

Sodium **644 mg**

Total Carbohydrate **37 g**

Dietary Fiber **1 g**

Protein **10 g**

Percent Calories from Fat **39%**

Percent Calories from Protein **13%**

Percent Calories from Carbohydrate **48%**

Prep Time: **5 minutes**

Cooking Time: **15 minutes**

Makes **6** *quesadillas*

cooking instructions

1. Preheat the oven to 350°F.

2. Heat the oil in a large sauté pan over medium-high heat. Add the peppers and scallions and season with salt and pepper. Cook until tender, about 5 minutes. Remove from heat and cool.

3. Stir together the pepper and scallion mixture with the remaining ingredients, except the tortillas and salsa. Taste and season with salt and pepper, if necessary.

4. Lay the tortillas out on a counter. Spread 1/6 of the vegetable mixture down the middle of each of the tortillas leaving a 2-inch border at the bottom edge. Spread a spoonful of salsa on top. Roll up the tortillas halfway, fold in the ends, and then continue rolling until they form a thick cylinder.

5. Set the quesadillas, seam side down on a baking sheet. Bake 5 minutes, flip the quesadillas, and cook an additional 5 to 10 minutes or until the cheese has melted. Serve warm or at room temperature.

Vegetarian Risotto with Three Bell Peppers

ingredients

4 cups low-sodium vegetable broth
1 tablespoon olive oil
1/2 cup diced onions
1 cup diced, mixed yellow, green, and red bell peppers
1 1/2 cups Arborio rice
1/2 cup freshly grated Parmesan cheese
salt to taste
freshly ground black pepper

nutrition facts
Serving Size about 1/2 cup

AMOUNT PER SERVING
Calories **300**
Total Fat **6 g**
Saturated Fat **2 g**
Cholesterol **9 mg**
Sodium **384 mg**
Total Carbohydrate **49 g**
Dietary Fiber **2 g**
Protein **10 g**
Percent Calories from Fat **18%**
Percent Calories from Protein **14%**
Percent Calories from Carbohydrate **68%**

Prep Time: **10 minutes**
Cooking Time: **40 minutes**
Serves **6**

cooking instructions

1. Heat the broth in a saucepan and keep hot over low heat.

2. Heat the olive oil over medium heat in a separate medium-size pot. Add the onions and peppers and cook for 2 to 3 minutes, until the onions turn translucent.

3. Add the rice to the onion mixture and stir.

4. Turn the heat to low, add about 1 cup of the hot broth to the rice mixture, and stir slowly until the broth is absorbed.

5. Continue to add the broth 1 cup at a time, stirring slowly, letting the rice absorb the broth before adding more.

6. The risotto is fully cooked when it is creamy on the outside and slightly firm (al dente) in the center, about 20 to 25 minutes in all. Stir in the Parmesan cheese. Season with salt and pepper to taste. If the risotto is too thick, add a little more broth until it becomes creamy.

Sautéed Sea Bass with Tomato and Mushroom Ragout

ingredients

FOR THE RAGOUT:

1 tablespoon olive oil

1 tablespoon chopped shallots

1 cup sliced white (or button) mushrooms

4 plum tomatoes, quartered

1 sprig tarragon, or 1/4 teaspoon dried tarragon

salt to taste

freshly ground black pepper

FOR THE SAUTÉED SEA BASS:

4 black or striped sea bass fillets, 4 to 5 ounces each

salt to taste

freshly ground black pepper

1 tablespoon canola oil

nutrition facts

Serving Size about 1 fillet with 2 tablespoons of ragout

AMOUNT PER SERVING

Calories **206**

Total Fat **10 g**

Saturated Fat **1 g**

Cholesterol **46 mg**

Sodium **394 mg**

Total Carbohydrate **8 g**

Dietary Fiber **2 g**

Protein **23 g**

Percent Calories from Fat **42%**

Percent Calories from Protein **44%**

Percent Calories from Carbohydrate **15%**

Prep Time: **15 minutes**

Cooking Time: **20 minutes**

Serves **4**

cooking instructions

For the ragout:

1. Heat the oil in a skillet over medium heat. Add the shallots and cook until they begin to soften, about 2 minutes.

2. Turn the heat to medium-high, add the mushrooms, and sauté 2 minutes more.

3. Add the tomatoes, tarragon, salt, and pepper. Heat thoroughly.

4. Adjust the salt and pepper to taste. (This can be made ahead and kept in the refrigerator for up to 2 days.)

For the sautéed sea bass:

1. Generously season the fillets with salt and pepper.

2. Heat the oil over medium-high heat in a pan large enough to accommodate all the fillets.

3. Sear the fillets for 3 to 4 minutes on each side, turning only once. (Thin fillets will take less time, thicker fillets take more.)

4. Serve the fish with 2 tablespoons of ragout spooned over the fish.

Chapter 7: Garlic, Onions, and Mushrooms

For centuries, people have been using garlic to treat everything from dog bites to the common cold. Once it was even thought to ward off vampires. Today, this much-loved vegetable seasons cuisines around the globe. The three most common types found in the market are hearty **American garlic**, **Mexican garlic**, and **Italian garlic**.

The ancient Greeks, Egyptians, and Romans thought garlic made them stronger. The Egyptian slaves laboring to build the great pyramids were fed garlic, and the Romans shipped it to the far reaches of their empire. Later, garlic was a popular antidote against the plague sweeping Europe, which many believed was caused by supernatural forces.

Another pantry staple is the onion. Onions come in many more varieties than garlic—from the common **yellow**, **red**, and **white onions** to more exotic varieties such as sweet **Vidalia, Bermuda**, and **Walla Walla**. Other popular foods are **mushrooms** (including **chanterelles**, **porcini**, **portobello**, **button**, and **shiitake,** among other varieties), **shallots**, **leeks**, and **scallions**. Like garlic, these foods often play a supporting role in recipes, enhancing the flavor of the main ingredients. However, they can all be stars in their own right, both because of their unique flavors and their healthful properties.

RECIPES IN THIS CHAPTER:

- Roasted Garlic and Soybean Hummus
- Red, Yellow, and Green Bell Pepper Salad with Roasted Garlic Vinaigrette
- Roasted Sugar Snap Peas with Shallots
- Grilled Vegetables
- Garlicky White Beans with Spinach and Red Onion
- Roasted Garlic and Scallion Mashed Potatoes
- White Pizza with Tomatoes, Onions, and Garlic
- Gambas Al Ajillo (Garlic Shrimp)
- Lemon, Rosemary, and Garlic Chicken
- Lamb Chops with Onion Relish and Tomato Vinaigrette

NUTRITION AND HEALTH

Rich in phytochemicals linked to lowering cholesterol, garlic is a wholesome low-fat, high-flavor cook's friend. Other members of the allium family, like onions and scallions, are also brimming with health-promoting phytochemicals.

You can turn to onions and scallions to increase your supply of vitamin C. Choose shallots for vitamin B6, and eat mushrooms for vitamins B2 and B3, as well as fiber.

WHAT TO LOOK FOR

To select garlic and onions that are fresh, pick bulbs that are plump and firm and have dry, papery skin. Avoid brown spots or green sprouts, which indicate aging.

Mexican and Italian garlic have a pinkish skin and a milder flavor than American garlic. Gigantic **elephant garlic**, which is actually a type of leek, has a milder flavor still.

Look for mushrooms that are dry and firm with a sweet earthy smell. If the caps are open, the gills should look fresh; they shouldn't be matted down. White button mushrooms should be rounded and plump and have closed caps. Chanterelles resemble a curving trumpet, and should be golden or orange-brown. Portobellos can be up to six inches wide, with open gills and large, flat caps. Shiitakes are umbrella-shaped and dark-colored.

Garlic, onions, and mushrooms are available year-round.

EASY STORAGE AND PREPARATION

Keep your garlic and onions in a cool, dry place. Uncut onions and whole garlic bulbs will last for up to two months. Once individual garlic cloves have been broken from the bulb, they are good for up to ten days. Preparing these vegetables is easy: Just peel the papery skin and cut or slice.

To store mushrooms, place them in a closed paper bag (or in a cardboard container) in the refrigerator. They should be eaten within a few days. If kept too long, they will turn slimy. To clean, wipe with a damp cloth. Do not soak in water to clean.

To use dried mushrooms, soak them in lukewarm water for at least 15 minutes to soften. Then rinse well, and remove the hard stems.

BEST USES

- Slicing, crushing, or pureeing garlic releases more of its essential oils and therefore produces a more robust flavor. You can keep a lid on garlic's intensity by using whole cloves. Be careful not to brown or burn garlic; it will result in a bitter flavor. Roasting garlic brings out its sweetness and mellows the flavor.

- Garlic is so pungent you can flavor a salad by merely rubbing the bowl with a raw clove just before you add the greens. The same essential oils that provide the garnish leave the telltale smell on a garlic eater's breath. Some say chewing on parsley will help beat the reek.
- You can use raw sweet onions in salads, while other varieties taste better cooked. A simple way to cook onions is to peel, chop, and sauté them in a small amount of olive oil for a few minutes for a delicious side dish. Peeled pearl onions can be boiled whole in salted water for 6 to 10 minutes.
- Mushrooms can act as the main ingredient or remain in the background; it's really up to you. Grilled portobellos make a great vegetarian alternative at a backyard barbecue and mushroom soup is hearty on a winter's day. Mushrooms add an earthy flavor to stews, and round out any pasta dish.

Garlic, onions, and mushrooms all come in different sizes and varieties, and they all add gusto to a vast array of foods. They complement meats, fish, and other vegetables well and can be used in every season. Try this selection of diverse, flavorful side dishes and main courses.

ABOUT HERBS AND SPICES

Oregano is a wild variety of the herb marjoram that has a stronger, more pungent taste. Look for fresh leaves and crumbled dried leaves. Oregano is a basic herb in Italian, Greek, and Mexican cooking. It's marvelous in tomato sauces and meat, poultry, and seafood dishes as well as eggplant and bean dishes. Oregano is also good in oil-and-vinegar salad dressings.

Paprika is a spice made by grinding sweet red pepper pods. The pungent flavor can be mild or hot. Spanish paprika is hot, although it's not labeled as such. Look for ground powder. Paprika adds a lively touch to potato and egg salads, fish, shellfish, and poultry. It's also a basic spice in Hungarian goulash and paprikash.

Roasted Garlic and Soybean Hummus

ingredients

1 1/2 cups dried or fresh soybeans
2 cloves garlic, peeled
1 tablespoon olive oil, plus extra
1 tablespoon roasted sesame tahini
1 tablespoon lemon juice
1/2 cup fresh parsley
salt to taste
1 to 2 tablespoons water or vegetable broth

nutrition facts
Serving Size about 2 tablespoons
AMOUNT PER SERVING
Calories **124**
Total Fat **7 g**
Saturated Fat **1 g**
Cholesterol **0 mg**
Sodium **54 mg**
Total Carbohydrate **8 g**
Dietary Fiber **3 g**
Protein **9 g**
Percent Calories from Fat **50%**
Percent Calories from Protein **27%**
Percent Calories from Carbohydrate **24%**

Prep Time: **10 minutes**
Cooking Time: **3 minutes** Plus Time to Prepare Beans
Serves 12

cooking instructions

1. If using dried soybeans, cover with fresh water, soak them in a large pot of water in the refrigerator overnight. Drain and simmer 2 1/2 to 3 hours, or until very tender. Drain. If using fresh soybeans, steam them for 20 minutes.

2. Preheat the broiler. Place the garlic cloves in an ovenproof dish, drizzle with olive oil, and roast for 5 to 10 minutes, or until they just begin to brown and can be pierced easily with a fork. Remove from broiler and let cool.

3. In a food processor, combine the garlic with the cooked soybeans, tahini, lemon juice, parsley, and 1 tablespoon of olive oil. Blend until smooth, adding salt to taste and water or broth until the desired consistency is reached. It can be made thick to spread on bread or crackers, or thin for use as a dip for veggies or chips.

Red, Yellow, and Green Bell Pepper Salad with Roasted Garlic Vinaigrette

ingredients

FOR THE ROASTED GARLIC VINAIGRETTE

1 bulb garlic
splash of olive oil
2 tablespoons Dijon mustard
2 tablespoons red wine vinegar
salt to taste
freshly ground black pepper
2 tablespoons extra virgin olive oil
4 tablespoons chicken stock
1 tablespoon finely chopped shallots
1 teaspoon freshly chopped basil

FOR THE SALAD

2 large red bell peppers, stems, seeds, removed and cut into 1/2" squares
2 large yellow bell peppers, stems and seeds removed and cut into 1/2" squares
2 large green bell peppers, stems and seeds removed and cut into 1/2" squares

nutrition facts

Serving Size about 3/4 cup of salad with vinaigrette

AMOUNT PER SERVING
Calories **217**
Total Fat **6 g**
Saturated Fat **1 g**
Cholesterol **0 mg**
Sodium **184 mg**
Total Carbohydrate **40 g**
Dietary Fiber **7 g**
Protein **7 g**
Percent Calories from Fat **22%**
Percent Calories from Protein **14%**
Percent Calories from Carbohydrate **67%**

Prep Time:
10 minutes
Cooking Time:
30 minutes
Serves **2**

cooking instructions

For the vinaigrette:

1. Preheat the oven to 350°F.

2. Slice off the top of the garlic bulb, just enough to barely expose the garlic inside each clove. Place the bulb in an ovenproof dish and drizzle with olive oil. Place the dish, uncovered, in the oven and cook the garlic until it is golden brown and soft, about 15 to 20 minutes. Let cool.

3. When the roasted garlic is cool enough to handle, squeeze the pulp from 6 of the cloves and mash with a mortar and pestle, or with a fork. (Store the remaining cloves in the refrigerator for up to 1 week.)

4. Put the garlic in a food processor and add the mustard, vinegar, salt, and pepper. Puree this mixture.

5. Slowly add the olive oil and stock through the feed tube, and continue to puree until the vinaigrette is creamy. If it is too thick, add a teaspoon of stock until the consistency is correct.

6. Add the shallots and basil. Adjust the salt and pepper to taste. (The vinaigrette can be made in advance and stored in the refrigerator for up to 5 days.)

For the salad:

1. Toss the peppers with the vinaigrette.

Roasted Sugar Snap Peas with Shallots

ingredients

2 pounds sugar snap peas, ends trimmed
1 tablespoon olive oil
salt to taste
1 tablespoon finely chopped shallots

Prep Time: **5 minutes**
Cooking Time: **10 minutes**
Serves **6**

cooking instructions

1. Preheat the oven to 450°F.
2. Spread the sugar snap peas out on a baking sheet. Brush them with olive oil and sprinkle with salt and shallots.
3. Roast the sugar snap peas on the top rack of the oven until they begin to get tender on the outside, about 5 minutes.
4. Remove from heat and serve immediately.

nutrition facts

Serving Size about 1/3 pound

AMOUNT PER SERVING
Calories **88**
Total Fat **3 g**
Saturated Fat **0 g**
Cholesterol **0 mg**
Sodium **94 mg**
Total Carbohydrate **13 g**
Dietary Fiber **4 g**
Protein **4 g**
Percent Calories from Fat **26%**
Percent Calories from Protein **17%**
Percent Calories from Carbohydrate **56%**

Grilled Vegetables

ingredients

1 eggplant, sliced 1/3" thick

1 summer squash, sliced 1/3" thick

1 green or red pepper, stem and seeds removed, and quartered

1 onion, sliced 1/3" thick

4 large whole mushrooms

1/2 cup Roasted Garlic Vinaigrette (page 62) or low-fat salad dressing

salt to taste

freshly ground black pepper

nutrition facts

Serving Size about 8 pieces of grilled vegetables

AMOUNT PER SERVING

Calories **124**

Total Fat **3 g**

Saturated Fat **0 g**

Cholesterol **0 mg**

Sodium **187 mg**

Total Carbohydrate **23 g**

Dietary Fiber **6 g**

Protein **4 g**

Percent Calories from Fat **19%**

Percent Calories from Protein **13%**

Percent Calories from Carbohydrate **68%**

Prep Time: **15 minutes**

Cooking Time: **5 minutes**

Serves **4**

cooking instructions

1. Preheat the grill.

2. Brush the vegetables on all sides with the Roasted Garlic Vinagrette.

3. Grill the vegetables on a hot grill for 2 minutes on each side. To keep the onions together, slide a spatula completely underneath to pick up all the rings. Turn the vegetables carefully. Season to taste with salt and pepper.

4. Serve hot or at room temperature.

Garlicky White Beans with Spinach and Red Onion

ingredients

2 tablespoons olive oil
1 red onion, peeled, halved, and sliced
salt to taste
freshly ground black pepper
2 cloves garlic, minced
2 15-ounce cans white beans (cannellini beans), rinsed and drained
2 bunches spinach (about 1 pound), washed
2 tablespoons balsamic vinegar

nutrition facts
Serving Size about 1 1/2 cups

AMOUNT PER SERVING
Calories **354**
Total Fat **8 g**
Saturated Fat **1 g**
Cholesterol **0 mg**
Sodium **250 mg**
Total Carbohydrate **55 g**
Dietary Fiber **12 g**
Protein **19 g**
Percent Calories from Fat **19%**
Percent Calories from Protein **21%**
Percent Calories from Carbohydrate **60%**

Prep Time: **10 minutes**
Cooking Time: **20 minutes**
Serves **4**

cooking instructions

1. Heat the olive oil in a large skillet over medium heat. Add the red onion, season lightly with salt and pepper, and cook for 2 minutes. Add the garlic and continue cooking until the onion softens, about 5 minutes. Turn up the heat and cook until the onion turns light brown on the edges.
2. Lower the heat to medium, add the white beans, and cook until the beans are thoroughly heated, about 5 minutes.
3. Add the spinach and balsamic vinegar. Continue cooking until the spinach is just wilted. Adjust the seasonings and serve.

Roasted Garlic and Scallion Mashed Potatoes

ingredients

6 cloves garlic, unpeeled
splash of olive oil
3 large potatoes (Idaho or russet)
2/3 cups low-sodium chicken broth
salt to taste
freshly ground black pepper
4 teaspoons freshly chopped scallions

nutrition facts
Serving Size about 1/2 cup

AMOUNT PER SERVING
Calories **86**
Total Fat **2 g**
Saturated Fat **0 g**
Cholesterol **1 mg**
Sodium **88 mg**
Total Carbohydrate **18 g**
Dietary Fiber **2 g**
Protein **3 g**
Percent Calories from Fat **16%**
Percent Calories from Protein **13%**
Percent Calories from Carbohydrate **71%**

Prep Time: **10 minutes**
Cooking Time: **30 minutes**
Serves **4**

cooking instructions

1. Preheat the oven to 350°F.

2. Place the garlic cloves in an ovenproof dish and drizzle with olive oil. Place the dish, uncovered, in the oven for 15 to 20 minutes until the garlic is golden brown and soft.

3. Remove from the oven and let cool.

4. Peel the potatoes and cut them in half. Place them in a pot and cover with cold water. Bring to a boil over high heat and simmer until the potatoes are tender when pricked with a fork, about 30 minutes depending on the size of the potatoes. Drain.

5. Bring the broth to a boil, and turn down to a simmer.

6. Squeeze the roasted garlic cloves to release each clove of garlic from its skin. Mash the garlic with a fork and throw the skins away.

7. Mash the potatoes with a potato masher or fork, or use a food mill. Add the roasted garlic. Slowly add the broth until the desired consistency is reached.

8. Adjust the salt and pepper to taste. Fold in the scallions.

Roasted Shallot Vinaigrette

ingredients

2 shallots
2 tablespoons extra virgin olive oil
1/2 teaspoon kosher salt
2 tablespoons Dijon mustard
2 tablespoons white wine vinegar
2 tablespoons red wine vinegar
4 tablespoons low-sodium chicken broth
1 tablespoon chopped chives
freshly ground black pepper

Prep Time:
10 minutes

Cooking Time:
30 minutes

Serves 8

cooking instructions

1. Preheat the oven to 350°F.
2. With the skin on, cut the shallots in half lengthwise. Spray a baking sheet with cooking spray. Drizzle the shallots with a bit of the olive oil and place them on the baking sheet cut side down.
3. Roast in the oven until the shallots are very soft, about 20 to 30 minutes. Remove from oven and let cool.
4. When the shallots are cool enough to handle, remove the skin and the root end. Puree the shallots and salt in a food processor.
5. Add the mustard and continue to puree. Add the vinegars by the tablespoon, pureeing after each addition.
6. With the motor running, add the olive oil and broth slowly through the feed tube.
7. Stir in the chives and pepper. Adjust the salt and pepper to taste.

nutrition facts

Serving Size about 2 tablespoons

AMOUNT PER SERVING
Calories **43**
Total Fat **4 g**
Saturated Fat **1 g**
Cholesterol **0 mg**
Sodium **217 mg**
Total Carbohydrate **2 g**
Dietary Fiber **0 g**
Protein **1 g**
Percent Calories from Fat **81%**
Percent Calories from Protein **5%**
Percent Calories from Carbohydrate **14%**

White Pizza with Tomatoes, Onions, and Garlic

ingredients

FOR THE PIZZA DOUGH:

3/4 cup warm water
1 tablespoon milk
4 teaspoons active dry yeast
2 cups all-purpose flour
1 teaspoon salt
1/2 teaspoon olive oil, plus extra

FOR THE TOPPING:

4 cloves garlic, chopped
2 tablespoons olive oil
1 cup fresh diced tomatoes, or use drained, canned tomatoes
4 ounces shredded mozzarella cheese
1 small yellow onion, sliced thinly into rings
1 teaspoon dried oregano
salt to taste
freshly ground black pepper
Roasted Garlic Vinaigrette (optional; see page 62)

nutrition facts
Serving Size about 2 slices

AMOUNT PER SERVING
Calories **409**
Total Fat **13 g**
Saturated Fat **4 g**
Cholesterol **16 mg**
Sodium **747 mg**
Total Carbohydrate **55 g**
Dietary Fiber **4 g**
Protein **17 g**
Percent Calories from Fat **29%**
Percent Calories from Protein **16%**
Percent Calories from Carbohydrate **54%**

Prep Time: **30 minutes**
Cooking Time: **15 minutes**
Serves **4**

cooking instructions

For the pizza dough:

1. Mix the water, milk, and yeast together in a large bowl and stir with a wooden spoon.

2. Add the flour, salt, and 1/2 teaspoon of olive oil. Mix together with a wooden spoon until the dough is too thick and sticky to stir.

3. Spread a little flour on a work surface and place the dough on top of the flour. Knead the dough by pulling the dough from the sides and folding it in the middle. Keep kneading until the dough becomes a smooth ball. If it sticks to the table or to your hands, add a little more flour.

4. Rub a clean bowl with the extra olive oil and put the dough in it. Cover the bowl with a towel and put it in a warm place. Let the dough rise for about 1 1/2 hours, or until doubled in volume.

5. Punch the raised dough down with your fist. Turn the dough over, form it into a ball again, cover, and let rise for another hour.

6. Preheat the oven to 450°F.

7. Roll out the dough with a rolling pin or use your hands to pat the dough into a circle about 12" to 14" across and 1/4"-thick. Place the dough on an oiled baking sheet.

White Pizza with Tomatoes, Onions, and Garlic (cont.)

For the topping:

1. Spread the garlic and olive oil over the rolled dough, then arrange the tomatoes on top. Sprinkle the mozzarella cheese, leaving the edge of the pizza free. Place the onions on top of the cheese. If desired, drizzle a little Roasted Garlic Vinaigrette on top of the pizza for added flavor.

2. Bake until nicely browned and crispy, about 15 minutes. Season with salt and pepper. Cut the pizza into 8 slices.

Gambas Al Ajillo (Garlic Shrimp)

Recipe by FoodFit Chef Joyce Goldstein, *cookbook author*

ingredients

2 tablespoons olive oil

4 large cloves garlic, finely minced

1 teaspoon hot pepper flakes

1 pound medium shrimp, peeled and deveined

2 tablespoons fresh lemon juice

2 tablespoons dry sherry

1 teaspoon paprika

salt and freshly ground black pepper

1 tablespoon chopped parsley

nutrition facts

Serving Size about 1/6 pound of shrimp

AMOUNT PER SERVING

Calories **106**

Total Fat **5 g**

Saturated Fat **0 g**

Cholesterol **107 mg**

Sodium **251 mg**

Total Carbohydrate **1 g**

Dietary Fiber **0 g**

Protein **12 g**

Percent Calories from Fat **44%**

Percent Calories from Protein **44%**

Percent Calories from Carbohydrate **7%**

Prep Time: **5 minutes**

Cooking Time: **5 minutes**

Serves **4 to 6**

cooking instructions

1. Heat the olive oil in a sauté pan over moderate heat. Add the garlic and hot pepper flakes and cook 1 minute.

2. Increase the heat to high. Add the shrimp, lemon juice, dry sherry, and paprika, stir well and sauté quickly, about 3 minutes. Sprinkle with salt, pepper, and parsley, and serve at once.

Lemon, Rosemary, and Garlic Roast Chicken

ingredients

1 whole chicken, about 5 pounds
salt to taste
freshly ground black pepper
2 lemons, one thinly sliced and one halved
2 medium onions, peeled and halved
8 cloves garlic, peeled
4 sprigs fresh rosemary
1 tablespoon butter, optional
1 teaspoon olive oil

nutrition facts

Serving Size about 1/4 chicken

AMOUNT PER SERVING
Calories **350**
Total Fat **11 g**
Saturated Fat **3 g**
Cholesterol **155 mg**
Sodium **179 mg**
Total Carbohydrate **17 g**
Dietary Fiber **4 g**
Protein **48 g**
Percent Calories from Fat **28%**
Percent Calories from Protein **53%**
Percent Calories from Carbohydrate **19%**

Prep Time:
15 minutes
Cooking Time:
1 hour 30 minutes
Serves **4**

cooking instructions

1. Preheat the oven to 350°F.

2. Rinse the chicken inside and out with cold water. Pat dry with paper towels.

3. Season the cavity of the chicken with salt and pepper and line it with the lemon slices. Add the onion halves, garlic, and rosemary to the cavity.

4. Squeeze the juice from the lemon halves all over the chicken and stuff the lemon halves into the cavity.

5. Place the chicken on a rack in a roasting pan. Run your finger under the skin of the breast and thigh to loosen it and then rub the butter evenly between the meat and skin (optional). Drizzle the olive oil over the skin.

6. Roast the chicken in the oven for 1 1/2 hours or until a thermometer inserted into the thickest part of the thigh registers 180°F.

7. Let the chicken rest for 15 minutes. Remove and discard the skin before carving.

Lamb Chops with Onion Relish and Tomato Vinaigrette

ingredients

FOR THE ONION RELISH:

1/2 large yellow onion
1/2 large red onion
3/4 teaspoon olive oil
1/8 teaspoon salt
freshly ground black pepper
2 tablespoons balsamic vinegar

FOR THE LAMB:

8 lamb chops, about 2 - 3 ounces each
salt to taste
freshly ground black pepper
1/2 cup Tomato Vinaigrette (see page 53)

nutrition facts
Serving Size 2 lamb chops with onion relish and tomato vinaigrette

AMOUNT PER SERVING
Calories **206**
Total Fat **9 g**
Saturated Fat **3 g**
Cholesterol **75 mg**
Sodium **237 mg**
Total Carbohydrate **6 g**
Dietary Fiber **1 g**
Protein **24 g**
Percent Calories from Fat **40%**
Percent Calories from Protein **48%**
Percent Calories from Carbohydrate **12%**

Prep Time: **20 minutes**
Cooking Time: **20 minutes**
Serves **4**

cooking instructions

1. Preheat the grill to medium-high heat.

2. Peel and slice the onions 1/2" thick. Rub the onion slices (trying to keep them intact) with the olive oil and sprinkle with salt and pepper.

3. Grill the onions until they are lightly charred and cooked through, about 3 to 4 minutes per side.

4. When the onions are cool enough to handle, chop them roughly and put them in a bowl. Add the balsamic vinegar. (This can be stored in the refrigerator for up to 1 week.)

5. Season the lamb chops with salt and pepper and grill for about 4 minutes on each side.

6. Re-warm the Tomato Vinaigrette.

7. To serve, spoon the onion relish on warmed plates and place 2 lamb chops on the relish. Top with about 2 tablespoons of the Tomato Vinaigrette.

Chapter 8: Sweet Potatoes and Root Vegetables

There's something about fall that beckons us to spend more time in the kitchen. The cooler weather makes it easy to cook with techniques like braising, wilting, roasting, mashing, pureeing, and caramelizing to create fragrant dishes from the season's freshest ingredients, such as root vegetables. Sweet potatoes are a star in this category, with a natural sweetness and a nutritional profile to match.

The sweet potato is actually part of the morning glory family and is native to tropical areas of the Americas. The Native Americans and colonists in the New World used the root extensively, and Columbus introduced the plant to Europe.

Varieties of sweet potatoes, such as **Jewel**, **Beauregard**, and **Garnet**, are often sold in the United States as yams. **Yams** are yet another unrelated root. Other root vegetables include **carrots**, **celery root** (sometimes called **celeriac**), **turnips**, **beets**, **rutabagas**, **radish**, **salsify**, **jicama**, and **parsnips**. **Potatoes** are actually not botanically root vegetables; they are tubers that pack a taste and nutrient punch. Potatoes are the world's most popular vegetable—Americans alone eat about 140 pounds per person every year!

RECIPES IN THIS CHAPTER:

- Celery Root Bisque with Stilton and Apple
- Chilled Baby Carrot Salad with Ginger-Soy Vinaigrette
- Mashed Sweet Potatoes with Toasted Pecans
- Roasted Root Vegetables
- Caramelized Turnips
- Celery Root, Rutabaga, and Pear Puree
- Potato Pancakes
- Sweet Potato Soufflé
- Four Seasons Vegetable Burgers
- Chicken Stewed with Garlic and Fall Vegetables

NUTRITION AND HEALTH

Sweet potatoes are a very nutrient-dense food. One medium-size sweet potato is brimming with beta-carotene, vitamins C, E, and B6, fiber, iron, and potassium—all for about 120 calories. (Most of the calories come from carbohydrates.) Be sure to eat the skin to get all the nutrients sweet potatoes have to offer.

Flavorful orange-colored foods like sweet potatoes, carrots, and yams are full of carotenoids—plant compounds that are responsible for their deep colors and offer many health benefits. Carrots are a fabulous source of beta-carotene and also supply fiber, potassium, B6, and iron.

Potatoes not only are a source of complex carbohydrates, they also supply protein, vitamins B6 and C, potassium, and iron. You can even get your fiber from the potato skins, as well as iron and calcium.

WHAT TO LOOK FOR

Look for firm, medium-size sweet potatoes with tapered ends. Avoid any root vegetables that have blemishes, sprouts, or other signs of decay.

Choose a celery root heavy for its size with unbruised skin. Don't pick roots larger than a softball because they are overgrown and will be woody inside.

Look for bright-colored carrots with a smooth texture. Avoid carrots with gnarled skins or those with cracked or bruised spots. Similarly, beets should be smooth and round with no bruised or soft spots.

Pick firm potatoes that smell sweet. Avoid potatoes with sprouted eyes or a greenish tint to the skin. With new potatoes, look for small potatoes with thin skins. New potatoes are not a particular variety, but refer to any potato harvested young.

EASY STORAGE AND PREPARATION

Roots such as sweet potatoes will keep for a week or more in a cool, dry place. Scrub and peel when ready to use. Don't store uncooked sweet potatoes or any other root vegetables in the refrigerator—cold temperatures make their flavors turn bitter.

Keep potatoes in a paper bag and away from any onions. Sunlight makes potatoes turn green, while refrigeration turns some of their starch into sugar. Cut away any sprouts or green spots on potatoes before cooking.

Store carrots in the refrigerator and scrub them well before using. If you purchase carrots that still have the green tops attached, cut the tops to about a 1" length before refrigerating.

If beet tops are intact, cut off at least 1" of the greens and store the greens for 1 to 2 days in the refrigerator.

ABOUT HERBS AND SPICES

Chili is a mix of ground chili peppers and other spices such as cumin and oregano. Look for ground powder. Chili energizes bean dishes, meat stews, soups, and egg and cheese dishes. Chili goes well with cilantro, basil, ginger, oregano, cinnamon, black pepper, cumin, fennel, and Italian (also known as flat-leaf) parsley.

BEST USES

- On cold winter days, take a tip from the Chinese and enjoy a hot sweet potato out of hand. Their sweet flavor needs no additions: Simply scrub skins and cut out any bruised spots. Bake unpeeled at 350°F for 30 to 45 minutes.
- Like white potatoes, you can also use sweet potatoes to make baked "fries." Cut them into wedges and toss in a bowl with a little olive oil, salt, and paprika or cayenne pepper if desired; bake on a cookie sheet until soft. Experiment further and sauté them cubed or grill them sliced.
- Celery root is delicious raw in coleslaw. Or try it in stews, braised with your roasts, or boiled and added to mashed potatoes for a new flavor.
- Carrots are delicious no matter how you prepare them. Raw, they make a great crunchy snack, and when you cook them they become even sweeter. (Cooking them actually improves their nutrient content; just take care not to overcook them.) Carrots pair well with herbs such as thyme and parsley, and their flavor is irresistible when combined with a pinch of orange zest or a splash of orange juice.
- Small beets make a wonderful raw, crunchy salad, while large beets are at their best when roasted. To prepare, just wrap them in foil and bake until tender, about 40 minutes in a 350°F oven. Peel the cooled beets and enjoy as a salad or a side dish. The sweet flavor of beets comes alive when paired with orange zest or juice.

Go beyond potatoes and carrots and experiment with other root vegetables. Celery root, turnips, and others are simple to prepare and are all chock-full of nutrients. During the cooler months, they are filling and comforting foods. Explore their possibilities with these recipes for salads, soups, sides, and even a soufflé.

Celery Root Bisque with Stilton and Apple

ingredients

2 tablespoons olive oil
1 cup chopped onion
1 cup chopped celery
2 shallots, peeled and diced
1/2 teaspoon fresh thyme or 1/4 teaspoon dried thyme
salt to taste
freshly ground black pepper to taste
1 1/2 pounds celery root (sometimes called celeriac)
8 cups low-sodium chicken broth
2 tart apples, such as Granny Smith
juice of 1 lemon
2 tablespoons crumbled blue cheese, such as Stilton

nutrition facts

Serving Size about 1 bowl of soup

AMOUNT PER SERVING
Calories **198**
Total Fat **8 g**
Saturated Fat **2 g**
Cholesterol **8 mg**
Sodium **315 mg**
Total Carbohydrate **29 g**
Dietary Fiber **5 g**
Protein **8 g**
Percent Calories from Fat **32%**
Percent Calories from Protein **14%**
Percent Calories from Carbohydrate **53%**

Prep Time:
10 minutes
Cooking Time:
1 hour
Serves **6**

cooking instructions

1. In a large soup pot, heat the olive oil over medium heat.

2. Add the onion and celery and cook until tender and translucent, about 10 minutes. Add the shallots and thyme, season lightly with salt and pepper, and cook a few minutes longer.

3. Meanwhile, peel and cube the celery root and add it to the pot along with the chicken broth. Bring to a boil. Reduce heat to a simmer and cook, covered, until celery root is tender, about 30 to 40 minutes.

4. Meanwhile, core and dice the apples and sprinkle them with lemon juice so that they do not discolor. Set aside for garnish.

5. Puree the soup in a blender.

6. Ladle the hot soup into bowls and serve garnished with diced apples and crumbled blue cheese.

Chilled Baby Carrot Salad with Ginger-Soy Vinaigrette

ingredients

2 pounds fresh baby carrots, trimmed
2 tablespoons rice vinegar
1 tablespoon soy sauce
1 tablespoon brown sugar
1 tablespoon finely chopped shallots
2 tablespoons sesame oil
1 tablespoon freshly grated ginger
salt to taste

nutrition facts

Serving Size about 3/4 cup of baby carrots with vinaigrette

AMOUNT PER SERVING
Calories **108**
Total Fat **5 g**
Saturated Fat **1 g**
Cholesterol **0 mg**
Sodium **142 mg**
Total Carbohydrate **16 g**
Dietary Fiber **5 g**
Protein **2 g**
Percent Calories from Fat **38%**
Percent Calories from Protein **6%**
Percent Calories from Carbohydrate **56%**

Prep Time: **10 minutes**
Cooking Time: **40 minutes**
Serves **6**

cooking instructions

1. Put about 2 inches of water in a large pot, insert a rack or steamer basket into the pot, and bring the water to a boil. Steam the baby carrots in the basket for about 6 to 8 minutes, or to desired tenderness. Remove the basket and run under cold water to stop the cooking process.

2. Meanwhile, in a small bowl, whisk the rice vinegar, soy sauce, and brown sugar together. Add the shallots and slowly whisk in the sesame oil and ginger. Season with salt to taste. (The vinaigrette can be made in advance and stored in the refrigerator for up to 5 days.)

3. Gently toss the baby carrots in the vinaigrette and serve at room temperature or chilled.

Mashed Sweet Potatoes with Toasted Pecans

ingredients

3 large sweet potatoes (or yams)
1 tablespoon unsalted butter
1 tablespoon brown sugar
pinch ground cinnamon
4 tablespoons toasted pecans

Prep Time: **10 minutes**

Cooking Time: **30 minutes**

Serves 4

nutrition facts

Serving Size about 1/2 cup

AMOUNT PER SERVING
Calories **181**
Total Fat **7 g**
Saturated Fat **2 g**
Cholesterol **8 mg**
Sodium **35 mg**
Total Carbohydrate **19 g**
Dietary Fiber **4 g**
Protein **2 g**
Percent Calories from Fat **34%**
Percent Calories from Protein **4%**
Percent Calories from Carbohydrate **61%**

cooking instructions

1. Peel the sweet potatoes and cut them in half. Place them in a pot and cover with cold water. Bring to a boil over high heat and simmer until the potatoes are tender when pricked with a fork, about 30 minutes depending on the size of the potatoes. Drain.

2. Mash the potatoes, butter, brown sugar, and cinnamon with a potato masher or fork, or use a food mill.

3. Transfer to a serving dish and top with the toasted pecans.

Roasted Root Vegetables

ingredients

1 1/2 pounds assorted root vegetables, such as parsnips, carrots, beets, rutabagas, and sweet potatoes

2 tablespoons olive oil

salt to taste

freshly ground black pepper

nutrition facts
Serving Size about 1/2 cup

AMOUNT PER SERVING
Calories **153**
Total Fat **3 g**
Saturated Fat **0 g**
Cholesterol **0 mg**
Sodium **178 mg**
Total Carbohydrate **31 g**
Dietary Fiber **6 g**
Protein **3 g**
Percent Calories from Fat **15%**
Percent Calories from Protein **7%**
Percent Calories from Carbohydrate **78%**

Prep Time:
15 minutes
Cooking Time:
20 minutes
Serves 4

cooking instructions

1. Preheat oven to 350°F.

2. Peel and cut vegetables into 1/2" cubes. Toss in olive oil and season with salt and pepper.

3. Place on a baking sheet and roast in the oven for 15 to 20 minutes. The vegetables are cooked when they are easily pierced by a fork.

Caramelized Turnips

Recipe by FoodFit Chef Alice Waters, Chez Panisse, Berkeley, CA

ingredients

8 small turnips
splash of olive oil
salt to taste
freshly ground black pepper

nutrition facts

Serving Size about 2 turnips

AMOUNT PER SERVING
Calories **159**
Total Fat **7 g**
Saturated Fat **1 g**
Cholesterol **0 mg**
Sodium **392 mg**
Total Carbohydrate **23 g**
Dietary Fiber **7 g**
Protein **3 g**
Percent Calories from Fat **38%**
Percent Calories from Protein **8%**
Percent Calories from Carbohydrate **54%**

Prep Time: **10 minutes**
Cooking Time: **30 minutes**
Serves 4

cooking instructions

1. Preheat oven to 425°F.

2. Turnips that are sufficiently young and tender need only be rinsed and dried before cooking; older purple-top turnips will need to be peeled. Cut small turnips in half. Larger turnips should be cut in half lengthwise and the halves sliced into wedges.

3. Toss the turnips in a bowl with a generous splash of olive oil, and salt and pepper to taste. Spread the turnips out in an even layer on a baking sheet and roast them for about 10 minutes. Toss them once (if tossed more frequently, they tend to break apart as they become tender).

4. Roast for 5 minutes more and check for doneness—depending on the water content of the turnips, they can take from 15 to 30 minutes. The turnips are done when they are fork tender and nicely caramelized (that is, when they turn golden brown).

Celery Root, Rutabaga, and Pear Puree

Recipe by FoodFit Chef Brian McBride, Melrose, Washington, DC

ingredients

4 large celery roots (celeriac)
2 large rutabagas
4 pears, peeled and cored
1/2 cup grapeseed oil
2 tablespoons honey
4 tablespoons lemon juice
salt to taste
freshly ground black pepper
4 tablespoons chopped parsley

nutrition facts
Serving Size about 1/4 cup

AMOUNT PER SERVING
Calories **260**
Total Fat **11 g**
Saturated Fat **1 g**
Cholesterol **0 mg**
Sodium **200 mg**
Total Carbohydrate **39 g**
Dietary Fiber **8 g**
Protein **4 g**
Percent Calories from Fat **38%**
Percent Calories from Protein **5%**
Percent Calories from Carbohydrate **57%**

Prep Time:
25 minutes
Cooking Time:
25 minutes
Serves **10**

cooking instructions

1. Peel the celery roots and rutabagas, place in a large pot, and cover with cold water.
2. Bring to a boil, reduce the heat, and simmer for 20 minutes.
3. Add the pears and simmer for 5 more minutes.
4. Drain and place in a food processor with all the remaining ingredients except the parsley.
5. Puree until smooth, adjust the seasoning, and fold in the parsley.
6. Serve hot.

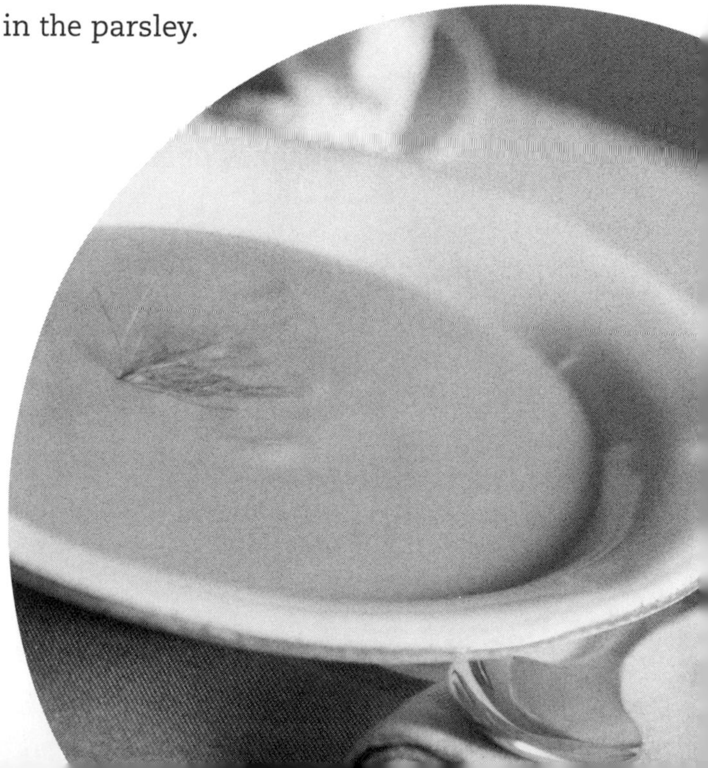

Potato Pancakes

ingredients

3 pounds Yukon gold potatoes
1 medium onion
1/3 cup flour
1/2 teaspoon baking powder
1 cup egg substitute, or 2 whole eggs plus 4 whites
pinch of salt
freshly ground black pepper
olive oil spray (or 2 tablespoons olive oil)

SERVE WITH:
non-fat or low-fat sour cream
applesauce

nutrition facts
Serving Size about 3 potato pancakes

AMOUNT PER SERVING
Calories **178**
Total Fat **1 g**
Saturated Fat **0 g**
Cholesterol **0 mg**
Sodium **159 mg**
Total Carbohydrate **37 g**
Dietary Fiber **4 g**
Protein **10 g**
Percent Calories from Fat **5%**
Percent Calories from Protein **20%**
Percent Calories from Carbohydrate **75%**

Prep Time:
20 minutes
Cooking Time:
15 minutes
Serves **8**

cooking instructions

1. Preheat a nonstick electric griddle to 450°F.
2. Peel the potatoes and onion and coarsely grate in a food processor fitted with a shredding disk, or on a box grater. Grab handfuls of the grated potatoes and squeeze tightly between your fingers to wring out as much liquid as possible.
3. Transfer the grated potatoes to a mixing bowl and stir in the flour, baking powder, egg substitute, and a pinch of salt and pepper. (The potato pancakes should be highly seasoned.)
4. Spray the hot griddle with oil (or drizzle the oil on it and spread with a wooden spoon.) Spoon small mounds of potato mixture onto a baking sheet to form 3" pancakes, leaving 1" between each. Fry the pancakes on the griddle until golden brown, 6 to 8 minutes per side, turning once with a spatula.
5. Transfer to plates or a platter and serve immediately with sour cream and/or applesauce.

Sweet Potato Soufflé

Recipe by FoodFit Chef Jeff Buben, Vidalia, Washington, DC

ingredients

4 large sweet potatoes
4 tablespoons butter
1/2 cup skim milk
1/2 cup dry sherry
1/2 cup brown sugar
1/2 cup frozen orange juice from concentrate
1 teaspoon ground nutmeg
1 teaspoon ground cloves
1 teaspoon ground cinnamon
1 pinch salt
4 large egg whites
2 tablespoons sugar
2 oranges cut in thin slices

nutrition facts

Serving Size about 1/10 of the soufflé

AMOUNT PER SERVING
Calories **224**
Total Fat **6 g**
Saturated Fat **4 g**
Cholesterol **15 mg**
Sodium **154 mg**
Total Carbohydrate **39 g**
Dietary Fiber **3 g**
Protein **3 g**
Percent Calories from Fat **21%**
Percent Calories from Protein **6%**
Percent Calories from Carbohydrate **65%**

Prep Time: **15 minutes**
Cooking Time: **45 minutes**
Serves **10**

cooking instructions

1. Preheat oven to 350°F.
2. In a large pot, cover the sweet potatoes with water and bring to a boil. Boil until tender.
3. Drain and peel the potatoes and place in a large mixing bowl. Mash well.
4. Add the butter, milk, sherry, brown sugar, orange juice, nutmeg, cloves, cinnamon, and salt. Beat well with a mixer.
5. Spoon mixture into a buttered, ovenproof gratin dish.
6. Bake until the potatoes are hot, about 25 minutes.
7. While the soufflé is cooking, make the meringue. In a clean bowl, whip egg whites until almost stiff. Gradually add the sugar and continue to beat until soft peaks form.
8. During the last five minutes of cooking the soufflé, top with the meringue mixture.
9. Return to oven and remove when the meringue is lightly browned. Garnish with the sliced oranges.

Four Seasons Vegetable Burgers

Recipe by FoodFit Chef Steven Raichlen, *cookbook author*

ingredients

2 teaspoons olive oil
1 cup finely chopped onion
1 cup coarsely grated turnips
1 cup coarsely grated zucchini
1/2 cup coarsely grated beets
2 cloves garlic, minced
1/2 teaspoon ground cumin
1/2 cup instant rolled oats, soaked in 1/2 cup water for 5 minutes then drained
1 1/2 cups mashed potatoes
1/2 cup cooked rice
1 tablespoon minced, fresh dill, tarragon, or basil
salt to taste
freshly ground black pepper

nutrition facts

Serving Size about 1 burger

AMOUNT PER SERVING
Calories **92**
Total Fat **2 g**
Saturated Fat **0 g**
Cholesterol **0 mg**
Sodium **172 mg**
Total Carbohydrate **17 g**
Dietary Fiber **2 g**
Protein **2 g**
Percent Calories from Fat **16%**
Percent Calories from Protein **10%**
Percent Calories from Carbohydrate **74%**

Prep Time: **15 minutes**
Cooking Time: **10 minutes**
Serves **8**

cooking instructions

1. Heat the olive oil in a large nonstick skillet. Add the grated vegetables, garlic, and cumin and cook over medium heat until the vegetables are tender and the liquid has evaporated, 10 to 15 minutes. Do not let the vegetables brown. Remove the pan from the heat and let cool.

2. Press the water out of the oats. Stir the oats into the vegetable mixture with the remaining ingredients. Add the salt and pepper to taste.

3. With wet hands, form the mixture into 8 thick burgers. Arrange the burgers on a plate spread with plastic wrap and chill for at least 3 hours.

4. Preheat the grill.

5. Spray the grill grate with cooking spray and grill the burgers over medium heat for about 5 minutes on each side. To broil, arrange the burgers on an oiled, nonstick baking sheet, lightly spray the tops with oil, and broil. To sauté, add 1 to 2 teaspoons of oil to a nonstick skillet. Cook the burgers over medium heat until crusty. Whichever method you use, you'll need about 4 to 6 minutes per side cooking time. Turn the burgers with a spatula as gently as you can.

6. Serve the burgers on rolls with onions, tomatoes, lettuce, and your favorite condiments.

Chicken Stewed with Garlic and Fall Vegetables

ingredients

2 tablespoons olive oil

1 1/4 pounds skinless, boneless chicken thighs

salt to taste

freshly ground black pepper

1/2 cup white wine

1 large yellow onion, sliced

1 stalk celery, finely chopped

3 cloves garlic, minced

2 carrots, peeled and sliced

2 parsnips, peeled and sliced into rounds

1 bay leaf

2 cups diced, canned Italian tomatoes with their juice

nutrition facts

Serving Size 1 bowl of chicken and vegetables

AMOUNT PER SERVING

Calories **373**
Total Fat **13 g**
Saturated Fat **2 g**
Cholesterol **118 mg**
Sodium **544 mg**
Total Carbohydrate **28 g**
Dietary Fiber **6 g**
Protein **32 g**
Percent Calories from Fat **30%**
Percent Calories from Protein **34%**
Percent Calories from Carbohydrate **30%**

Prep Time: **15 minutes**

Cooking Time: **40 minutes**

Serves **4**

cooking instructions

1. Heat the olive oil in a large skillet over medium-high heat. While the oil heats, season the chicken with salt and pepper. Add the chicken to the pan and brown on all sides. As the chicken pieces finish browning, transfer them to a plate and set aside.

2. Add the wine to the skillet, letting it boil rapidly for a minute and then stir with a wooden spoon and loosen any browned bits that may be stuck to the pan.

3. Turn the heat to medium and add the onion and celery. Cook, stirring occasionally, until the onion begins to wilt, about 5 minutes. Add the garlic and cook for 2 more minutes.

4. Return the chicken to the skillet and add the carrots, parsnips, bay leaf, and canned tomatoes with juice. Adjust the heat so that the mixture simmers slowly and place a lid, slightly ajar, over the skillet. Cook until the chicken is completely tender, about 25 minutes. Taste the cooking liquid and adjust the salt and pepper.

5. Serve the chicken and vegetables in warm bowls.

Chapter 9: Acorn and Other Winter Squash

RECIPES IN THIS CHAPTER:

- Acorn Squash and Apple Soup
- Roasted Pumpkin Soup with Pepitas
- Spiced Acorn Squash
- Farro with Butternut Squash
- Acorn Squash and Shiitake Mushroom Risotto
- Pumpkin Muffins with Candied Ginger
- Pumpkin Cookies
- Pumpkin Crème Caramel

Winter squash are wonderfully versatile. These deep-colored, unusual-looking vegetables can be teamed with grains, star in a soup, or make fabulous muffins. Plus, they make festive table arrangements and spooky jack o' lanterns! Winter squash are packed with nutrients and have a deeply satisfying flavor and stick-to-your-ribs quality. You can build a meal on winter squash—they are true comfort food.

Acorn squash, an edible gourd, is thought to be one of the first foods cultivated by Native American Indians. Squash seeds have been found in ancient Mexican archeological digs dating back to between 9,000 and 4,000 B.C.

The other winter squash have familiar names: **pumpkin**, **Hubbard**, **banana**, **butternut**, the pale gold-and-green-striped **delicata**, the dark green **kabocha**, the red **kuri**, the orange-and-gold **turban**, and the oval, pale green **spaghetti squash**. Members of the Cucurbitaceae family and relatives of both the melon and the cucumber, most winter squash have inedible hard, thin skin, and firm flesh.

NUTRITION AND HEALTH

Winter squash are well-known for their nutritional value. Virtually fat-free, they are rich in vitamins and minerals and are a great source of fiber. In just one cup of baked acorn squash, there are 11 grams of fiber!

Acorn squash is rich in vitamin C and potassium, and contains a good amount of folate and vitamin B1.

Pumpkin and butternut squash are especially high in beta-carotene. In general, winter squash are far more nutritious than summer squash and higher in complex carbohydrates.

WHAT TO LOOK FOR

When choosing winter squash in general, look for vegetables that are firm, heavy, smooth, and free of blemishes. They should have a deep color as well. Leave behind any that have spots of mold. If possible, choose squash with their stems still attached.

Acorn squash has a harvest green skin speckled with orange patches and pale yellow-orange flesh. Butternut squash is shaped like a large pear with cream-colored skin, deep orange-colored flesh, and a sweet flavor. Hubbard squash is a larger-sized squash that can be dark green, gray-blue or orange-red in color; the Hubbard's flavor is less sweet than many other varieties.

EASY STORAGE AND PREPARATION

There's no worry about using this fresh produce within a week—acorn and other winter squash can be kept for a month in a dry, cool place.

Winter squash are incredibly versatile, but releasing maximum flavor and softening the flesh requires slower cooking methods. The squash can be peeled, the seeds removed, and then sliced or diced and sautéed, or baked whole or halved in the oven in their shells. It's generally easier to bake the squash whole and then cut them halfway through cooking, after they have softened up a bit.

BEST USES

- Baked squash is wonderful to have on hand to eat as a meal, or liven up other dishes. After halving the squash, remove the seeds and sprinkle with salt, pepper, and olive oil. Roast in a 350°F oven for 30 to 45 minutes until the flesh is tender.
- Cut cooked squash into cubes and serve in a grain dish, or puree it with orange marmalade for a sweet and nutritious spread for bread.
- Add cooked squash to soups and risotto to give them a richer flavor.
- For a nutritious snack, try roasted pumpkin seeds (pepitas). To prepare, halve the pumpkin, remove seeds, wash them under running water, and dry on paper towels. Sprinkle with salt, pepper, and olive oil. To cook, preheat the oven to 250°F. Lightly oil a baking sheet and spread the seeds over it. Bake the seeds until completely dried, at least 1 hour, shaking the pan occasionally. Turn the heat up to 350°F and brown the seeds lightly, about five minutes. Cool, and store in an airtight container.

As temperatures cool down, winter squash begin to appear in markets. Pumpkins decorate porches and provide a taste of autumn in seasonal and holiday dishes. The following recipes add the wonderful fragrances and flavors of spices such as cinnamon, nutmeg, and ginger to winter squash and offer options from soups to desserts.

ABOUT HERBS AND SPICES

Allspice is actually made of small berries, which are called allspice because they taste like a mix of cloves, cinnamon, and nutmeg. Look for whole dried berries or ground powder. Allspice is great added to spice cakes, cookies, and fruit pies. It's also good in marinades for fish, meat, and poultry. For better flavor, buy whole berries and grind them as needed rather than using ground allspice. A pepper mill works well, as does a mortar and pestle.

Acorn Squash and Apple Soup

ingredients

2 acorn squash, about 2 to 2 1/2 pounds total
1 tablespoon olive oil
1 onion, chopped
1 stalk celery, chopped
2 tart apples, such as Granny Smith, peeled, cored, and chopped
salt to taste
freshly ground black pepper
1/4 teaspoon ground cumin
1/2 teaspoon curry powder
2 tablespoons dry sherry or white wine
4 cups low-sodium chicken broth
1/4 cup low-fat sour cream

nutrition facts
Serving Size 8 ounces

AMOUNT PER SERVING
Calories **159**
Total Fat **4 g**
Saturated Fat **1 g**
Cholesterol **3 mg**
Sodium **288 mg**
Total Carbohydrate **30 g**
Dietary Fiber **4 g**
Protein **5 g**
Percent Calories from Fat **18%**
Percent Calories from Protein **10%**
Percent Calories from Carbohydrate **69%**

Prep Time: **15 minutes**
Cooking Time: **30 minutes**
Serves **6**

cooking instructions

1. Cut the acorn squash in half and microwave on high until tender and easily pierced with a fork, about 15 minutes. Let cool.

2. Meanwhile, heat the oil in a large soup pot over medium heat. Add the onion, celery, and apples, and cook until soft and translucent, about 5 minutes.

3. Season lightly with salt and pepper, add the cumin and curry powder, and cook for 2 more minutes.

4. Remove the seeds from the squash and discard them. Scoop the squash pulp out of the skin with a spoon and add it to the soup pot along with the sherry or white wine and cook for 2 or 3 minutes more.

5. Puree this mixture in a blender in batches, being careful not to overfill the blender and adding broth as needed. Strain the blended mixture through a colander to remove any remaining fiber or seeds.

6. Reheat the soup and add the remaining broth to adjust the consistency. Season with salt and pepper.

7. Serve the soup in warm bowls with a dollop of sour cream.

Roasted Pumpkin Soup with Pepitas

Recipe by FoodFit Chef Nora Pouillon, *Restaurant Nora, Washington, DC*

ingredients

1 pumpkin, about 2 to 2 1/2 pounds
2 teaspoons canola oil
1 onion, chopped
1 celery rib, chopped
2 cups low-fat milk
2 cups water
2 tablespoons fresh lemon juice
1/4 teaspoon ground cumin
1 pinch allspice
2 tablespoons dry sherry or Marsala wine
sea salt to taste
freshly ground black pepper
2 tablespoons pumpkin seeds, for garnish

nutrition facts
Serving Size 2 cups

AMOUNT PER SERVING
Calories **142**
Total Fat **4 g**
Saturated Fat **1 g**
Cholesterol **4 mg**
Sodium **94 mg**
Total Carbohydrate **24 g**
Dietary Fiber **2 g**
Protein **6 g**
Percent Calories from Fat **20%**
Percent Calories from Protein **14%**
Percent Calories from Carbohydrate **60%**

Prep Time:
15 minutes
Cooking Time:
1 hour
Serves 4

cooking instructions

1. Preheat the oven to 350°F.

2. Cut the pumpkin in half, scrape out the seeds and set them aside, and place it, cut side down, on a baking sheet. Bake for about 40 minutes or until tender and easily pierced with a fork. Allow the pumpkin to cool about 10 minutes before proceeding, as it will be easier to handle when it is not so hot.

3. While the pumpkin is baking, heat the oil in a small sauté pan and sauté the onion and celery for about 3 minutes or until softened and translucent. Remove from the heat and set aside.

4. When the pumpkin has cooled, scoop the pulp with a large spoon, put it into a large bowl, and add the onion, celery, milk, and water. Stir to combine. Ladle some of this mixture into a blender and puree it in batches, being careful not to overfill the blender. Strain the soup through a colander to remove any remaining fiber or seeds. Add the lemon juice, cumin, allspice, and sherry or Marsala wine. Season to taste with salt and pepper.

5. Spread the pepitas (roasted pumpkin seeds) on a baking sheet and roast in the oven for 10 minutes or until toasted.

6. Reheat the soup, divide it among 4 warmed soup bowls, and sprinkle with the pepitas.

Spiced Acorn Squash

ingredients

2 medium-size acorn squash
1 tablespoon lemon juice
cinnamon to taste
1 teaspoon brown sugar
1 pinch nutmeg

nutrition facts
Serving Size about 1/2 cup

AMOUNT PER SERVING
Calories **93**
Total Fat **0 g**
Saturated Fat **0 g**
Cholesterol **0 mg**
Sodium **7 mg**
Total Carbohydrate **24 g**
Dietary Fiber **3 g**
Protein **2 g**
Percent Calories from Fat **2%**
Percent Calories from Protein **7%**
Percent Calories from Carbohydrate **91%**

Prep Time:
5 minutes
Cooking Time:
40 minutes
Serves 4

cooking instructions

1. Preheat the oven to 350°F.

2. Prick the squash skin with a fork and place in the microwave on high for about 3 minutes. Remove from the microwave and let cool for a few minutes. Cut the squashes in half and place the cut side down in a baking dish for about 40 minutes. Check for doneness by piercing with a fork; there should be little resistance.

3. Scoop the squash flesh from the skin into a bowl and mash with a potato masher or fork, or use a food mill.

4. Add the lemon juice and stir well. Add the cinnamon, brown sugar, and nutmeg, to taste.

Farro with Butternut Squash

Recipe by FoodFit Chef Joyce Goldstein, cookbook author

ingredients

2 cups farro, rinsed or soaked in cold water for an hour

6 cups water

1 1/2 teaspoons salt

2 cups cooked, diced butternut squash, tender but still firm

salt to taste

freshly ground pepper

butter to taste

2 tablespoons chopped fresh sage

nutrition facts
Serving Size about 3/4 cup

AMOUNT PER SERVING
Calories **111**
Total Fat **2 g**
Saturated Fat **1 g**
Cholesterol **5 mg**
Sodium **965 mg**
Total Carbohydrate **21 g**
Dietary Fiber **3 g**
Protein **3 g**
Percent Calories from Fat **16%**
Percent Calories from Protein **10%**
Percent Calories from Carbohydrate **73%**

Prep Time: **15 minutes**

Cooking Time: **20 minutes**

Serves **6**

cooking instructions

1. To cook the farro, simmer it with the water and salt. It doubles in volume after cooking. Start checking for doneness after 20 minutes. When cooked, it will be soft but still have some firmness at the center. If all the water has not been absorbed, simply drain the cooked farro in a strainer.

2. Season with salt and pepper and toss with butter.

3. Fold in the cooked, diced butternut squash and the chopped sage. Cooked farro will keep for up to 4 days in the refrigerator.

Acorn Squash and Shiitake Mushroom Risotto

ingredients

1 small acorn squash, about 1 pound
4 cups low-sodium chicken broth
2 teaspoons olive oil
1/3 cup diced onion
salt to taste
freshly ground black pepper
1 cup sliced shiitake mushrooms
1 teaspoon minced garlic
1 teaspoon minced, fresh thyme
1 cup Arborio rice
1/3 cup freshly grated Parmesan cheese

nutrition facts
Serving Size about 1/2 cup

AMOUNT PER SERVING
Calories **302**
Total Fat **6 g**
Saturated Fat **2 g**
Cholesterol **9 mg**
Sodium **176 mg**
Total Carbohydrate **49 g**
Dietary Fiber **2 g**
Protein **10 g**
Percent Calories from Fat **19%**
Percent Calories from Protein **14%**
Percent Calories from Carbohydrate **67%**

Prep Time: **10 minutes**
Cooking Time: **40 minutes**
Serves **4**

cooking instructions

1. Cut the squash in half and remove the seeds. Place it, cut surface up, in the microwave. Microwave on high until it is tender, about 15 minutes. Cool slightly, scoop out the flesh in tablespoon-size pieces, and reserve. Discard the skin.

2. Meanwhile, heat the chicken broth in a saucepan and keep hot over low heat.

3. Heat the olive oil over medium heat in a separate, medium-size pot. Add the onion and cook until it turns translucent, about 5 minutes. Season lightly with salt and pepper. Add the mushrooms and cook until the mushrooms become tender, about 8 minutes. Add the garlic and thyme and cook 2 minutes more.

4. Add the rice to the onion mixture, stir and turn the heat to low. Add about 1 cup of the hot broth to the rice mixture, and stir slowly until the broth is absorbed.

5. Continue to add the broth 1 cup at a time, stirring slowly, letting the rice absorb the broth before adding more.

6. The risotto is cooked when it is creamy on the outside and slightly firm (al dente) in the center, about 20 to 25 minutes in all. Stir in half of the Parmesan cheese. Gently stir in the squash chunks just to reheat without crushing. Remove from the heat. Season with salt and pepper to taste. If the risotto is too thick, add a little more broth until it becomes creamy.

7. Divide the risotto into serving dishes, sprinkle with the remaining cheese, and serve immediately.

Pumpkin Muffins with Candied Ginger

ingredients

cooking spray
1/4 cup (1/2 stick) unsalted butter, at room temperature
1/2 cup brown sugar, firmly packed
1 large egg
1/2 cup canned pumpkin puree
1 teaspoon freshly grated ginger root
1 cup all-purpose flour
1/4 teaspoon baking soda
1 teaspoon baking powder
1/4 teaspoon salt
1/4 teaspoon ground cinnamon
1/4 teaspoon ground nutmeg
1/4 teaspoon ground allspice
1/3 cup low-fat buttermilk
1/2 cup minced crystallized ginger

nutrition facts
Serving Size 1 muffin

AMOUNT PER SERVING
Calories **137**
Total Fat **4 g**
Saturated Fat **3 g**
Cholesterol **28 mg**
Sodium **126 mg**
Total Carbohydrate **23 g**
Dietary Fiber **1 g**
Protein **2 g**
Percent Calories from Fat **28%**
Percent Calories from Protein **6%**
Percent Calories from Carbohydrate **67%**

Prep Time:
10 minutes
Cooking Time:
25 minutes
Serves 12

cooking instructions

1. Preheat the oven to 350°F and spray 12 muffin tins with cooking spray.

2. Place the butter in a mixing bowl and beat at high speed with an electric mixer for 30 seconds. Gradually add the brown sugar and continue to beat until the mixture is very fluffy.

3. Add the egg and mix on low speed to combine. Add the pumpkin puree and grated ginger root and mix again.

4. Sift the flour, baking soda, baking powder, salt, cinnamon, nutmeg, and allspice together.

5. Fold in half of the flour mixture into the butter mixture. Stir in the buttermilk. Fold in the remaining flour mixture and the crystallized ginger. The batter should be smooth, but be careful to not overmix.

6. Fill the prepared tins halfway with the batter. Bake until the muffins are golden brown and a toothpick inserted into the center of a muffin comes out clean, about 25 minutes.

7. Transfer the muffin tins to a wire rack and cool for 10 minutes before removing the muffins.

Pumpkin Cookies

ingredients

vegetable cooking spray
3/4 cup canned pumpkin puree
3/4 cup light brown sugar, packed
1/2 cup plain low-fat yogurt
2 tablespoons vegetable oil
1 teaspoon vanilla extract
2 cups cake flour, sifted
1/2 teaspoon ground cinnamon
1/2 teaspoon ground ginger
1/4 teaspoon ground allspice
1/2 teaspoon baking soda
1/2 teaspoon salt
1 cup golden raisins

nutrition facts
Serving Size 2 cookies

AMOUNT PER SERVING
Calories **77**
Total Fat **1 g**
Saturated Fat **0 g**
Cholesterol **mg**
Sodium **93 mg**
Total Carbohydrate **15 g**
Dietary Fiber **0 g**
Protein **1 g**
Percent Calories from Fat **16%**
Percent Calories from Protein **7%**
Percent Calories from Carbohydrate **76%**

Prep Time: **15 minutes**
Cooking Time: **15 minutes**
Makes 42 **cookies**

cooking instructions

1. Preheat the oven to 350°F. Spray 2 baking sheets with vegetable cooking spray.

2. In a large bowl, whisk together the pumpkin puree, sugar, yogurt, oil, and vanilla extract until smooth.

3. In a medium-size bowl, combine the flour, cinnamon, ginger, allspice, baking soda, and salt. Stir the dry ingredients into the wet and mix until just blended. Fold in the raisins.

4. Drop the batter by tablespoonfuls onto the baking sheets, leaving 1 1/2 inches between cookies. Bake until lightly golden, about 15 minutes.

5. Place the baking sheets on wire racks. Cool for 5 to 10 minutes. Remove the cookies with a spatula and cool completely. (These cookies can be made ahead and stored in an airtight container for up to 2 weeks.)

Pumpkin Crème Caramel

Recipe by FoodFit Chef Kate Jansen, Firehook Bakery, Washington, DC

ingredients

FOR THE CARAMEL BASE:

3/4 cup superfine granulated sugar
3 tablespoons water

FOR THE FLAN:

1 1/2 cups pumpkin puree (canned or fresh)
1 12-ounce can evaporated skim milk
3/4 cup egg substitute
1 tablespoon vanilla extract
1 cup superfine granulated sugar
1 teaspoon ground cinnamon
1/4 teaspoon ground ginger
1/8 teaspoon ground nutmeg
1/8 teaspoon ground cardamom
1/8 teaspoon salt

nutrition facts
Serving Size 1 slice

AMOUNT PER SERVING
Calories **200**
Total Fat **1 g**
Saturated Fat **0 g**
Cholesterol **2 mg**
Sodium **108 mg**
Total Carbohydrate **43 g**
Dietary Fiber **2 g**
Protein **6 g**
Percent Calories from Fat **3%**
Percent Calories from Protein **11%**
Percent Calories from Carbohydrate **84%**

Prep Time:
15 minutes
Cooking Time:
1 hour
Serves **10**

cooking instructions

1. Preheat the oven to 350°F.

For the caramel base:

1. Melt sugar with water in a small copper or heavy-gauged saucepan over moderate heat. Stir occasionally to melt sugar.
2. Let the mixture boil without stirring for at least 5 minutes until the liquid turns golden brown.
3. Immediately pour into a 9" baking dish.

For the flan:

1. Mix the pumpkin, evaporated milk, egg substitute, and vanilla extract in a bowl by hand or mixer.
2. Add the dry ingredients and blend well.
3. Pour the mixture into the baking dish prepared with the caramel base.
4. Place the dish in a larger pan and pour hot water into the larger pan until the water comes halfway up the edge of the baking dish.
5. Bake for 1 hour or until it is set. If you shake it gently, it will jiggle but no longer be liquidy.
6. Cool to room temperature then refrigerate for at least 4 hours and up to 1 day before serving.
7. Before serving, run a sharp knife around the edge of the flan and invert onto a platter, making sure that the caramel runs down the top and sides.

PART III

Fruit

Chapter 10: Pears, Apples, and Avocados

RECIPES IN THIS CHAPTER:

- Avocado, Kumquat, and Grapefruit Salad with Bibb Lettuce and Watercress
- Apple and Walnut Chicken Salad
- Pan-Seared Pork Chops with Caramelized Apples and Onions
- Roasted Pears and Grapes
- Pear Compote with Frozen Yogurt
- Sour Cream–Apple Muffins
- Apple-Walnut Cookies

Pears, one of the world's oldest cultivated fruits, date back several thousand years. Their sweet taste prompted Homer to proclaim them "gifts from the gods." Since then, more than 5,000 varieties of pears have been grown throughout the world. Look forward to the yellow-green **Bartlett**, the slender **Bosc**, and the red-blushed **d'Anjou** appearing in the fall at a store or farmer's market near you.

In addition, Asian pears have begun to make an appearance. They are usually round and taste more like apples than pears. Two main varieties of Asian pears are sold in the United States: **20th Century** and **Hosui**.

The pear is a member of the pome fruit family. In botany, a pome is a type of fruit of a flowering plant. The pear's relatives include **apples**, **pomegranates**, **quince**, **avocado** (yes, it's technically a fruit, sometimes called an alligator pear), and **loquats**. While the many varieties of the apple are familiar friends, some of the other members of the pome family are less well-known. Quince, which tastes like a cross between an apple and a pear, comes in two varieties: **perfumed** and **pineapple**. Avocados are native to Latin America, but today the bulk of the crop comes from California. The two most common varieties are **Hass** and **Fuerte**.

NUTRITION AND HEALTH

The many varieties of pears are loaded with fiber, offering almost four grams per piece of fruit—twice as much as a piece of whole-wheat bread. Pears also offer vitamin C.

In general, pears, apples, and other pomes contain more sugar, in the form of fructose and glucose, than other fruits.

These monosaccharides are simple carbohydrates, which make up 98% of the energy provided by a pear. Like most other fruits, pears are fat-free.

An apple a day is still a pretty good idea. One medium apple supplies about 15 percent of a day's worth of vitamin C and is only 80 calories. And whether they're green, golden, or red, leave the skin on your pears and apples—it provides extra fiber. Quince provide vitamin C and fiber. Avocados are full of folate fiber, potassium, and vitamin C, and are rich in heart-healthy monounsaturated fat.

WHAT TO LOOK FOR

Bartlett pears are one of the few varieties that signal ripeness by a change in color. Yellow Bartletts, at first green, turn bright yellow as they ripen. Red Bartletts change from a dark red color to a brighter red, often with some light vertical striping. Look for firm pears that are free of bruises and blemishes.

Asian pears will still feel hard when ripe, so smell the fruit and choose the ones that are most aromatic. 20th Century Asian pears should be smooth, round, and green-yellow in color with a sweet, mild taste and lots of juice. Hosui should be golden brown in color and very, very juicy.

Apples also should be very firm, with no bruises or broken skin. Similarly, pick quince that are firm and yellow. Quince bruise easily but the marks don't affect the quality or taste. The perfumed quince is shaped a bit like a football, while the pineapple quince is rounder and more pear-shaped.

Choose firm avocados without any bruises or mushy spots. Both Hass and Fuerte avocados have creamy, pale green flesh; the difference is only skin-deep. Hass avocados, available year-round, have green, pebbly skin that turns purplish-black when ripe, while Fuerte avocados, in season from late fall through spring, have a thin, green skin that's easy to peel.

EASY STORAGE AND PREPARATION

Most pears in the store will need to ripen for a few days at room temperature. When ripening, pears need to be exposed to circulating air so ripen them on the counter, not in a plastic bag. A pear ripens from its core outward, so don't let a pear sit on the counter until the outside is soft—it will be overripe. Refrigerate ripe pears.

Store Asian pears in paper bags in the produce bin of your refrigerator. They will last several weeks.

You can store apples at room temperature for up to a week or in the refrigerator for up to 6 weeks.

Because they ripen best off the tree, most avocados you'll find in the grocery store will be as hard as rocks. It's easy to ripen them on your kitchen counter or in a paper bag. Remember—they're delicate, so handle them gently. Avocados discolor when the flesh is exposed to air. If you're not going to eat them right away or you are tossing them in a salad, sprinkle the peeled fruit with lemon juice to prevent it from browning.

ABOUT HERBS AND SPICES

Cinnamon is a spice that comes from the dried bark of an evergreen tree. Cinnamon has a sweet, mildly hot taste. Look for hollow brown sticks and ground powder. Cinnamon is used in sweets and savories. It's delicious in cakes, pies, and buns, and, at the same time, it enhances most meat stews.

BEST USES

- Served raw, pears are an elegant addition to salads and alongside cheese. Pears are also delicious cooked. Combine diced pears, wild rice, cubed smoked turkey, and pecans for a tantalizing side dish. Sautéed Asian pears make a wonderful condiment for pork.
- Nothing could be more fall-like than a simple baked apple. Apples are also terrific in cakes, pies, or tarts, as well as pureed into applesauce.
- Quince are best cooked and this is why they are often used in jams. The flesh turns a beautiful purple color, becoming softer and sweeter when cooked.
- Guacamole is the signature dish of avocados—and rightly so. The smooth, green puree highlights their creamy flavor like no other recipe. But avocados are also delicious simply mashed and spread on bread with a dash of salt and lemon juice; try using mashed avocado instead of mayonnaise on your sandwich.

The variety of choices in this fruit family can be enjoyed in many ways. From pear vinaigrette to caramelized apples, the following recipes allow you to explore the range of healthful possibilities provided by crispy, colorful apples and pears, creamy avocados, and others.

Avocado, Kumquat, and Grapefruit Salad with Bibb Lettuce and Watercress

ingredients

4 kumquats
1 head bibb lettuce
1 bunch watercress, large stems removed
2 grapefruits, peeled and sectioned
1 avocado
1/2 cup Sherry Vinaigrette (see page 22)

nutrition facts
Serving Size about 1 cup of salad with 2 tablespoons vinaigrette

AMOUNT PER SERVING
Calories **455**
Total Fat **26 g**
Saturated Fat **4 g**
Cholesterol **0 mg**
Sodium **204 mg**
Total Carbohydrate **58 g**
Dietary Fiber **23 g**
Protein **7 g**
Percent Calories from Fat **48%**
Percent Calories from Protein **6%**
Percent Calories from Carbohydrate **47%**

Prep Time:
15 minutes
Cooking Time:
5 minutes
Serves **2**

cooking instructions

1. Bring a small pot of water to a boil.
2. Add the kumquats to the boiling water and cook for about 20 seconds. Remove, pat dry, and slice thinly.
3. Gently wash and dry the bibb lettuce and watercress leaves.
4. Peel the grapefruit and remove the sections.
5. Peel the avocado and slice into sections.
6. Gently toss the watercress, bibb lettuce, and fruit with Sherry Vinaigrette.
7. Make a bed of bibb lettuce and watercress leaves on each plate. Arrange the grapefruit and avocado sections on top. Place the kumquat slices in the center and serve immediately.

Apple and Walnut Chicken Salad

ingredients

1/2 cup dry white wine, such as Sauvignon Blanc
pinch of salt
10 black peppercorns
juice of 1 lemon
2 sprigs fresh thyme
4 boneless, skinless chicken breasts about 4 ounces each
1/2 cup non-fat sour cream
2 apples, cored and chopped
1/2 cup diced celery
1/4 cup diced red onion
1 tablespoon chopped, fresh parsley
salt to taste
freshly ground black pepper
8 cups mixed salad greens
1/4 cup chopped walnuts, toasted

nutrition facts
Serving Size 1 salad

AMOUNT PER SERVING
Calories **420**
Total Fat **7 g**
Saturated Fat **1 g**
Cholesterol **136 mg**
Sodium **552 mg**
Total Carbohydrate **24 g**
Dietary Fiber **5 g**
Protein **60 g**
Percent Calories from Fat **15%**
Percent Calories from Protein **56%**
Percent Calories from Carbohydrate **22%**

Prep Time:
15 minutes
Cooking Time:
20 minutes
Serves **4**

cooking instructions

1. In a large saucepan combine the wine, salt, peppercorns, lemon juice, and thyme. Add the chicken breasts and enough water to cover them. Bring the liquid to a boil, reduce the heat, and simmer for 10 minutes. Remove from the heat and let the chicken cool in the liquid.

2. In a large bowl, mix the sour cream, apples, celery, red onion, and parsley together.

3. When the chicken breasts are cool enough to handle, remove them from the liquid. (Discard the liquid.) Cut the chicken into small pieces, add it to the sour cream mixture, and toss. Season to taste with salt and pepper. Refrigerate until ready to serve.

4. Divide the salad greens among 4 plates. Top the greens with the chicken salad and garnish with walnuts.

Corn and Avocado Relish

ingredients

1 ear corn, shucked
2 tablespoons lime juice
1 tablespoon extra virgin olive oil
2 tablespoons balsamic vinegar
2 tablespoons chopped red onion
2 tablespoons chopped scallions
1/2 tablespoon seeded, chopped jalapeño pepper
1/2 teaspoon chopped, fresh cilantro
1/2 avocado
salt to taste
freshly ground black pepper

Prep Time:
20 minutes

Cooking Time:
10 minutes

Serves **4**

cooking instructions

1. Preheat the grill or oven to 450°F.
2. Roast the corn on the grill or in the oven until it begins to turn golden, about 10 minutes.
3. Meanwhile, mix the lime juice, olive oil, vinegar, red onion, scallions, jalapeño, and cilantro together in a bowl.
4. When the corn is cool enough to handle, cut the kernels from the cob and add them to the bowl. Pit, skin, and chop the avocado and add that to the bowl.
5. Season with salt and pepper.

nutrition facts

Serving Size 1/4 cup

AMOUNT PER SERVING
Calories **108**
Total Fat **7 g**
Saturated Fat **1 g**
Cholesterol **0 mg**
Sodium **82 mg**
Total Carbohydrate **12 g**
Dietary Fiber **3 g**
Protein **2 g**
Percent Calories from Fat **54%**
Percent Calories from Protein **7%**
Percent Calories from Carbohydrate **39%**

Pan-Seared Pork Chops with Caramelized Apples and Onions

ingredients

2 teaspoons olive oil

4 pork loin chops, about 4 to 6 ounces each

salt to taste

freshly ground black pepper

1 medium yellow onion, peeled, halved, and thinly sliced

1 sprig fresh thyme, or 1/2 teaspoon dried thyme

1 cup apple cider

3 tart apples, peeled (optional), cored, and sliced

nutrition facts

Serving Size 1 pork chop with apples and onions

AMOUNT PER SERVING

Calories **311**
Total Fat **10 g**
Saturated Fat **3 g**
Cholesterol **78 mg**
Sodium **303 mg**
Total Carbohydrate **24 g**
Dietary Fiber **3 g**
Protein **32 g**
Percent Calories from Fat **29%**
Percent Calories from Protein **41%**
Percent Calories from Carbohydrate **31%**

Prep Time: **10 minutes**

Cooking Time: **20 minutes**

Serves **4**

cooking instructions

1. Heat the olive oil in a large skillet over medium-high heat.

2. Season the pork chops with salt and pepper and sear them on both sides until just cooked through, about 4 to 6 minutes per side depending on the thickness of the chops. (Thinner chops will take less time; thicker chops will take a bit longer.) Transfer the pork chops to a platter and keep warm.

3. In the same pan, add the onion and thyme and turn the heat down to medium. Season with salt and pepper and cook until the onions begin to wilt, about 3 minutes. Turn the heat to high, and cook until the onions are golden brown.

4. Add the apple cider and apples and cook until the cider has reduced and slightly thickened and the apples are tender, about 6 minutes.

5. Remove the thyme sprig. Serve the pork chops topped with the apple-onion mixture.

Roasted Pears and Grapes

Recipe by FoodFit Chef Lidia Bastianich, Felidia, New York, NY

ingredients

2 cups seedless red grapes
1 cup sugar
2 lemons, juiced
2/3 cup moscato (or other dessert wine)
1/2 vanilla bean, split lengthwise
2 tablespoons apricot jam
3 firm, but ripe Bosc pears

nutrition facts

Serving Size 1/2 pear and grapes

AMOUNT PER SERVING
Calories **234**
Total Fat **1 g**
Saturated Fat **0 g**
Cholesterol **0 mg**
Sodium **163 mg**
Total Carbohydrate **56 g**
Dietary Fiber **2 g**
Protein **1 g**
Percent Calories from Fat **2%**
Percent Calories from Protein **1%**
Percent Calories from Carbohydrate **88%**

Prep Time: **10 minutes**
Cooking Time: **50 minutes**
Serves **6**

cooking instructions

1. Preheat the oven to 375°F.

2. Place the grapes in an 11" x 17" baking dish.

3. Combine sugar, lemon juice, moscato, vanilla bean, and apricot jam in a bowl and stir until blended.

4. Pour over the grapes.

5. Cut the pears in half through the core and remove the cores and seeds.

6. Nestle the pear halves, cut side up, into the grapes.

7. Bake until the pears are tender and the liquid around the grapes is thick and syrupy, about 50 minutes.

8. Serve the pears with some of the grapes and their liquid spooned around them.

Pear Compote with Frozen Yogurt

ingredients

2/3 cup sugar (more or less depending on taste)

1/3 cup water

one 1/4" slice lemon zest (yellow part only)

2 2/3 cups peeled, cored, and sliced pears

1 pint low-fat vanilla frozen yogurt

nutrition facts
Serving Size about 1/2 cup

AMOUNT PER SERVING
Calories **277**
Total Fat **0 g**
Saturated Fat **0 g**
Cholesterol **0 mg**
Sodium **80 mg**
Total Carbohydrate **67 g**
Dietary Fiber **2 g**
Protein **4 g**
Percent Calories from Fat **1%**
Percent Calories from Protein **6%**
Percent Calories from Carbohydrate **93%**

Prep Time:
10 minutes

Cooking Time:
20 minutes

Serves 4

cooking instructions

1. Bring the sugar, water, and lemon zest to a boil over high heat. Simmer for 5 minutes. This will extract flavor from the peel, dissolve the sugar, and make a syrup.

2. Add the pears and continue to cook for about 5 to 10 minutes until just tender.

3. Remove the pears from the juice and set aside. Discard the lemon zest.

4. Reduce the juice over medium-high heat for about 5 minutes until it becomes syrupy. Pour the reduced syrup over the cooked pears.

5. Scoop the frozen yogurt into 4 bowls. Spoon the warm pears and syrup over the yogurt and serve.

Sour Cream–Apple Muffins

ingredients

cooking spray
6 tablespoons softened (room temperature) butter
1 cup sugar
2 eggs
1 1/2 teaspoons vanilla extract
1 cup all-purpose flour
1 cup whole-wheat flour
1/2 teaspoon baking powder
1/2 teaspoon baking soda
1/2 teaspoon salt
1/3 cup applesauce
2/3 cup non-fat sour cream
2 Gala or Granny Smith apples, peeled, cored, and sliced

nutrition facts
Serving Size 1 muffin

AMOUNT PER SERVING
Calories **228**
Total Fat **7 g**
Saturated Fat **4 g**
Cholesterol **51 mg**
Sodium **185 mg**
Total Carbohydrate **38 g**
Dietary Fiber **2 g**
Protein **5 g**
Percent Calories from Fat **27%**
Percent Calories from Protein **8%**
Percent Calories from Carbohydrate **65%**

Prep Time:
15 minutes
Cooking Time:
40 minutes
Serves 12

cooking instructions

1. Preheat the oven to 350°F and spray a muffin tin with cooking spray.
2. Beat the butter and sugar together with an electric mixer on high speed until the mixture is light in color and fluffy.
3. Reduce the speed to low and add the eggs one at a time. Add the vanilla extract.
4. In a separate bowl, combine the flours, baking powder, baking soda, and salt.
5. Fold half of the dry ingredients into the butter mixture using a rubber spatula or wooden spoon. Stir in the applesauce and sour cream. Fold in the remaining dry ingredients.
6. Fill the muffin tins halfway with batter. Add a few apple slices to each muffin and spoon the remaining batter over the apples.
7. Bake on the center rack until the muffins are golden brown and springy to the touch, about 35 to 40 minutes.

Apple-Walnut Cookies

ingredients

cooking spray
1 cup rolled oats
1/2 cup walnuts, chopped
1 cup whole-wheat pastry flour
1/2 teaspoon baking soda
1/4 teaspoon baking powder
1/4 teaspoon salt
1/2 teaspoon ground cinnamon
1/4 teaspoon ground ginger
2 egg whites
1 Granny Smith apple, peeled, cored, and grated
1/4 cup unsweetened applesauce
1/2 cup light brown sugar, packed
3 tablespoons white sugar
2 tablespoons vegetable oil
1/2 teaspoon vanilla extract
1/2 cup raisins

nutrition facts

Serving Size 2 cookies

AMOUNT PER SERVING
Calories **106**
Total Fat **4 g**
Saturated Fat **0 g**
Cholesterol **mg**
Sodium **84 mg**
Total Carbohydrate **16 g**
Dietary Fiber **2 g**
Protein **2 g**
Percent Calories from Fat **32%**
Percent Calories from Protein **9%**
Percent Calories from Carbohydrate **58%**

Prep Time: **20 minutes**
Cooking Time: **20 minutes**
Serves **36**

cooking instructions

1. Heat the oven to 375°F. Spray 2 baking sheets with cooking spray.

2. Place the oats and nuts on a separate, unsprayed baking sheet and toast until golden, about 8 minutes. Set aside.

3. Combine the flour, baking soda, baking powder, salt, cinnamon, and ginger in a medium bowl.

4. Combine the egg whites, grated apple, applesauce, brown sugar, white sugar, oil, and vanilla extract in a large bowl. Stir in the dry ingredients until just combined. Add the raisins and toasted oats and walnuts.

5. Drop the dough onto the prepared baking sheets by tablespoonfuls, about 2 inches apart.

6. Bake the cookies until golden, about 10 to 12 minutes. Cool on wire racks for 3 minutes before removing them from the baking sheet. Cool cookies completely before serving. (These cookies can be made ahead and stored in an airtight container for up to 2 days.)

Chapter 11: Peaches and Stone Fruit

Peaches are a sweet delight, blissful plucked straight from the fruit bowl, great on the grill, yummy in salsas, and other condiments, and a summer dessert mainstay. Since a medium-size peach has only 40 calories, it's also a fantastic, fit snack.

Peaches originally came from China and were brought to the New World by Spanish explorers. The peach is a sacred plant in the Taoist religion and symbolizes hope and longevity. Nowadays, peaches are mainly grown in the United States, South Africa, and Australia.

Like peaches, **nectarines**, **plums**, **apricots**, and **cherries** are all commonly referred to as "stone fruits." That's because they all contain a large hard stone pit surrounding the seed. When it comes to stone fruits, local is often better. If peaches are picked too early and kept in cold storage, even for a couple of weeks, they have a woolly texture.

NUTRITION AND HEALTH

Low in calories and fat, peaches and other stone fruit provide fiber and vitamin C.

Most stone fruits also contain vitamin E, which is often hard to find in a fat-free food. The orange-gold color of apricots is a tell-tale sign that the fruit is rich in beta-carotene, which the body converts to vitamin A. Apricots are also a good source of potassium. Cherries owe their deep red color to anthocyanins and are a significant source of these and other disease-fighting phytochemicals.

RECIPES IN THIS CHAPTER:
- Grilled Chicken with Ginger-Peach Glaze
- Moroccan Pork Tenderloins with Dried Plums
- Muesli with Dried Apricots and Raisins
- Apricot Yogurt Dip with Pistachios
- Cold Peach Soup with Frozen Yogurt
- Apricot, Date, and Nut Bars
- Blackberry-Peach Cobbler
- Almond Angel Cake with Nectarine Compote

WHAT TO LOOK FOR

Pick peaches that are fragrant and fairly firm. The skin between the red spots should be yellow or cream-colored, but keep in mind that the amount of red blush doesn't indicate how ripe the fruit is. Hard fruit with green color will never ripen. Also skip very soft peaches or those with any flattened bruises or signs of decay, which starts as a pale tan spot, expands in a circle and slowly turns darker.

Pick deep yellow apricots with a pink blush and no sign of green. Apricots should be plump and firm with tender, velvety skin.

Look for firm, plump, shiny cherries that still have their green stems. Avoid those with soft spots, bruises, and splits. Red cherries are ripe when deep red. White and yellow varieties are ripe when flushed with pink.

EASY STORAGE AND PREPARATION

Peaches will keep at room temperature for a few days. To ripen peaches, put them in a paper bag that has a few holes in it. Once the fruit is ripe, you can keep it in the refrigerator in a plastic bag for up to a couple of days. Peaches do have one pitfall, however—they can go from unripe, to ripe, to mushy in a heartbeat. Peaches also bruise easily, so handle them carefully.

Apricots can be stored at room temperature or in the refrigerator. Use them within a day or two. To bring out their flavor, poach under-ripe fruit in sugar and water to soften.

Cherries keep best in the refrigerator. Remove stems and pits just before using. Once the stem is removed, the cherry will deteriorate rapidly.

BEST USES

- Very ripe peaches peel with ease. Otherwise, blanching is a good option. Cut a small X in the end opposite the stem and plunge into boiling water for 30 seconds, then swiftly transfer to ice water. The skin will peel away easily afterward. Rub or sprinkle with lemon juice to prevent the peaches from browning.
- Grilling is a great way to prepare slightly under-ripe peaches. Simply halve them, remove the pit, and place the peach on the grill rack. Grill for about 4 minutes per side.
- Raw cherries (sweet varieties only) are great in salads, smoothies, and sorbets. Cooked, they're perfect for compotes, cobblers, pies, and sauces for poultry, especially duck.
- Raw apricots are excellent in salads and sorbets. Cooked apricots make excellent jams and tarts and are tasty accompaniments to meats and poultry.

ABOUT HERBS AND SPICES

Ginger is a sweet, peppery spice. Look for fresh, whole dried, ground powder, and crystallized ginger. Ginger is a versatile herb that's especially good in Asian and Indian dishes. Ground dried powder is delicious in baked goods, rice dishes, and marinades. Use crystallized ginger in baking; fresh ginger in marinades, or with fish, meat, and vegetable dishes.

Nutmeg is the spice seed from a tropical evergreen. It has a delicate, warm, spicy, sweet taste and aroma. Look for whole seeds and ground seeds. Terrific in cream sauces and soups and with vegetables, especially spinach, nutmeg is a wonderful addition to all kinds of desserts and, of course, eggnog. Add freshly grated nutmeg at the end of cooking because heat diminishes the flavor.

These summer fruits are favorites for eating out of hand or for dessert, but they are also wonderful ingredients to use in many light, seasonal dishes. Add a taste of sunshine by incorporating the fruits in sauces, grilling them with meats, mixing them with grains, or making them into dip.

Grilled Chicken with Ginger-Peach Glaze

ingredients

FOR THE GINGER-PEACH GLAZE:

1 tablespoon red wine vinegar
1 tablespoon sugar
1 teaspoon freshly grated ginger
1 clove garlic, crushed
1/4 cup peach jam or preserves
1 teaspoon low-sodium soy sauce
salt to taste
freshly ground black pepper

FOR THE CHICKEN:

2 boneless, skinless chicken breasts, 4 to 6 ounces each
salt to taste
freshly ground black pepper
1 1/2 teaspoons olive oil

nutrition facts

Serving Size 1 glazed chicken breast

AMOUNT PER SERVING
Calories **314**
Total Fat **5 g**
Saturated Fat **1 g**
Cholesterol **82 mg**
Sodium **450 mg**
Total Carbohydrate **37 g**
Dietary Fiber **0 g**
Protein **33 g**
Percent Calories from Fat **14%**
Percent Calories from Protein **41%**
Percent Calories from Carbohydrate **44%**

Prep Time: **5 minutes**
Cooking Time: **20 minutes**
Serves **2**

cooking instructions

For the ginger-peach glaze:

1. In a small saucepan, heat the vinegar and sugar over medium heat until the mixture boils and the sugar dissolves. Add the ginger and garlic and cook for another minute. Add the peach jam or preserves, whisk the mixture together, and bring it to a boil. Remove from heat.

2. Add the soy sauce and season with salt and pepper.

For the chicken:

1. Preheat the grill to medium-high.

2. Sprinkle the chicken with salt and pepper and drizzle with olive oil.

3. Place the chicken on the grill and cook until the juices run clear, 6 to 8 minutes per side.

4. Place the chicken on a serving platter, brush it with the ginger-peach glaze, and serve immediately.

Moroccan Pork Tenderloins with Dried Plums

ingredients

FOR THE PORK TENDERLOINS:

3 pork tenderloins, silver skin removed
1/2 cup cider vinegar
1/2 teaspoon ground cayenne pepper
1/2 teaspoon ground cumin
1/2 teaspoon cracked black pepper
1 teaspoon dried thyme leaves

FOR THE DRIED PLUMS:

1 tablespoon butter
1 cup chopped onions
1 shallots, finely chopped
1 teaspoon fresh, chopped thyme or parsley
salt to taste
freshy ground black pepper
1 cup dried plums (prunes), pitted and chopped
1 cup apple cider

nutrition facts

Serving Size 1/2 pork tenderloin with dried plums

AMOUNT PER SERVING
Calories **436**
Total Fat **11 g**
Saturated Fat **6 g**
Cholesterol **154 mg**
Sodium **298 mg**
Total Carbohydrate **26 g**
Dietary Fiber **3 g**
Protein **48 g**
Percent Calories from Fat **30%**
Percent Calories from Protein **45%**
Percent Calories from Carbohydrate **24%**

Prep Time: **20 minutes**
Cooking Time: **20 minutes**
Serves **6**

cooking instructions

1. Place the pork tenderloins in a shallow bowl. In a medium bowl, whisk together the vinegar, cayenne pepper, cumin, cracked black pepper, and dried thyme leaves, and pour over the tenderloins. Marinate the pork tenderloin for 30 minutes in the refrigerator.

2. While the pork is marinating, melt the butter in a skillet over medium heat and add the onions, shallots, fresh thyme or parsley, salt, and pepper. Cook until the onions are soft, about 5 minutes. Turn off the heat and set aside in the pan.

3. Preheat the oven to 350°F.

4. Remove the tenderloins from the marinade and pat them dry. Season with salt and freshly ground black pepper. Heat a large ovenproof skillet over medium-high heat. Sear the tenderloins on all sides and finish cooking in the oven until the pork is just cooked through, about 12 to 15 minutes.

5. Place the tenderloins on a cutting board and let them rest 2 to 3 minutes before slicing.

6. Meanwhile, place the onion mixture over medium heat and add the dried plums. Cook for 1 minute and add the apple cider. Bring to a boil and cook until the cider reduces a little and becomes syrupy, about 2 to 3 minutes.

7. Slice the pork, place a few slices on each plate along with some of the dried plum mixture, and a drizzle of the syrupy liquid.

Muesli with Dried Apricots and Raisins

ingredients

1 cup rolled oats
1/2 cup skim milk
1/3 cup chopped dried apricots
1/3 cup raisins

Prep Time:
5 minutes

Serves 4

cooking instructions

1. Place the oats in a bowl. Add the milk. Cover and refrigerate overnight.

2. Stir in the apricots and raisins just before serving.

nutrition facts

Serving Size 2 ounces

AMOUNT PER SERVING
Calories **165**
Total Fat **1 g**
Saturated Fat **0 g**
Cholesterol **1 mg**
Sodium **19 mg**
Total Carbohydrate **34 g**
Dietary Fiber **3 g**
Protein **5 g**
Percent Calories from Fat **8%**
Percent Calories from Protein **12%**
Percent Calories from Carbohydrate **80%**

Peach Sizzle

ingredients

1 teaspoon butter
2 cups pitted, peeled, and sliced peaches
1/2 cup maple syrup
dash nutmeg

Prep Time:
5 minutes
Cooking Time:
5 minutes
Serves 2

cooking instructions

1. In a small skillet, melt the butter over medium heat. Add the fruit and cook until it begins to soften slightly, about 2 to 3 minutes.

2. Add the maple syrup and nutmeg. Bring to a boil, then pour over pancakes.

nutrition facts

Serving Size about 1/2 cup

AMOUNT PER SERVING
Calories **135**
Total Fat **1 g**
Saturated Fat **1 g**
Cholesterol **3 mg**
Sodium **13 mg**
Total Carbohydrate **32 g**
Dietary Fiber **1 g**
Protein **0 g**
Percent Calories from Fat **7%**
Percent Calories from Protein **1%**
Percent Calories from Carbohydrate **92%**

Apricot Yogurt Dip with Pistachios

ingredients

2 cups plain low-fat yogurt
1 cup dried apricots
2 tablespoons sugar
1 tablespoon crushed pistachio nuts

nutrition facts
Serving Size 3 tablespoons

AMOUNT PER SERVING
Calories **90**
Total Fat **1 g**
Saturated Fat **0 g**
Cholesterol **5 mg**
Sodium **39 mg**
Total Carbohydrate **17 g**
Dietary Fiber **1 g**
Protein **3 g**
Percent Calories from Fat **12%**
Percent Calories from Protein **15%**
Percent Calories from Carbohydrate **73%**

Prep Time: **10 minutes**
Cooking Time: **5 minutes**
Serves **8**

cooking instructions

1. Place a strainer over a deep bowl. Add the yogurt to the strainer, cover and refrigerate overnight. The yogurt will drain and thicken overnight. Discard the liquid. (This can be done in advance and stored for up to one week in the refrigerator.)
2. Place the apricots and sugar in a small saucepan and add just enough water to cover. Bring to a simmer and cook until the apricots are very soft, about 10 minutes. Let cool.
3. Drain the apricots and puree them in a food processor. Add the drained yogurt and process to combine. Chill for at least one hour. (This can be made in advance and stored in the refrigerator for up to 3 days.)
4. Garnish with the pistachios. Serve with fresh or dried fruits or Brown Sugar Meringues (below).

Brown Sugar Meringues

ingredients

1/2 cup egg whites (about 4 large eggs)
pinch of salt
1 cup light brown sugar

cooking instructions

1. Preheat the oven to 300°F. Line 2 cookie sheets with parchment or wax paper.
2. With an electric mixer, beat the egg whites and salt on high speed until soft peaks form.
3. Continue mixing on high speed while adding 1/2 cup of the sugar. Add the remaining sugar by the tablespoon. Beat for another 1 to 2 minutes, until the mixture is stiff and shiny.
4. Drop by the spoonful, onto the cookie sheets. Flatten each cookie slightly with the back of a spoon.
5. Bake until golden brown, about 30 minutes. Let cool.

Prep Time: **15 minutes**
Cooking Time: **30 minutes**
Makes **36** *Cookies*

nutrition facts
Serving Size 1 cookie

AMOUNT PER SERVING
Calories **25**
Total Fat **0 g**
Saturated Fat **0 g**
Cholesterol **0 mg**
Sodium 9 mg
Total Carbohydrate **6 g**
Dietary Fiber **0 g**
Protein **0 g**
Percent Calories from Fat **0%**
Percent Calories from Protein **6%**
Percent Calories from Carbohydrate **94%**

Cold Peach Soup with Frozen Yogurt

ingredients

6 peaches, skinned and pitted
1/3 cup sugar
juice of half a lemon
1 pint low-fat frozen yogurt

Prep Time:
10 minutes
Serves 4

cooking instructions

1. Puree the peaches in a blender. Blend in the sugar and lemon until a pleasant balance of sweetness and tartness is reached.

2. Strain, pressing with a rubber spatula to release the juices. Discard the fibrous pulp. (This can be made ahead and stored in the refrigerator for one or two days.)

3. Ladle the soup into 4 bowls. Place a scoop of frozen yogurt in each bowl.

nutrition facts

Serving Size about 1/2 cup soup and 1/2 cup of frozen yogurt

AMOUNT PER SERVING
Calories **258**
Total Fat **1 g**
Saturated Fat **1 g**
Cholesterol **22 mg**
Sodium **63 mg**
Total Carbohydrate **56 g**
Dietary Fiber **3 g**
Protein **7 g**
Percent Calories from Fat **5%**
Percent Calories from Protein **10%**
Percent Calories from Carbohydrate **85%**

Georgia Peach Cooler

ingredients

4 cups silken or soft tofu, drained
2 cups of peaches, pitted and chopped
1 cup apple juice, chilled
1/2 banana, peeled
juice of 1 lime
6 sprigs fresh mint, washed

cooking instructions

1. Place the tofu, peaches, apple juice, banana, and lime juice in a blender and process for 10 seconds. Serve immediately in frosted tall glasses garnished with mint sprigs.

Recipe by FoodFit Chef Bill Wavrin, *Miraval Resort and Spa, Catalina, AZ*

Prep Time:
5 minutes
Serves 6

nutrition facts

Serving Size about 9 ounces

AMOUNT PER SERVING
Calories **156**
Total Fat **6 g**
Saturated Fat **0 g**
Cholesterol **0 mg**
Sodium **13 mg**
Total Carbohydrate **16 g**
Dietary Fiber **1 g**
Protein **11 g**
Percent Calories from Fat **33%**
Percent Calories from Protein **27%**
Percent Calories from Carbohydrate **40%**

Apricot, Date, and Nut Bars

ingredients

cooking spray
1/3 cup dates, pitted and chopped
1/3 cup dried apricots, chopped
3/4 cup flour
1/3 cup golden raisins
1 cup pecans, chopped
3 eggs
1 1/2 cups firmly packed brown sugar
3/4 teaspoon baking powder
1/4 teaspoon salt

Prep Time: **15 minutes**
Cooking Time: **20 minutes**
Serves **15 bars**

nutrition facts
Serving Size 1 bar

AMOUNT PER SERVING
Calories **217**
Total Fat **6 g**
Saturated Fat **1 g**
Cholesterol **43 mg**
Sodium **74 mg**
Total Carbohydrate **39 g**
Dietary Fiber **1 g**
Protein **3 g**
Percent Calories from Fat **26%**
Percent Calories from Protein **5%**
Percent Calories from Carbohydrate **69%**

cooking instructions

1. Preheat the oven to 350°F and spray a 10" x 10" pan with cooking spray.
2. Toss the dates and apricots with 1 tablespoon of flour. Add the raisins and pecans and set aside.
3. Place the eggs in a mixing bowl and whip them with an electric mixer until frothy. Gradually add the brown sugar and continue whipping until the mixture is thick, about 5 minutes.
4. Combine the remaining flour, baking powder, and salt in a separate bowl and fold it into the egg mixture. Fold in the fruit-and-nut mixture.
5. Spread the batter into the prepared pan and bake until golden brown and springy to the touch, about 20 minutes.
6. Let cool completely, cut into bars, and store in an airtight container for up to 5 days.

Blackberry-Peach Cobbler

ingredients

3/4 cup light brown sugar
2 tablespoons cornstarch
6 large peaches, peeled, pitted, and sliced
1/2 pint fresh blackberries
1 1/2 cups all-purpose flour
2 tablespoons sugar
1/2 teaspoon baking soda
1/2 teaspoon salt
4 tablespoons very cold unsalted butter, cut into small cubes
1/3 cup non-fat buttermilk
4 cups vanilla non-fat frozen yogurt (optional)

nutrition facts
Serving Size about 1 cup with crust

AMOUNT PER SERVING
Calories **239**
Total Fat **5 g**
Saturated Fat **3 g**
Cholesterol **10 mg**
Sodium **163 mg**
Total Carbohydrate **48 g**
Dietary Fiber **3 g**
Protein **3 g**
Percent Calories from Fat **16%**
Percent Calories from Protein **6%**
Percent Calories from Carbohydrate **78%**

Prep Time: **15 minutes**
Cooking Time: **40 minutes**
Serves **8**

cooking instructions

1. Preheat the oven to 350°F degrees.

2. In a small bowl, mix the brown sugar and cornstarch together.

3. Place the peaches and blackberries in a medium-size saucepan and stir in the brown sugar mixture. Bring the mixture to a simmer and cook for 2 minutes, stirring frequently. Pour the mixture into a 2-quart baking dish and set aside.

4. In a food processor, combine the flour, sugar, baking soda, and salt. Add the butter and process until the butter is the size of small peas. With the motor running, add the buttermilk in a steady stream and process for 5 seconds.

5. Turn the dough out onto a lightly floured surface and knead gently until the dough comes together in a ball. Roll out the dough until it is about 1/3" thick and is wide enough to cover the top of the baking dish. Place the dough on top of the fruit mixture and, using a sharp paring knife, cut the dough to fit just inside the dish.

6. Cut a few slits (air vents) in the dough, place the dish on a cookie sheet, and bake until the crust is golden brown, about 30 to 40 minutes. Let cool.

7. Serve the cobbler warm or at room temperature, with or without frozen yogurt.

Almond Angel Cake with Nectarine Compote

ingredients

1 cup cake flour
1 1/2 cups superfine granulated sugar
1 1/4 cups egg whites (about 10 large eggs whites), at room temperature
1 1/4 teaspoons cream of tartar
1/4 teaspoon salt
1 teaspoon vanilla extract
1/4 teaspoon almond extract
1 recipe Nectarine Compote (see page 120)

nutrition facts
Serving Size 1 slice (1/14 of cake)

AMOUNT PER SERVING
Calories **294**
Total Fat **0 g**
Saturated Fat **0 g**
Cholesterol **0 mg**
Sodium **78 mg**
Total Carbohydrate **71 g**
Dietary Fiber **2 g**
Protein **4 g**
Percent Calories from Fat **1%**
Percent Calories from Protein **5%**
Percent Calories from Carbohydrate **93%**

Prep Time:
10 minutes
Cooking Time:
1 hour
Serves **6**

cooking instructions

1. Preheat the oven to 350°F.
2. Sift the flour with 1/2 cup of the sugar.
3. With an electric mixer on high speed, beat the egg whites, cream of tartar, and salt until soft peaks form when the mixer is removed from the batter.
4. Add half of the remaining sugar and beat for 1 minute. Add the remaining sugar, 2 tablespoons at a time, beating after each addition.
5. Stir in the vanilla and almond extracts.
6. Fold the flour-and-sugar mixture into the egg whites, 1/4 cup at a time, just until incorporated.
7. Put the batter in an ungreased 10" tube pan and bake until the cake is light golden brown and springy to the touch, about 1 hour. Invert the pan and let the cake cool completely before removing from the pan.
8. Slice the cake into 14 slices. Place 6 slices on serving plates. (Reserve the remaining 8 slices in an airtight container to eat on its own.) Spoon the Nectarine Compote over the cakes.

Nectarine Compote

ingredients

1 cup sugar (more or less, depending on taste)

1/2 cup water

one 1/2" slice lemon zest (yellow part only)

4 cups peeled and pitted nectarines

Prep Time: **10 minutes**

Cooking Time: **20 minutes**

Serves **6**

cooking instructions

1. Bring the sugar, water, and lemon zest to a boil over high heat. Simmer for 5 minutes. This will extract flavor from the peel, dissolve the sugar, and make a syrup.
2. Add the fruit and continue to cook for about 5 minutes, until just tender.
3. Remove the fruit from the juice and set aside. Discard the lemon zest.
4. Reduce the juice over medium-high heat for about 5 minutes, until it becomes syrupy. Pour the syrup over the cooked fruit.
5. Serve warm over Whole-Wheat Griddle Cakes (page 179) for a weekend breakfast or over Honey Vanilla Frozen Yogurt (page 267) for a low-fat dessert. For safekeeping, cool the compote. Refrigerate up to 5 days.

nutrition facts

Serving Size about 1/2 cup

AMOUNT PER SERVING

Calories **174**
Total Fat **0 g**
Saturated Fat **0 g**
Cholesterol **0 mg**
Sodium **0 mg**
Total Carbohydrate **44 g**
Dietary Fiber **1 g**
Protein **1 g**
Percent Calories from Fat **2%**
Percent Calories from Protein **2%**
Percent Calories from Carbohydrate **96%**

Chapter 12: Oranges and Citrus Fruit

The bright flavor and sweet taste of citrus fruits are a welcome relief during the winter months. There's nothing like a juicy **orange** to conjure up the pleasure of a sun-drenched beach. Sensational taste is just one thing citrus fruits have going for them; they are also rich in vitamins, particularly cold-fighting vitamin C. Citrus fruits are available all year- round, but the most fragrant fruits debut each year during the winter months.

Today, markets are filled with so many different kinds of zesty oranges, it's tough to choose. Loose-skinned oranges like **tangerines** and **clementines** are especially popular with kids because they're often seedless and are easy to peel. Other varieties include **mandarin**, **blood**, **Jaffa**, **Satsumas**, **temple**, **valencia**, and the hardy **navel orange**.

Other refreshing members of the citrus family are **grapefruit**, **lemons**, and **limes**, plus the lesser-known **tangelos** and **kumquats**. Citrus fruits were first cultivated in Asia thousands of years ago, and came to the Americas with the Spanish explorers. Today, citrus fruits are grown in sunny climates around the globe from Florida to Israel.

RECIPES IN THIS CHAPTER:

- Beet Salad with Orange Vinaigrette
- Baby Greens with Mandarin Oranges, Almonds, and Ginger-Soy Vinaigrette
- Herbed Lemony Swiss Chard
- Pan-Roasted Scallops with Mandarins and Chickpeas
- Lemon-Basil Stuffed Chicken Breasts
- Grilled Pork Chops with Orange-Rosemary Relish
- Caramelized Grapefruit
- Pink Grapefruit Sorbet

NUTRITION AND HEALTH

Oranges, the most popular member of the citrus family, are unusually rich in nutrients. One medium-size orange is bursting with vitamin C and also supplies healthful fiber, folate, and potassium. As a bonus for your bones, they also contain a modest amount of calcium. Eating the fruit is more nutritious than drinking it because orange juice does not offer fiber.

The membranes between citrus segments provide pectin, a fiber that helps control blood cholesterol levels. Other citrus fruits are also brimming with vitamin C and other carotenoids.

WHAT TO LOOK FOR

Thick-skinned oranges are best for eating; for juicing, choose firm, thin-skinned oranges. When choosing mandarin oranges, pick ones that are heavy for their size.

For tangerines, you should also select ones that are heavy for their size, free of bruises and brown spots. Color is not always an indicator, since some dark areas can be a sign of good, strong flavor.

Again, grapefruit should be heavy for their size, firm, and thin-skinned. Skin color varies from yellow to ruby red.

EASY STORAGE AND PREPARATION

You can store oranges at room temperature for up to 1 week, or even longer in the refrigerator. The zest of the orange—the outermost colored part of the peel—contains aromatic oils that add tang to everything from stews to baked goods. If grating the zest, avoid the white pith, which tends to be bitter.

Drink fresh-squeezed orange juice within 2 days while it still has the maximum amount of vitamin C, and store juice made from frozen concentrate in a glass pitcher with a lid. For even more nutrients, you can now find calcium-fortified orange juice.

Citrus fruits will keep for at least 2 weeks and in some cases up to 6 weeks in the refrigerator. Unfortunately, once they've been squeezed or cut, the vitamin content in many citrus fruits begins to decrease.

BEST USES

- Oranges complement the flavors of onions, olives, and cucumbers. Raw orange slices make a wonderful addition to savory salads, and add a brightness to fruit salads.
- Orange zest is an easy way to add flavor to baked goods, as well as pancakes and crêpes.
- Lemons are rarely eaten alone due to their tartness, but are frequently used to season fish, vegetables, salads, and tea. When added to vegetables that contain sulfur compounds, such as broccoli or cauliflower, the flavor of the vegetable improves dramatically.
- Like lemons, limes are usually used as a flavoring agent. They also tenderize and heighten the flavors of other foods, especially fish and poultry. Squeeze a wedge of lime over fish or chicken tacos to brighten the flavor.

- Although raw grapefruit is usually found on the breakfast table, broiled grapefruit makes a nice change. Grapefruit segments also add a tangy twist to fruit salads and fruit salsas.

Cooking with citrus is a pleasure. These fruits are fragrant, fat-free, flavor enhancers. A splash of fresh lemon, lime, or orange juice can bring a salad dressing to life or draw out the flavor in other fresh fruits. All of the members of the citrus family make great additions to salads, desserts, and entrées, especially those that feature seafood and chicken.

Beet Salad with Orange Vinaigrette

Recipe by FoodFit Chef Anne Quatrano, Bacchanalia, Atlanta, GA

ingredients

FOR THE ORANGE VINAIGRETTE:

3 shallots, diced
salt to taste
freshly ground black pepper
1/2 cup raspberry vinegar
1/4 cup honey
1/2 cup grapeseed oil
zest of 1 orange, chopped

FOR THE BEET SALAD:

4 medium beets
1/4 cup raspberry vinegar
1 tablespoon honey
1 tablespoon butter
6 cups baby greens, washed and drained

nutrition facts
Serving Size 1 salad

AMOUNT PER SERVING
Calories **130**
Total Fat **8 g**
Saturated Fat **2 g**
Cholesterol **5 mg**
Sodium **203 mg**
Total Carbohydrate **14 g**
Dietary Fiber **1 g**
Protein **2 g**
Percent Calories from Fat **55%**
Percent Calories from Protein **5%**
Percent Calories from Carbohydrate **40%**

Prep Time: **10 minutes**
Cooking Time: **1 hour**
Serves **6**

cooking instructions

For the vinaigrette:

1. Whisk the shallots, salt, pepper, raspberry vinegar, and honey together in a mixing bowl. Slowly drizzle the grapeseed oil in while whisking. Add the orange zest.

For the beet salad:

1. Preheat the oven to 350°F.
2. Remove the tops and tails from the beets. Place them in an ovenproof casserole dish with 1/4 cup of the raspberry vinegar, 1 tablespoon of the honey, and the butter. Add water until the liquid covers about half of the beets. Cover with foil and bake for about an hour (longer if beets are larger). The beets should be tender throughout when pierced with a knife.
3. While the beets are still warm, peel and cut them into eighths. (The beets can be stored in the refrigerator for up to 5 days.)
4. Toss the beets with about 1/3 cup of the vinaigrette. (Reserve any remaining vinaigrette in the refrigerator for up to 1 week.)
5. Arrange the beets on a platter and garnish with baby greens.

Baby Greens with Mandarin Oranges, Almonds, and Ginger-Soy Vinaigrette

ingredients

FOR THE VINAIGRETTE:

1 tablespoon finely chopped shallots
4 tablespoons red wine vinegar
1 teaspoon freshly grated ginger
1 tablespoon soy sauce
2 tablespoons olive oil
salt to taste
freshly ground black pepper

FOR THE SALAD:

6 cups baby greens, washed and drained
12 mandarin oranges, peeled and separated into segments
2 tablespoons sliced almonds

nutrition facts

Serving Size 1 cup of salad with 2 tablespoons of vinaigrette

AMOUNT PER SERVING
Calories **75**
Total Fat **3 g**
Saturated Fat **0 g**
Cholesterol **0 mg**
Sodium **153 mg**
Total Carbohydrate **12 g**
Dietary Fiber **3 g**
Protein **2 g 4**
Percent Calories from Fat **33%**
Percent Calories from Protein **58%**
Percent Calories from Carbohydrate **9%**

Prep Time:
20 minutes
Serves 4

cooking instructions

For the vinaigrette:

1. Place the shallots, red wine vinegar, ginger, soy sauce, and olive oil in a container with a tight-fitting lid. Shake well.
2. Add the salt and pepper to taste.

For the salad:

1. Toss the greens with the vinaigrette in a bowl.
2. Transfer to a serving plate and garnish with the mandarin orange segments and almonds.

Herbed Lemony Swiss Chard

ingredients

2 pounds Swiss chard, washed
1/2 cup low-sodium chicken broth
1 tablespoon minced shallots
salt to taste
freshly ground black pepper
2 tablespoons fresh lemon juice
2 teaspoons olive oil
1 tablespoon chopped, fresh tarragon

nutrition facts
Serving Size about 1/2 cup

AMOUNT PER SERVING
Calories **72**
Total Fat **3 g**
Saturated Fat **0 g**
Cholesterol **0 mg**
Sodium **126 mg**
Total Carbohydrate **10 g**
Dietary Fiber **4 g**
Protein **5 g**
Percent Calories from Fat **31%**
Percent Calories from Protein **22%**
Percent Calories from Carbohydrate **47%**

Prep Time:
15 minutes
Cooking Time:
10 minutes
Serves 4

cooking instructions

1. Slice the chard into 2" pieces.

2. In a large skillet, heat the chicken broth and add the shallots and the stems of the chard. Simmer for about 3 minutes and add the chard leaves. Continue to cook until the chicken broth is reduced and the chard is tender, about 5 more minutes.

3. Remove from the heat and toss the chard with the lemon juice and olive oil. Taste and add salt and pepper. Sprinkle with tarragon.

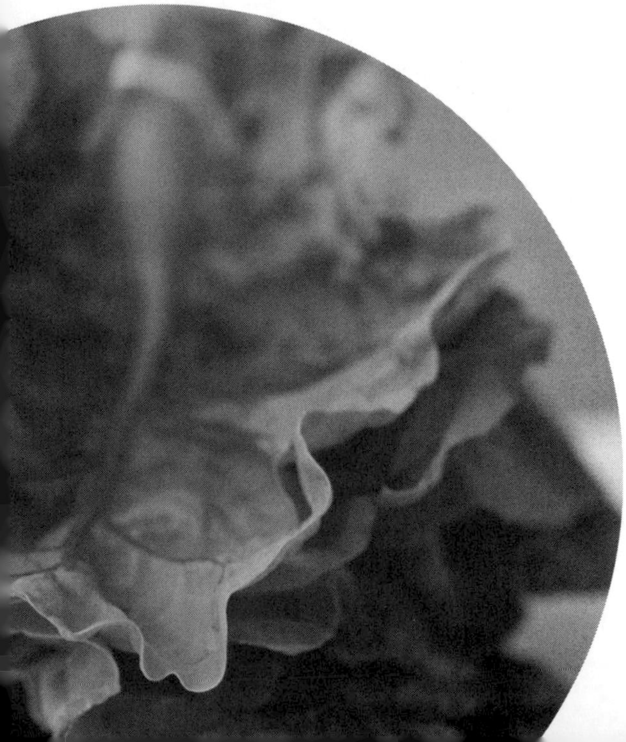

Pan-Roasted Scallops with Mandarins and Chickpeas

Recipe by FoodFit Chef Allen Susser, *Chef* Allen's, *Aventura, FL*

ingredients

4 large mandarin oranges or clementines
1 pound bay scallops
1/4 teaspoon ground cinnamon
1/2 teaspoon ground allspice
3 tablespoons olive oil
1/2 teaspoon chopped garlic
1 cup cooked chickpeas (garbanzo beans)
1 medium European or English cucumber
salt to taste
freshly ground black pepper

nutrition facts

Serving Size about 4 ounces scallops

AMOUNT PER SERVING
Calories **407**
Total Fat **13 g**
Saturated Fat **1 g**
Cholesterol **37 mg**
Sodium **270 mg**
Total Carbohydrate **43 g**
Dietary Fiber **9 g**
Protein **31 g**
Percent Calories from Fat **29%**
Percent Calories from Protein **29%**
Percent Calories from Carbohydrate **42%**

Prep Time:
15 minutes
Plus Marinating Time

Cooking Time:
5 minutes

Serves 4

cooking instructions

1. Peel and segment 2 of the oranges, reserving 2 tablespoons of the peel, sliced into thin pieces.

2. Juice the remaining 2 oranges and reserve the juice.

3. In a large stainless steel bowl, combine the scallops, orange peel, cinnamon, allspice, and olive oil. Cover and refrigerate for 1 hour.

4. Cut the cucumbers in half lengthwise, and scoop out the cucumber into rounds or balls with a small melon baller.

5. Heat a sauté pan over high heat. Drain the scallops and sauté for 2 minutes. Add the garlic, chickpeas, cucumber rounds or balls, and reserved orange juice. Heat thoroughly and adjust salt and pepper to taste.

6. Add the reserved mandarin segments to the scallop sauté and remove from heat. Serve immediately.

Lemon-Basil Stuffed Chicken Breasts

ingredients

4 boneless, skinless chicken breasts, about 4 to 6 ounces each

1 lemon, cut into 8 slices

2 tablespoons chopped, fresh basil

1/2 cup chopped spinach

1 1/2 tablespoons olive oil

1/4 cup balsamic vinegar

3/4 cup low-sodium chicken broth

salt to taste

freshly ground black pepper

nutrition facts

Serving Size 1 chicken breast

AMOUNT PER SERVING

Calories **223**

Total Fat **7 g**

Saturated Fat **1 g**

Cholesterol **83 mg**

Sodium **120 mg**

Total Carbohydrate **4 g**

Dietary Fiber **0 g**

Protein **34 g**

Percent Calories from Fat **30%**

Percent Calories from Protein **62%**

Percent Calories from Carbohydrate **8%**

Prep Time: **10 minutes**

Cooking Time: **15 minutes**

Serves 4

cooking instructions

1. Cut a deep, horizontal pocket in the side of each chicken breast. Make the pocket as large as you can without piercing the top or bottom of the breast. Place 2 lemon wedges, 1/2 tablespoon of the basil, and 1/4 of the spinach in the pocket of each chicken breast.
2. Close the pocket with toothpicks, threading along the side of the breasts.
3. Heat the oil in a heavy skillet over medium-high heat. Add the chicken to the skillet and cook on each side until golden brown, about 4 minutes per side.
4. Add the vinegar and chicken broth and bring to a boil. Lower the heat and gently simmer the chicken for 4 to 6 minutes until cooked through.
5. Remove the chicken breasts from the skillet and keep warm. Continue to cook the sauce until it is reduced to a thick syrup, approximately 5 minutes.
6. Taste the sauce and season with the salt and pepper. Spoon the sauce over each chicken breast and serve.

Grilled Pork Chops with Orange-Rosemary Relish

ingredients

3 oranges, peeled and cut into sections (remove all membranes)
juice of 1 lemon
1 teaspoon chopped, fresh rosemary
1 tablespoon canola oil
6 center-cut, boneless pork loin chops, about 1" thick
salt to taste
freshly ground black pepper

nutrition facts
Serving Size 1 pork chop with relish

AMOUNT PER SERVING
Calories **195**
Total Fat **7 g**
Saturated Fat **2 g**
Cholesterol **62 mg**
Sodium **162 mg**
Total Carbohydrate **11 g**
Dietary Fiber **4 g**
Protein **22 g**
Percent Calories from Fat **33%**
Percent Calories from Protein **45%**
Percent Calories from Carbohydrate **23%**

Prep Time: **15 minutes**
Cooking Time: **8 minutes**
Serves **6**

cooking instructions

1. Preheat the grill.

2. To make the orange relish, combine the orange sections in a mixing bowl with the lemon juice and rosemary and set aside. (This can be made in advance and stored in the refrigerator for a day or two. The relish should be served at room temperature.)

3. Brush the pork chops with oil and season generously with salt and pepper.

4. Grill the pork chops for 5 to 8 minutes on each side, turning only once. (Thin chops will take less time; thicker chops will take more.)

5. Place the chops on warmed plates, top with orange relish, and serve.

Caramelized Grapefruit

ingredients

1 grapefruit, halved
2 tablespoons brown sugar

Prep Time:
5 minutes
Cooking Time:
5 minutes
Serves **2**

cooking instructions

1. Preheat the broiler to high.

2. Place the grapefruit halves in a baking dish and sprinkle with brown sugar.

3. Broil about 5" away from the heat source, until the sugar deepens in color and has a caramel-like consistency, about 5 minutes.

4. Transfer to individual dishes and serve.

nutrition facts

Serving Size 1/4 grapefruit

AMOUNT PER SERVING
Calories **87**
Total Fat **0 g**
Saturated Fat **0 g**
Cholesterol **0 mg**
Sodium **5 mg**
Total Carbohydrate **22 g**
Dietary Fiber **1 g**
Protein **1 g**
Percent Calories from Fat **1%**
Percent Calories from Protein **3%**
Percent Calories from Carbohydrate **96%**

Pink Grapefruit Sorbet

Recipe by Chef Gale Gand, Tru, Chicago, IL

ingredients

1 3/4 cups freshly squeezed pink grapefruit juice
1/4 cup freshly squeezed lemon juice
2 cups water
1 1/2 cups sugar
6 black peppercorns

nutrition facts

Serving Size about 1/2 cup

AMOUNT PER SERVING
Calories **168**
Total Fat **0 g**
Saturated Fat **0 g**
Cholesterol **0 mg**
Sodium **1 mg**
Total Carbohydrate **43 g**
Dietary Fiber **0 g**
Protein **0 g**
Percent Calories from Fat **0%**
Percent Calories from Protein **1%**
Percent Calories from Carbohydrate **99%**

Prep Time: **10 minutes**
Cooking Time: **5 minutes**
Serves **8**

cooking instructions

1. In a medium bowl, combine the fruit juices and set aside.

2. In a medium saucepan, make a syrup by bringing the water, sugar, and peppercorns to a boil over medium heat. Allow to cool slightly, then fish the peppercorns out with a spoon.

3. Stir most of the syrup into the fruit juice mixture and taste for sweetness. Add more syrup if needed.

4. Freeze the sorbet mixture in an ice-cream maker according to the manufacturer's instructions.

5. Serve in frosted glasses.

Chapter 13: Blueberries and Other Berries

RECIPES IN THIS CHAPTER:

- Summer Fruit Salad
- Baby Greens with Grilled Turkey, Cranberries, and Roasted Shallot Vinaigrette
- Cranberry, Butternut Squash, and Roasted Shallot Couscous
- Classic Strawberry-Rhubarb Shortcakes
- Balsamic Strawberries with Strawberry Sorbet
- Fruit Kebabs
- Rustic Fresh Blueberry-Peach Tart

It's nice to know that something that tastes so good is so good for you. Blueberries are one of the richest sources of antioxidants of all fresh fruits and vegetables. Blueberries grow wild in Scandinavia, the British Isles, Russia, and North and South America. Surprisingly, blueberries weren't grown on farms until the early 1900s. Cultivated berries are larger than their wild cousins, but all blueberries have that beloved sweet, juicy taste.

Native Americans believed that the "Great Spirit" sent blueberries to feed their children during famines. Blueberries were an important part of their cooking and were also used for medicinal purposes. They weren't the only ones who loved blueberries: Some species of bears will eat nothing but wild blueberries when in season, and will travel up to 15 miles a day to find a blueberry patch.

The rainbow of berries that appears in summer markets is a treasure trove of antioxidants and other nutrients. Eat your fill of **raspberries**, **blackberries**, **cranberries**, **gooseberries**, **huckleberries**, **currants**, or the always-popular **strawberries** and **grapes**.

NUTRITION AND HEALTH

What gives blueberries their lovely indigo color and their healthful antioxidant powers are anthocyanin pigments. Some scientists believe they help the body fight aging, cancer, and heart disease, and improve vision. Besides antioxidants, blueberries are a great source of vitamin C and a good source of fiber. And a cup of blueberries has a mere 80 calories.

Blackberries are also full of vitamin C and fiber and contain folate and iron. Next to blueberries, blackberries have one of the highest levels of anthocyanins. Raspberries are high in fiber and offer a good amount of vitamin C. Super-nutritious strawberries abound in vitamin C and fiber. Strawberries are also a great source of health-promoting antioxidants, including anthocyanins, which give the berries their deep-red color.

WHAT TO LOOK FOR

Fresh blueberries (and their close relative, huckleberries) should be dark blue and have a silvery cast. Choose berries that are fully colored, plump, firm, the same size, dry, and free of stems or leaves. Avoid soft, mushy, or moldy berries or juice-stained containers.

When choosing blackberries, look for firm fruit with a rich, dark black color and a pleasing aroma. Bigger is better. The drupelets—the little sacs that make up the berry—should be large and plump. That way you know the fruit wasn't picked too early. Skip blackberries that have hulls, another sign they were picked before their time.

Look for raspberries that are firm, plump, and fully colored.

Cranberries should be shiny and not shriveled. A brown or a deep red color signals freshness. A good, fresh berry should be hard and bounce if dropped on a hard surface.

Strawberries should have a strong red color and an intact green, leafy hull. Avoid berries with soft or brown spots. Huge berries often have hollow centers and little flavor or juice.

EASY STORAGE AND PREPARATION

Blueberries won't ripen after you buy them, so plan to eat them within a couple of days. Store at room temperature or refrigerate in a single layer. Use within a day or two. Handle the fragile fruit tenderly; wash just before eating.

Cranberries will keep for up to two weeks in the refrigerator. Sort and rinse in cold water before using. Store strawberries at room temperature or refrigerate in a single layer. Use within a day or two. Wash before removing green tops and only when ready to use.

Blackberries should be an immediate pleasure. They don't travel well. You can keep them for a day or two. Store blackberries at room temperature or refrigerate in a single layer. Wait to wash your berries until just before eating.

Raspberries, strawberries, and gooseberries should all be stored at room temperature or refrigerated in a single layer. Use within a day or two. Wash when ready to use.

BEST USES

- Blueberries are delicious by the handful. Popping the sweet, button-like fruit into your mouth is one of summer's pleasures. They're dynamite paired with sliced peaches or strawberries.
- Blueberries pair well with poultry—add them to your next chicken salad. Blueberries are also great in fruit salad, or sprinkled over cereal or yogurt.
- For dessert, blueberries are a natural in cobblers, crisps, and pies. If you're baking, a squeeze of lemon enhances the fruit's flavor.
- Cranberries are unpleasantly tart on their own, but they're excellent for flavoring a sauce, in a stuffing, and in cakes and breads.
- Strawberries, blackberries, and raspberries are all naturals fresh in fruit tarts, salads, smoothies, sorbets, and cooked in jams, cobblers, and pies.
- To enjoy berries year-round, buy organic frozen berries or freeze fresh berries yourself. Scatter a single layer of unwashed, fresh berries on a cookie tray. Once they're frozen, transfer them to an airtight plastic bag or container. Remember to wash before using.

Berries are lively fruits that perk up any dish. Their sweet flavor shines through whether they are raw or cooked, eaten alone or incorporated into a healthy dish. These recipes showcase berries in surprisingly wonderful ways, from strawberries with balsamic vinegar to couscous with cranberries.

Summer Fruit Salad

ingredients

1 cup mixed berries
1 mango, peeled, pitted, and cubed
1 nectarine, pitted and sliced
2 tablespoons orange juice

Prep Time:
10 minutes
Serves 4

cooking instructions

1. Mix the fruit in a bowl. Sprinkle with the orange juice.

2. Serve for breakfast over yogurt, as a side dish with lunch or dinner or for dessert over sorbet or low-fat frozen yogurt.

nutrition facts

Serving Size about 2/3 cup

AMOUNT PER SERVING
Calories **71**
Total Fat **0 g**
Saturated Fat **0 g**
Cholesterol **0 mg**
Sodium **2 mg**
Total Carbohydrate **18 g**
Dietary Fiber **2 g**
Protein **1 g**
Percent Calories from Fat **5%**
Percent Calories from Protein **4%**
Percent Calories from Carbohydrate **91%**

Baby Greens with Grilled Turkey, Cranberries, and Roasted Shallot Vinaigrette

ingredients

FOR THE GRILLED TURKEY:

4 turkey cutlets, about 4 ounces each
2 teaspoons olive oil
salt and pepper to taste

FOR THE GREEN SALAD:

1/2 cup Roasted Shallot Vinaigrette (see page 67)
8 cups fresh baby greens, washed and drained
1/2 cup dried cranberries

nutrition facts

Serving Size 1 turkey cutlet with salad

AMOUNT PER SERVING
Calories **283**
Total Fat **7 g**
Saturated Fat **1 g**
Cholesterol **98 mg**
Sodium **317 mg**
Total Carbohydrate **17 g**
Dietary Fiber **4 g**
Protein **36 g**
Percent Calories from Fat **24%**
Percent Calories from Protein **52%**
Percent Calories from Carbohydrate **25%**

Prep Time: **20 minutes**
Cooking Time: **20 minutes**
Serves **4**

cooking instructions

For the grilled turkey:

1. Preheat the grill to medium-high.

2. Brush the cutlets with olive oil and season with salt and pepper.

3. Grill the turkey for about 4 to 6 minutes on each side, depending on the thickness, until it is cooked through. Remove from the grill and place on a cutting board to rest. Cut the turkey into strips. (The turkey can be grilled in advance and stored in the refrigerator for up to 2 days.)

For the green salad:

1. Place the turkey strips in a mixing bowl, add the dried cranberries and half of the vinaigrette.

2. Place the lettuce in a separate salad bowl and toss it with the remaining vinaigrette. Arrange the turkey and cranberry mixture on top.

Cranberry, Butternut Squash, and Roasted Shallot Couscous

Recipe by FoodFit Chef Jimmy Schmidt, The Rattlesnake Club, Detroit, MI

ingredients

1 large butternut squash, cut in half, seeds removed
4 cups peeled, whole shallots
2 tablespoons olive oil or corn oil
salt to taste
freshly ground black pepper
1 pound fresh cranberries
2 cups water
1 cup granulated sugar
about 3 cups unsweetened cranberry juice
1 pound couscous
1/2 cup snipped, fresh chives
1 tablespoon chopped, fresh rosemary

nutrition facts
Serving Size 1 cup

AMOUNT PER SERVING
Calories **243**
Total Fat **2 g**
Saturated Fat **0 g**
Cholesterol **0 mg**
Sodium **132 mg**
Total Carbohydrate **51 g**
Dietary Fiber **4 g**
Protein **5 g**
Percent Calories from Fat **8%**
Percent Calories from Protein **8%**
Percent Calories from Carbohydrate **84%**

Prep Time:
15 minutes
Cooking Time:
1 hour
Serves **8**

cooking instructions

1. Preheat the oven to 400°F.

2. In an ovenproof dish, place the butternut squash cut side down. In a small bowl, combine the shallots and oil, and season with salt and pepper, mixing well. Place the shallots around the squash and bake until very tender and slightly caramelized, about 45 minutes to 1 hour. Remove from the oven and allow to cool. Cut the shallots into large dice. Spoon the squash from the skin and cut into large dice. Reserve the dice and discard the skin.

3. While the squash is baking, combine the cranberries, water, and sugar in a large saucepan. Bring to a boil over high heat, then turn down to simmer, and cook until the cranberries are tender, about 30 minutes. Transfer to a colander, drain the cranberries, and reserve the cooking liquid. Add enough additional cranberry juice to the cooking liquid to measure 4 cups and return to the saucepan.

4. Bring the cranberry liquid to a simmer over medium-high heat. Add the couscous and cover with a tight-fitting lid. Stir occasionally, cooking until tender, about 20 minutes. Remove from the heat and transfer to a large ovenproof casserole. Add the cooked cranberries, roasted shallots, squash, chives, and rosemary. Season with salt and pepper. Cover with a lid or foil and keep warm in the oven until serving.

Classic Strawberry-Rhubarb Shortcakes

Recipe by FoodFit Chef Michael Lomonaco, *Gustavino's, New York, NY*

ingredients

FOR THE SHORTCAKES:

1 cup all-purpose flour, sifted
3 tablespoons sugar
1 teaspoon baking powder
1/4 teaspoon salt
3 tablespoons cold unsalted butter, cut into small pieces
1/4 cup buttermilk
1/4 cup heavy cream
2 tablespoons unsalted butter, melted

FOR THE TOPPING:

2 cups water
1 cup sugar
10 stalks rhubarb, sliced
1 cup heavy cream
4 teaspoons confectioners' sugar
2 teaspoons vanilla extract
2 quarts strawberries, washed and sliced

Prep Time:
40 minutes

Cooking Time:
35 minutes

Serves **8**

cooking instructions

For the shortcakes:

1. In a large bowl, combine the flour, sugar, baking powder, and salt. Stir thoroughly with a wooden spoon to combine.

2. Add the pieces of cold butter and stir to coat the small pieces with flour so that they do not stick together.

3. Add the buttermilk and cream. Stir briefly to combine, leaving the mixture as lumpy as possible.

4. Pour the lumpy dough onto a lightly floured surface. Flatten gently with a rolling pin into a squarish shape approximately 1" thick.

5. Cut into 4 equal squares. Place the squares on a baking sheet and brush with melted butter. Put the entire baking sheet into the refrigerator for 20 minutes while you preheat the oven to 375°F.

6. Bake the chilled shortcakes until nicely browned, about 20 to 25 minutes.

Classic Strawberry-Rhubarb Shortcakes (cont.)

For the topping:

1. In a saucepan, bring the water, sugar, and rhubarb to a low boil. Cook, uncovered, until the rhubarb falls apart and the mixture thickens slightly to about the consistency of applesauce. Let cool.

2. Place the cream, confectioners' sugar, and vanilla extract in a bowl and whisk until soft peaks form.

3. Split each shortcake in half. Spread 1 side with the whipped cream. Top the cream with strawberries. Spoon 1 tablespoon of the rhubarb mixture on top of the strawberries. Top with the other half of the shortcake.

nutrition facts
Serving Size 1 shortcake with topping

AMOUNT PER SERVING
Calories **421**
Total Fat **22 g**
Saturated Fat **12 g**
Cholesterol **66 mg**
Sodium **91 mg**
Total Carbohydrate **60 g**
Dietary Fiber **2 g**
Protein **3 g**
Percent Calories from Fat **43%**
Percent Calories from Protein **3%**
Percent Calories from Carbohydrate **53%**

Mixed Berry Smoothie

ingredients

1 cup orange juice
2 cups plain, low-fat yogurt
3/4 cup raspberries, washed
3/4 cup blackberries, washed
3/4 cup blueberries, washed
honey to taste

cooking instructions

1. Place the orange juice, yogurt, raspberries, blackberries, and blueberries in a blender. Blend on high speed until smooth, adding honey to adjust the sweetness to taste.

Prep Time: **5 minutes**
Serves **2**

nutrition facts
Serving Size about 1 cup

AMOUNT PER SERVING
Calories **139**
Total Fat **0 g**
Saturated Fat **0 g**
Cholesterol **3 mg**
Sodium **70 mg**
Total Carbohydrate **31 g**
Dietary Fiber **3 g**
Protein **6 g**
Percent Calories from Fat **3%**
Percent Calories from Protein **16%**
Percent Calories from Carbohydrate **81%**

Balsamic Strawberries with Strawberry Sorbet

ingredients

1 quart fresh strawberries, washed, hulls removed

1/2 cup balsamic vinegar

freshly ground black pepper (optional)

6 scoops of strawberry sorbet

nutrition facts

Serving Size 3/4 cup strawberries with a scoop of sorbet

AMOUNT PER SERVING

Calories **177**
Total Fat **1 g**
Saturated Fat **0 g**
Cholesterol **0 mg**
Sodium **7 mg**
Total Carbohydrate **43 g**
Dietary Fiber **4 g**
Protein **1 g**
Percent Calories from Fat **3%**
Percent Calories from Protein **2%**
Percent Calories from Carbohydrate **95%**

Prep Time:
10 minutes

Cooking Time:
10 minutes

Serves **6**

cooking instructions

1. Slice the strawberries in half if they are large or keep whole if they are small. Place in a bowl.

2. Heat the vinegar in a small pan over medium heat. Cook for about 5 to 10 minutes until the vinegar is reduced to a thick syrup.

3. Just before serving, ladle the syrup over the strawberries and gently toss to coat them. If desired, sprinkle with freshly ground black pepper for a spicy addition.

4. Serve with a scoop of strawberry sorbet.

Fruit Kebabs

Recipe by FoodFit Chef Jody Adams, Rialto, Boston, MA

ingredients

4 strawberries
16 large blueberries
12 grapes
4 1" pieces of pineapple
4 1" pieces of watermelon
4 narrow plastic straws or wooden skewers

Prep Time:
10 minutes

Serves **4**

instructions

1. Wash the berries and grapes and dry them well. Skewer the fruit on the straws or skewers in an appealing pattern. Wrap in plastic and refrigerate until ready to serve.

nutrition facts

Serving Size 1 skewer

AMOUNT PER SERVING
Calories **30**
Total Fat **0 g**
Saturated Fat **0 g**
Cholesterol **0 mg**
Sodium **1 mg**
Total Carbohydrate **7 g**
Dietary Fiber **0 g**
Protein **0 g**
Percent Calories from Fat **8%**
Percent Calories from Protein **4%**
Percent Calories from Carbohydrate **88%**

Rustic Fresh Blueberry-Peach Tart

ingredients

1 cup flour
6 tablespoons sugar
1/4 teaspoon salt
6 tablespoons very cold butter
3 tablespoons ice cold water
1 cup blueberries
1 cup peeled, sliced peaches

nutrition facts
Serving Size 1/8 of the tart

AMOUNT PER SERVING
Calories **189**
Total Fat **9 g**
Saturated Fat **5 g**
Cholesterol **23 mg**
Sodium **76 mg**
Total Carbohydrate **26 g**
Dietary Fiber **1 g**
Protein **2 g**
Percent Calories from Fat **41%**
Percent Calories from Protein **4%**
Percent Calories from Carbohydrate **54%**

Prep Time: **10 minutes**
Cooking Time: **30 minutes**
Serves **8**

cooking instructions

1. Preheat the oven to 400°F.
2. Place the flour, salt, butter, and 2 tablespoons sugar in a food processor fitted with blade attachment.
3. Process the mixture until the butter is the size of small peas.
4. With the motor running, add the water and process it for 15 seconds.
5. Turn the crumbly dough onto a work surface and form it into a disk. Chill for several hours.
6. Roll the dough out to a 9" or 10" shell.
7. Put the dough on a baking sheet and pile the blueberries and peaches toward the center. Sprinkle the fruit with the remaining sugar.
8. Gently fold the edges of the dough to contain the fruit.
9. Bake until the crust is lightly golden, about 20 to 30 minutes.

Chapter 14: Cantaloupes and Melons

RECIPES IN THIS CHAPTER:

Named for a castle in Italy, cantaloupes have orange flesh and a distinctive, sweet, and succulent taste. Truth be told, cantaloupes are only grown in Europe. The American fruits are actually muskmelons, but both are delicious.

Cantaloupes were cultivated in Egypt as early as 2400 BCE. Egyptian paintings dating back to that period include fruits that are identified as melons. There were also Roman manuals that gave specific directions on how to cultivate melons. Brought to the New World by Christopher Columbus, cantaloupes became a major crop in the United States after the Civil War.

Sweet, juicy, thirst-quenching, refreshing—melons have just what you want on a hot summer day. **Cantaloupes**, **honeydews**, and **watermelons** are all ideal for summertime enjoyment. Plus, they're fat-free, full of vitamins, and fun to eat, especially for kids. You can also try more exotic melons like **Crenshaw** and **casaba**, two varieties that really come into their own in the fall. Casabas are not as flavorful as other melons, but they last longer. The fragrant Crenshaw, on the other hand, tastes exquisite.

NUTRITION AND HEALTH

Cantaloupes and other melons are low in calories, and their high water content make them a good choice when you are watching your weight.

Packed with vitamins C, folate, and potassium, cantaloupes of all the melons are the most nutritious. Beta-carotene, a carotenoid thought to reduce the risk of chronic diseases, gives cantaloupes their orange color.

Watermelons offer vitamin C and, most importantly, are full

of lycopene, a cancer-fighting carotenoid, while honeydews contain zeaxanthin, another major carotenoid that can help maintain healthy cells and tissues in your eyes. Honeydews are also loaded with vitamin C.

WHAT TO LOOK FOR

Contrary to common belief, shaking cantaloupes isn't a good way to tell if they're ripe. Pick cantaloupes that feel heavy for their size, smell fragrant, are well-netted, and don't have any sign of a stem (that means they were picked too early).

Similarly, honeydews should feel heavy for their size and be well-rounded. Watermelon should have a symmetrical pattern, and be free of dents or bruises. The underside of the melon, where it sat on the ground, should be creamy yellow, not pale green or white.

Casaba melons are teardrop-shaped, and should have a deep yellow skin color and no dark or moist patches. The casaba's skin is coarse and has a thick, ridged rind; its flesh is creamy white to yellow. Crenshaw melons have a mottled, green-yellow ridged rind and orange-pink flesh.

EASY STORAGE AND PREPARATION

Most cantaloupes are sold before they're ready to eat. To ripen, put the melon in a loosely closed paper bag. Be sure it's whole; the fruit won't ripen once you've sliced into it. To store the cut, ripe fruit, it's important to wrap it tightly in plastic before putting it in the refrigerator, because cantaloupe easily absorbs the flavor of the foods around it as well as transfers its flavor to other foods!

Crenshaw and casaba melons are best at room temperature, and can be stored at room temperature for two to three days. Similarly, watermelon and honeydew can be stored at room temperature for several days, but should then be refrigerated after cutting.

A word to the wise—always be careful to wash your melons before you cut into them. Disease-causing bacteria may be clinging to the outer rind, and can be transferred to the flesh of the fruit when cut.

BEST USES

- Fresh melon is wonderful eaten on its own and is best at room temperature. A squeeze of lemon juice on the fruit can be a great way to draw out the flavor.
- Melons, especially sweet honeydew melons, are a great addition to fruit salads, salsas, smoothies, and sorbets.
- Blueberries and cantaloupe are a sweet match made in heaven.
- The Italians often pair melon with prosciutto, a salt-cured ham.
- In Egypt and Israel, watermelon is often served with savory feta cheese. The sweet and salty combination is truly delectable.

Luscious, ripe melon is easy to love. While it is commonly enjoyed at its most simple—sliced for breakfast or dessert—it also adds a refreshing splash of sweetness to soups, salads, and sauces. These recipes provide creative ways to use this healthful fruit, including melon kebabs and cantaloupe smoothies.

Fresh Cantaloupe Soup

Recipe by FoodFit Chef John Ash, Fetzer Vineyards, Napa Valley, CA

ingredients

8 cups cantaloupe, seeded and cut into 1/2" chunks

1 cup plain low-fat yogurt

1 cup fruity Gewurztraminer or Riesling white wine

1 tablespoon fresh lime juice

1 tablespoon honey (or to taste)

1/2 teaspoon freshly grated nutmeg

1 tablespoon finely chopped fresh mint

salt to taste

drops of hot sauce to taste

Garnish: a swirl of pureed and strained raspberries or blackberries

mint leaves and edible flower petals, if desired

nutrition facts

Serving Size 1 cup

AMOUNT PER SERVING

Calories **129**
Total Fat **1 g**
Saturated Fat **0 g**
Cholesterol **1 mg**
Sodium **343 mg**
Total Carbohydrate **25 g**
Dietary Fiber **2 g**
Protein **4 g**
Percent Calories from Fat **6%**
Percent Calories from Protein **10%**
Percent Calories from Carbohydrate **63%**

Prep Time: **10 minutes**

Serves **6**

instructions

1. In a food processor or blender, puree all of the ingredients (except the garnish) until smooth.

2. Pour into a bowl and chill for at least 2 hours for flavors to blend. (This can be made up to a day ahead.)

3. Garnish with berry puree, mint leaves, and flowers.

Cold Cucumber and Honeydew Melon Soup with Crab

Recipe by FoodFit Chef John Ash, Fetzer Vineyards, Napa Valley, CA

ingredients

2 quarts roughly chopped, peeled English cucumbers, seeds removed

1 quart roughly chopped, peeled ripe honeydew melon, seeds removed

3 tablespoons fresh lemon juice

1 tablespoon sugar

1/3 cup heavy cream

salt to taste

1/8 teaspoon hot sauce

10 ounces fresh crabmeat

3/4 cup diced yellow and/or red tomato, seeds removed

1/2 cup diced ripe (yet still firm) avocado

2 teaspoons chopped fresh chives

2 teaspoons chopped fresh tarragon (or basil)

Garnish: fresh herb sprigs

nutrition facts

Serving Size 1 cup

AMOUNT PER SERVING

Calories **186**
Total Fat **8 g**
Saturated Fat **3 g**
Cholesterol **60 mg**
Sodium **220 mg**
Total Carbohydrate **20 g**
Dietary Fiber **3 g**
Protein **13 g**
Percent Calories from Fat **35%**
Percent Calories from Protein **25%**
Percent Calories from Carbohydrate **40%**

Prep Time: **20 minutes**

Serves **6**

cooking instructions

1. Add the cucumbers, melon, 2 tablespoons of the lemon juice, and the sugar to a food processor and puree until smooth.

2. Strain through a medium strainer pushing down on the solids with a rubber spatula to extract as much liquid as possible.

3. Stir the cream into the liquid and season to taste with salt and hot sauce. You should end up with about 1 quart of soup. Cover and refrigerate for at least 1 hour.

4. Gently combine the crab, tomato, avocado, and herbs. Season to taste with salt, hot sauce, and lemon juice.

5. Gently press the crab mixture into a 1/4-cup measuring cup and unmold in the center of a large, flat soup plate. Ladle the chilled cucumber mixture around and garnish with herbs.

Light Cantaloupe Smoothie

ingredients

1 cup orange juice
1 cup peeled, cubed cantaloupe, seeds removed
honey to taste
1 cup ice

Prep Time:
5 minutes
Serves **2**

instructions

1. Place the juice, melon, and honey in a blender. Blend on high speed for 30 seconds. Add ice and blend until smooth. Pour into tall glasses and serve.

nutrition facts
Serving Size about 1 1/4 cups

AMOUNT PER SERVING
Calories **84**
Total Fat **0 g**
Saturated Fat **0 g**
Cholesterol **0 mg**
Sodium **8 mg**
Total Carbohydrate **20 g**
Dietary Fiber **1 g**
Protein **2 g**
Percent Calories from Fat **5%**
Percent Calories from Protein **7%**
Percent Calories from Carbohydrate **88%**

Watermelon Juice

ingredients

2 cups watermelon chunks, seedless
2 tablespoons sugar
1/2 cup cold water
5 ice cubes
juice of 1 lime (optional)

cooking instructions

1. Combine all of the ingredients in a blender and puree until smooth. Serve over ice.

Prep Time:
5 minutes
Serves **2**

Recipe by FoodFit Chefs Mary Sue Milliken and Susan Feniger, Border Grill, Santa Monica, CA

nutrition facts
Serving Size 1 tall glass

AMOUNT PER SERVING
Calories **105**
Total Fat **1 g**
Saturated Fat **0 g**
Cholesterol **0 mg**
Sodium **3 mg**
Total Carbohydrate **26 g**
Dietary Fiber **1 g**
Protein **1 g**
Percent Calories from Fat **5%**
Percent Calories from Protein **4%**
Percent Calories from Carbohydrate **91%**

Melon Kebabs with Yogurt Dipping Sauce

ingredients

1 cup plain low-fat yogurt
1 tablespoon fresh lime juice
1 tablespoon sugar (or to taste)
1 teaspoon chopped fresh cilantro leaves
1 1/2 cups cubed seedless watermelon (about 1" cubes)
1 1/2 cups cubed cantaloupe (about 1" cubes)
1 1/2 cups cubed honeydew (about 1" cubes)
8 metal or bamboo skewers

nutrition facts
Serving Size 2 fruit kebabs

AMOUNT PER SERVING
Calories **107**
Total Fat **1 g**
Saturated Fat **1 g**
Cholesterol **5 mg**
Sodium **50 mg**
Total Carbohydrate **22 g**
Dietary Fiber **1 g**
Protein **4 g**
Percent Calories from Fat **10%**
Percent Calories from Protein **14%**
Percent Calories from Carbohydrate **77%**

Prep Time:
20 minutes
Serves 4

cooking instructions

1. In a small mixing bowl, stir the yogurt, lime juice, sugar, and cilantro together.

2. Transfer the yogurt mixture to a small serving dish, cover and refrigerate until ready to serve.

3. Thread the cubes of watermelon, cantaloupe, and honeydew melon onto the skewers.

4. Serve the melon kebabs with the yogurt dipping sauce.

Watermelon-Lime Granita

Recipe by FoodFit Chef Gale Gand, Tru, Chicago, IL

ingredients

6 limes, juiced
1/2 cup water
1/4 cup sugar
4 cups watermelon cubes, seeds removed
1/8 teaspoon pure vanilla extract
40 dried currants

nutrition facts
Serving Size 1/2 cup

AMOUNT PER SERVING
Calories **100**
Total Fat **0 g**
Saturated Fat **0 g**
Cholesterol **0 mg**
Sodium **2 mg**
Total Carbohydrate **26 g**
Dietary Fiber **2 g**
Protein **0 g**
Percent Calories from Fat **3%**
Percent Calories from Protein **2%**
Percent Calories from Carbohydrate **95%**

Prep Time: **10 minutes**
Cooking Time: **5 minutes**
Serves **8**

cooking instructions

1. Warm the limes in the microwave for 30 seconds to slightly soften them (this will make them easier to juice) and then squeeze the juice from them.

2. Make a syrup by combining the water, sugar and 2 of the lime skulls (the peel after juicing) in a saucepan and bring to a boil. Boil until the sugar dissolves. Set aside to cool and remove the skulls.

3. Puree the watermelon cubes in a food processor or blender, then strain through a coarse strainer into the bowl containing the lime juice. Stir in the vanilla extract and cooled sugar syrup.

4. Pour into ice cube trays and freeze overnight. (The recipe can be made up to this point and kept frozen up to 3 days in advance.)

5. When ready to serve, place the watermelon ice cubes into a food processor fitted with a metal blade. Pulse the machine until the granita has the texture of crushed ice. Dot with the currants, making them look like watermelon seeds. Serve immediately or keep frozen until ready to serve.

Melon Gelato

Recipe by FoodFit Chef Alice Waters, Chez Panisse, Berkeley, CA

ingredients

1 small cantaloupe or muskmelon (about 2 1/2 pounds)
6 egg yolks
1/3 cup plus 1 tablespoon sugar
5 ounces (1/2 cup plus 1 tablespoon) light corn syrup
1/3 cup heavy cream
4 egg whites
1 tablespoon lemon juice

nutrition facts

Serving Size 1/2 cup

AMOUNT PER SERVING
Calories **214**
Total Fat **8 g**
Saturated Fat **4 g**
Cholesterol **173 mg**
Sodium **73 mg**
Total Carbohydrate **35 g**
Dietary Fiber **1 g**
Protein **4 g**
Percent Calories from Fat **31%**
Percent Calories from Protein **8%**
Percent Calories from Carbohydrate **61%**

Prep Time:
30 minutes
Serves **8**

cooking instructions

1. Cut the melon in half, scoop out the seeds, peel off the rind, and cut the flesh into small pieces. Puree until smooth in a blender or food processor.
2. Beat together the egg yolks and 1/3 cup sugar until thick.
3. Warm the corn syrup over low heat. Whisk the egg yolks and sugar into the syrup and cook over low heat, whisking just until warmed through. Remove from the heat and strain through a sieve.
4. Whip the cream until it begins to mound up and peak softly, and fold it into the egg-yolk mixture.
5. Beat the egg whites and 1 tablespoon sugar until they form soft peaks, fold into the yolk-and-cream mixture.
6. Stir in the melon puree and lemon juice and freeze according to the instructions for your ice-cream maker.

Cantaloupe, Yogurt, and Granola Parfaits with Blueberry Sauce

ingredients

FOR THE GRANOLA:

2 cups rolled oats
1/4 cup sliced almonds
1/4 cup honey
1/4 cup molasses
2 tablespoons water
1 1/2 tablespoons vegetable oil
1/4 teaspoon cinnamon
3/4 cup raisins

FOR THE BLUEBERRY SAUCE:

1 cup blueberries fresh or frozen
juice of 1/2 lemon
sugar (2 to 4 tablespoons, to taste)

FOR THE PARFAITS:

2 cups fresh cantaloupe, cubed, seeds removed
4 cups plain, nonfat yogurt

Prep Time: **30 minutes**

Cooking Time: **35 minutes**

Serves **8**

cooking instructions

For the granola:

1. Heat the oven to 375°F.

2. Combine the oats and almonds in a medium bowl.

3. In a small saucepan combine the honey, molasses, water, vegetable oil, and cinnamon and heat through, stirring for about 1 minute. Pour over the oat mixture and stir to blend.

4. Spread the granola onto a baking sheet and toast, stirring every 10 minutes until golden-crisp, about 30 minutes.

5. Remove from the oven and add the raisins. Cool completely before serving.

6. The granola can be made ahead and stored in an airtight container for up to three weeks in the refrigerator or at room temperature.

Cantaloupe, Yogurt, and Granola Parfaits with Blueberry Sauce (cont.)

For the blueberry sauce:

1. Puree the berries in a blender with the lemon juice. Blend in the sugar by the tablespoonful, tasting after each addition, until the desired degree of sweetness is reached.

2. Strain through a fine strainer, pressing with a rubber spatula to release the juices.

For the parfaits:

1. Layer the granola, cantaloupe, and yogurt in tall glasses and drizzle with blueberry sauce.

nutrition facts
Serving Size 1 parfait

AMOUNT PER SERVING
Calories **325**
Total Fat **5 g**
Saturated Fat **1 g**
Cholesterol **3 mg**
Sodium **86 mg**
Total Carbohydrate **64 g**
Dietary Fiber **4 g**
Protein **10 g**
Percent Calories from Fat **14%**
Percent Calories from Protein **74%**
Percent Calories from Carbohydrate **11%**

Ginger-Melon Marinade

ingredients

1/2 cup pureed cantaloupe (or other melon), seeds removed
1 tablespoon freshly grated ginger
2 tablespoons olive oil
2 tablespoons lemon juice
salt and pepper

Prep Time:
10 minutes

Seasons 4 chicken breasts or scallops

instructions

1. Whisk all the ingredients together in a bowl. Marinate in the refrigerator for at least 30 minutes or overnight.

Note: Use to marinate chicken breasts or scallops.

nutrition facts
Serving Size about 2 tablespoons

AMOUNT PER SERVING
Calories **20**
Total Fat **2 g**
Saturated Fat **0 g**
Cholesterol **0 mg**
Sodium **1 mg**
Total Carbohydrate **1 g**
Dietary Fiber **0 g**
Protein **0 g**
Percent Calories from Fat **75%**
Percent Calories from Protein **2%**
Percent Calories from Carbohydrate **23%**

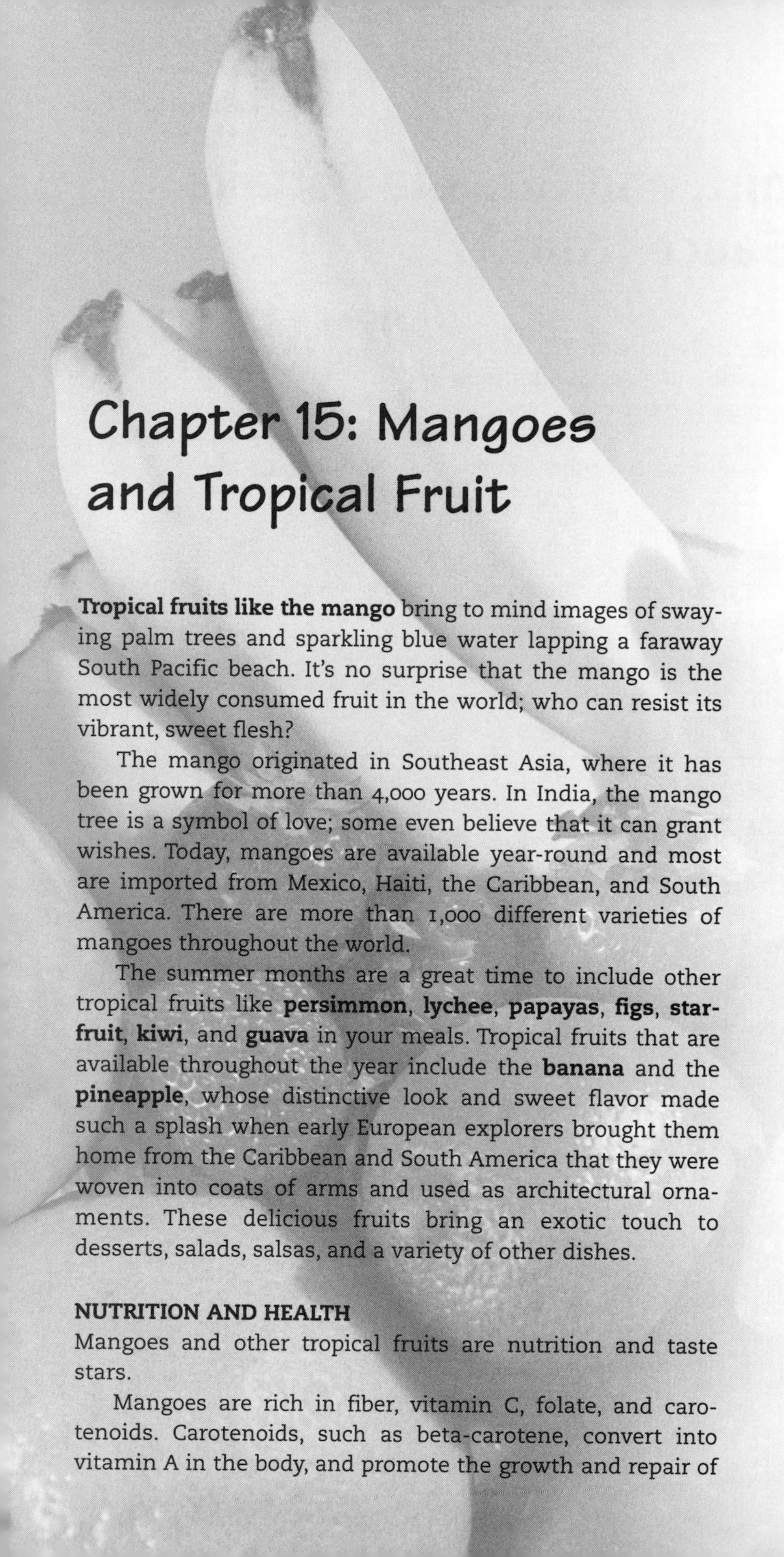

Chapter 15: Mangoes and Tropical Fruit

RECIPES IN THIS CHAPTER:

- Cucumber, Mango, and Red Onion Salad
- Mangospacho
- Pan-Roasted Red Snapper with Orange-and-Mango Salsa
- Salmon Teriyaki with Pineapple Salsa
- Thai Curried Chicken with Coconut and Mango
- Stir-Fry of Tropical Fruits in Spiced Crêpes
- Carrot-Pineapple Sweet Bread
- Banana Bran Muffins

Tropical fruits like the mango bring to mind images of swaying palm trees and sparkling blue water lapping a faraway South Pacific beach. It's no surprise that the mango is the most widely consumed fruit in the world; who can resist its vibrant, sweet flesh?

The mango originated in Southeast Asia, where it has been grown for more than 4,000 years. In India, the mango tree is a symbol of love; some even believe that it can grant wishes. Today, mangoes are available year-round and most are imported from Mexico, Haiti, the Caribbean, and South America. There are more than 1,000 different varieties of mangoes throughout the world.

The summer months are a great time to include other tropical fruits like **persimmon**, **lychee**, **papayas**, **figs**, **starfruit**, **kiwi**, and **guava** in your meals. Tropical fruits that are available throughout the year include the **banana** and the **pineapple**, whose distinctive look and sweet flavor made such a splash when early European explorers brought them home from the Caribbean and South America that they were woven into coats of arms and used as architectural ornaments. These delicious fruits bring an exotic touch to desserts, salads, salsas, and a variety of other dishes.

NUTRITION AND HEALTH

Mangoes and other tropical fruits are nutrition and taste stars.

Mangoes are rich in fiber, vitamin C, folate, and carotenoids. Carotenoids, such as beta-carotene, convert into vitamin A in the body, and promote the growth and repair of body tissue and maintain a strong immune system.

Bananas provide vitamin B6, fiber, and potassium, which helps keep blood pressure under control. Kiwis have a lot of vitamin C, fiber, and potassium, plus folate and vitamin E. Pineapples offer ample vitamin C, plus vitamin B1, which helps the body convert food into energy, among other key functions.

WHAT TO LOOK FOR

Smaller mangoes have the most flavor. Choose the fruit with smooth skins that are yellow-red and yield to slight pressure. They should also have a sweet aroma.

Similarly, pineapples and papayas should have a sweet aroma. Most tropical fruits should yield to gentle pressure and like bananas, have a vibrant color and be free of brown or black specks. Avoid any fruit with bruises or soft spots.

Kiwis should have brown skin that yields to slight pressure with no soft spots. They should also have a fragrant aroma. Unripe kiwis can be placed in a paper bag with an apple for 1 to 2 days to ripen.

When choosing guavas, look for those with knobby skin that ranges from yellow to purple. Guavas are usually 2 to 4 inches in diameter.

Choose figs that are firm but yield to slight pressure. The color can vary according to the variety, from pale green-yellow to almost black.

EASY STORAGE AND PREPARATION

Keep mangoes at room temperature, where the fruit will continue to ripen. To prepare, remove the skin and pit. Work over a bowl to save the juice. Ripe mangoes should be stored in the refrigerator. Handle mangoes carefully: The fruits are related to poison ivy and some people have a mild reaction after touching them.

Persimmons, which are winter fruits, should be kept in the refrigerator. Otherwise, most tropical fruits do best at room temperature.

Pineapple, however, should be put in the refrigerator once it's been cut. To peel the prickly exterior of a pineapple, place it on its side and lop off the frond top and the bottom. Next, stand it upright on the stem end and trim off the prickly exterior. The "eyes" or little brown nubs underneath will follow a diagonal pattern. Take a thin paring knife and slice down each side of the "eyes" to remove.

Figs will keep at room temperature for a few days or longer in the refrigerator.

BEST USES

- Mangoes are ideal for fruit salsas. Just peel a few mangoes, along with a mix of pears, peaches, kiwi, and pineapple. In a small bowl, combine the fruits, with one teaspoon of each lemon and lime juice, a quarter cup of chopped red onion, and a tablespoon of chopped cilantro. Refrigerate until ready to use.
- Raw mangoes are a nice addition to salads, smoothies, and sorbets. Mangoes also pair well with poultry and fish.
- Cooked mango is used in chutneys and relishes.
- Pineapple is a tasty contribution to fruit salads, salsas, sorbets, and smoothies. Cooked, it's a perfect partner for ginger, curry, coconut, rum, or black pepper. Or sizzle it under the broiler for a hot dessert.
- Bananas also make a fantastic dessert when brushed with orange juice and broiled. Spritz the banana with lemon juice after slicing to prevent discoloration. Use overripe bananas in banana bread or muffins.

Tropical fruits like the mango have become more readily available in local markets, making it possible to enjoy their sweet, sunny taste in entrées, desserts, and side dishes. Although they are perfect fresh, you will be wowed by the zing they bring to these recipes for salads, breads, and more.

ABOUT HERBS AND SPICES

Cilantro is a leafy, green herb that has a strong smell and a distinctive, refreshing taste. Look for fresh leaves. (Dried seeds are called coriander.) Cilantro is a popular addition to Mexican, South American, and Asian dishes and is great with ground meat, rice, and beans. Add fresh leaves at the last minute to fish, salads, salsas, and vegetables.

Cucumber, Mango, and Red Onion Salad

Recipe by FoodFit Chef Alice Waters, *Chez Panisse, Berkeley, CA*

ingredients

1 medium cucumber, peeled and thinly sliced

1 mango, pitted and cut into large dice

1 red onion, sliced into thin rounds

2 tablespoons lime juice

salt to taste

3 tablespoons fresh cilantro leaves

Prep Time:
15 minutes

Serves 4

instructions

1. Place the cucumber, mango, and red onion in a medium bowl.

2. Season to taste with the lime juice and salt.

3. Garnish generously with cilantro leaves.

nutrition facts

Serving Size about 1/2 cup

AMOUNT PER SERVING

Calories **58**
Total Fat **0 g**
Saturated Fat **0 g**
Cholesterol **0 mg**
Sodium **76 mg**
Total Carbohydrate **14 g**
Dietary Fiber **2 g**
Protein **1 g**
Percent Calories from Fat **3%**
Percent Calories from Protein **9%**
Percent Calories from Carbohydrate **88%**

Mangospacho

Recipe by FoodFit Chef Steven Raichlen, *cookbook author*

ingredients

3 large or 5 to 6 small mangoes, peeled and very finely diced (about 6 cups)

1 cucumber, peeled, seeded, and very finely diced

1/2 red bell pepper, very finely diced

1/2 small red onion, very finely diced

1 cup cold water, or as needed

3 tablespoons rice vinegar, or to taste

2 to 3 tablespoons olive oil

1 teaspoon Asian hot sauce, such as Thai Sriracha

1 to 2 tablespoons brown sugar, or to taste

1/4 cup finely chopped, fresh cilantro

pinch of salt (optional)

2 tablespoons finely chopped, fresh chives or cilantro

nutrition facts

Serving Size about 1 cup

AMOUNT PER SERVING

Calories **137**
Total Fat **5 g**
Saturated Fat **1 g**
Cholesterol **0 mg**
Sodium **153 mg**
Total Carbohydrate **25 g**
Dietary Fiber **3 g**
Protein **1 g**
Percent Calories from Fat **29%**
Percent Calories from Protein **4%**
Percent Calories from Carbohydrate **67%**

Prep Time: **30 minutes**

Serves **6**

cooking instructions

1. Combine the diced mangoes, cucumber, pepper, and onion in a mixing bowl and toss to combine. Place 2/3 of the mixture in a food processor (reserve the remaining 1/3 for later) and grind to a smooth puree. Add in the water, vinegar, oil, hot sauce, and sugar. If the mixture is too tart, add more sugar. If too thick, add more water.

2. Strain the mixture into a bowl and stir in the cilantro and the reserved diced mango, cucumber, bell pepper, and onion. Correct the seasoning, adding vinegar or sugar to taste, or even a pinch of salt. The soup can be served right away, but it will taste better if you refrigerate it for 1 hour to allow the flavors to blend.

3. To serve, ladle the mangospacho into bowls and garnish each with a sprinkling of chives or cilantro.

Pan-Roasted Red Snapper with Orange-and-Mango Salsa

Recipe by FoodFit Chef Allen Susser, Chef Allen's, Aventura, FL

ingredients

FOR THE SALSA:

2 large oranges, peeled, segmented, and diced
1 large mango, peeled, pitted, and diced
1/2 cup diced red onion
1 jalapeño pepper, seeded, and diced
2 tablespoons chopped, fresh cilantro
1/2 tablespoon olive oil
1 tablespoon freshly squeezed lime juice
1 teaspoon kosher salt
1/4 teaspoon freshly ground black pepper

FOR THE FISH:

4 6-ounce red snapper fillets
1 teaspoon kosher salt
1/4 teaspoon freshly ground black pepper
1 1/2 tablespoons olive oil
1 clove garlic, minced
1 cup fresh orange juice
1 tablespoon chopped, fresh cilantro

nutrition facts
Serving Size 1 fillet plus 1/2 cup salsa

AMOUNT PER SERVING
Calories **344**
Total Fat **10 g**
Saturated Fat **2 g**
Cholesterol **63 mg**
Sodium **1170 mg**
Total Carbohydrate **29 g**
Dietary Fiber **5 g**
Protein **36 g**
Percent Calories from Fat **26%**
Percent Calories from Protein **42%**
Percent Calories from Carbohydrate **33%**

Prep Time: **20 minutes**
Cooking Time: **10 minutes**
Serves **4**

cooking instructions

For the salsa:

1. In a stainless steel bowl, combine all the salsa ingredients and mix well. Set aside.

For the fish:

1. Season the snapper fillets with salt and pepper, then drizzle with olive oil.
2. Place a sauté pan large enough to accommodate all the fillets over medium-high heat. Add the snapper fillets and lower the heat to medium. Cook until well-browned on one side, about 3 minutes. Turn the fillets over and cook 1 more minute.
3. Add the garlic and orange juice to the pan. Bring to a low simmer, then remove the fish and place on a warm platter. Continue to simmer the juice for 3 to 4 minutes to reduce. Add the cilantro.
4. Place each fillet in the center of a warm plate. Pour the orange-flavored cooking juice over the fish and serve the salsa on the side.

Salmon Teriyaki with Pineapple Salsa

ingredients

FOR THE SALMON TERIYAKI:

3 tablespoons soy sauce
3 tablespoons mirin (rice wine)
3 tablespoons rice vinegar
3 tablespoons sugar
2 teaspoon freshly grated ginger
1/2 cup beer
4 salmon fillets, 4 to 6 ounces each

FOR THE SALSA:

2/3 cup diced, fresh or canned pineapple
3 teaspoons diced red onion
1/3 cup diced red pepper
1/2 jalapeño pepper, seeded and diced
2 teaspoons chopped cilantro
4 teaspoons orange juice

nutrition facts
Serving Size 1 salmon filet with salsa

AMOUNT PER SERVING
Calories **283**
Total Fat **9 g**
Saturated Fat **1 g**
Cholesterol **78 mg**
Sodium **322 mg**
Total Carbohydrate **16 g**
Dietary Fiber **1 g**
Protein **29 g**
Percent Calories from Fat **30%**
Percent Calories from Protein **42%**
Percent Calories from Carbohydrate **28%**

Prep Time:
30 minutes
Plus Marinating Time

Cooking Time:
10 minutes

Serves **4**

cooking instructions

For the salsa:

1. Combine the pineapple, onion, red pepper, jalapeño pepper, cilantro, and orange juice in a small mixing bowl. (This can be done in advance and stored in the refrigerator for up to 3 days.)

For the salmon teriyaki:

1. For the teriyaki marinade, combine the soy sauce, mirin, vinegar, sugar, ginger, and beer in a small saucepan. Cook over high heat until the mixture reduces by half. Let cool.

2. Marinate the salmon in the teriyaki marinade, cover and refrigerate for 15 to 30 minutes in the refrigerator.

3. Preheat the grill or broiler to medium-high.

4. Grill or broil the salmon on each side until it is cooked through, about 4 to 6 minutes per side, depending on thickness.

5. Serve a few spoonfuls of salsa on top of each salmon filet.

Thai Curried Chicken with Coconut and Mango

ingredients

1 to 2 teaspoons yellow curry paste (available at Asian markets), to taste
1 12 ounce-can light coconut milk
1 firm mango, peeled, pitted, and chopped
1 tablespoon olive oil
1 small onion, chopped
1 teaspoon minced garlic
2 cups chicken stock
1 medium eggplant (preferably Japanese), chopped into 1" cubes
4 grilled chicken breasts, sliced (about 4 to 6 ounces each before grilling)
salt to taste
freshly ground black pepper

nutrition facts
Serving Size about 1 1/2 cupS

AMOUNT PER SERVING
Calories **402**
Total Fat **12 g**
Saturated Fat **4 g**
Cholesterol **84 mg**
Sodium **178 mg**
Total Carbohydrate **25 g**
Dietary Fiber **7 g**
Protein **38 g**
Percent Calories from Fat **29%**
Percent Calories from Protein **43%**
Percent Calories from Carbohydrate **28%**

Prep Time: **15 minutes**
Cooking Time: **20 minutes**
Serves **4**

cooking instructions

1. Combine the curry paste, coconut milk, and mango in a small skillet. Bring to a boil, stirring occasionally, then turn down the heat and simmer.

2. Meanwhile, heat the oil in a large skillet over medium heat. Add the onion and cook until it turns translucent, about 5 minutes. Add the garlic and cook 1 minute more. Add chicken stock, by the tablespoonful, as needed to keep the mixture from sticking and burning.

3. Add the eggplant and the remaining chicken stock. Simmer until the eggplant becomes tender, about 10 minutes.

4. Add the sliced chicken and heat thoroughly.

5. Stir in the curry mixture, season to taste with salt and pepper, and serve.

Stir-Fry of Tropical Fruits in Spiced Crêpes

Recipe by FoodFit Chef Norman Van Aken, *Norman's, Coral Gables, Florida*

ingredients

FOR THE STIR-FRY:

3 tablespoons canola oil or grapeseed oil

1 carambola (star fruit), thinly sliced and cut into quarters

1/4 pineapple, peeled and diced

1 cup watermelon, peeled, seeds removed, and diced

1 banana, peeled and cut into small cubes (best done at last moment)

3 tablespoons spiced rum

1 cup apple cider (or juice)

juice of one lemon

1/2 cup honey

FOR THE CRÊPE BATTER:

3 eggs, beaten

1 cup skim milk

1 cup flour

1/8 teaspoon salt

1 teaspoon ground cinnamon

1 teaspoon ground cloves

2 tablespoons melted butter

nutrition facts

Serving Size 2 crepes with fruit

AMOUNT PER SERVING

Calories **420**
Total Fat **14 g**
Saturated Fat **4 g**
Cholesterol **117 mg**
Sodium **109 mg**
Total Carbohydrate **66 g**
Dietary Fiber **3 g**
Protein **8 g**
Percent Calories from Fat **29%**
Percent Calories from Protein **7%**
Percent Calories from Carbohydrate **61%**

Prep Time: **20 minutes**

Cooking Time: **15 minutes**

Serves **6**

cooking instructions

For the stir-fry:

1. Heat 3 tablespoons of the cooking oil in a large skillet or wok. When the oil is hot, add the fruits and cook for about 2 minutes. Now add the rum, cider, lemon juice, and honey. Allow the fruits to just get soft and then transfer them with a slotted spoon to a mixing bowl.

2. Heat the remaining liquid until it is reduced to a syrup. Strain it into a small saucepan. Keep warm. (If this mixture gets too thick, just whisk in a tiny bit more cider.) Reserve.

For the crêpes:

1. Whisk the eggs and milk together in a large bowl. Beat in the flour, salt, cinnamon, cloves and melted butter. Reserve.

2. Heat a nonstick crêpe pan over medium-high heat. Pour a few tablespoons of batter into the pan while tilting the pan so that the batter covers the bottom of the pan in a thin layer. When the crêpe is golden brown, flip it and cook the other side until golden brown, about 45 seconds.

3. Spoon some of the warmed fruit compote into 1 quadrant of each crêpe. Fold the crêpe in half and then spoon fruit into another quadrant.

4. Serve 2 crêpes per plate or a shallow soup plate and then with a spoon-drizzle some of the warm fruit syrup over the folded crêpe. Serve immediately.

Carrot-Pineapple Sweet Bread

ingredients

1/4 cup unsalted butter
2 medium eggs
3/4 cup sugar
pinch of cinnamon
1/2 teaspoon freshly ground black pepper
1/2 teaspoon grated orange zest
3/4 cup grated carrot
1 cup all purpose flour
1 1/4 teaspoons baking powder
pinch of salt
6 tablespoons drained, canned, crushed pineapple
1/4 cup toasted walnuts, chopped
cooking spray

nutrition facts
Serving Size 1 slice of bread

AMOUNT PER SERVING
Calories **154**
Total Fat **6 g**
Saturated Fat **3 g**
Cholesterol **37 mg**
Sodium **60 mg**
Total Carbohydrate **23 g**
Dietary Fiber **1 g**
Protein **2 g**
Percent Calories from Fat **35%**
Percent Calories from Protein **6%**
Percent Calories from Carbohydrate **59%**

Prep Time: **25 minutes**
Cooking Time: **36 minutes**
Serves 12

cooking instructions

1. Preheat the oven to 350°F. Remove the butter and the eggs from the refrigerator to allow them to come to room temperature.

2. Place the butter in a mixing bowl and beat at high speed with an electric mixer for 30 seconds. Gradually add the sugar and continue to beat until the mixture is pale yellow and very fluffy.

3. Add the eggs one at a time, mixing on low speed.

4. Stir in the cinnamon, black pepper, orange zest, and carrots.

5. Sift the flour, baking powder, and salt together.

6. Stir half the flour mixture into the butter-and-egg mixture. Stir in the pineapple and walnuts. Stir in the rest of the flour mixture. The batter should be smooth, but do not overmix.

7. Coat a 9" loaf pan with cooking spray. Pour the batter into the pan.

8. Bake until the loaf is golden brown and set in the center (test with a toothpick), about 30 to 35 minutes.

Banana Bran Muffins

ingredients

cooking spray
2 1/2 cups flour
3/4 cups sugar
1 1/2 teaspoons baking soda
1/4 teaspoon salt
2 large eggs, at room temperature
1 1/2 cups buttermilk
1 1/2 cups bran
1 cup mashed, ripe bananas

nutrition facts

Serving Size 1 muffin

AMOUNT PER SERVING
Calories **100**
Total Fat **1 g**
Saturated Fat **0 g**
Cholesterol **18 mg**
Sodium **125 mg**
Total Carbohydrate **21 g**
Dietary Fiber **2 g**
Protein **3 g**
Percent Calories from Fat **7%**
Percent Calories from Protein **12%**
Percent Calories from Carbohydrate **80%**

Prep Time:
15 minutes

Cooking Time:
25 minutes

Serves **24**

cooking instructions

1. Preheat oven to 350°F. Coat two 12-cup muffin pans with cooking spray.

2. Sift the flour, sugar, baking soda, and salt together.

3. Whisk together the eggs, buttermilk, and bran. Let stand for 10 minutes.

4. Make a well in the center of the dry ingredients and add the egg mixture all at once. Stir with a wooden spoon until the dry ingredients are just moistened.

5. Fold in the mashed bananas. (Be careful to keep the mixing to a minimum—a light stirring that leaves some lumps is fine. The dough should not be mixed to the point of pouring, but should break into coarse globs.) Fill the muffin pans two-thirds full, being careful not to drip the batter on the edge of the pans where it will burn and cause sticking.

6. Bake for about 25 minutes. The muffins are done when a knife inserted in the center of a muffin comes out dry.

Mango Liquado

ingredients

4 cups cubed, ripe mango
3 cups water
1/4 cup sugar, or to taste
juice of 1 lemon
lime wedges for garnish

instructions

1. In a blender, combine the mango and water and puree at high speed until smooth. Thin with more water, if desired. Add sugar and lemon juice to taste. Blend again and serve in tall glasses over ice with a wedge of lime.

nutrition facts

Serving Size 1 tall glass

AMOUNT PER SERVING
Calories **106**
Total Fat **0 g**
Saturated Fat **0 g**
Cholesterol **0 mg**
Sodium **2 mg**
Total Carbohydrate **28 g**
Dietary Fiber **2 g**
Protein **1 g**
Percent Calories from Fat **2%**
Percent Calories from Protein **2%**
Percent Calories from Carbohydrate **96%**

Prep Time:
5 minutes

Serves **6**

Recipe by FoodFit Chefs Mary Sue Milliken and Susan Feniger, *Border Grill, Santa Monica, CA*

PART IV

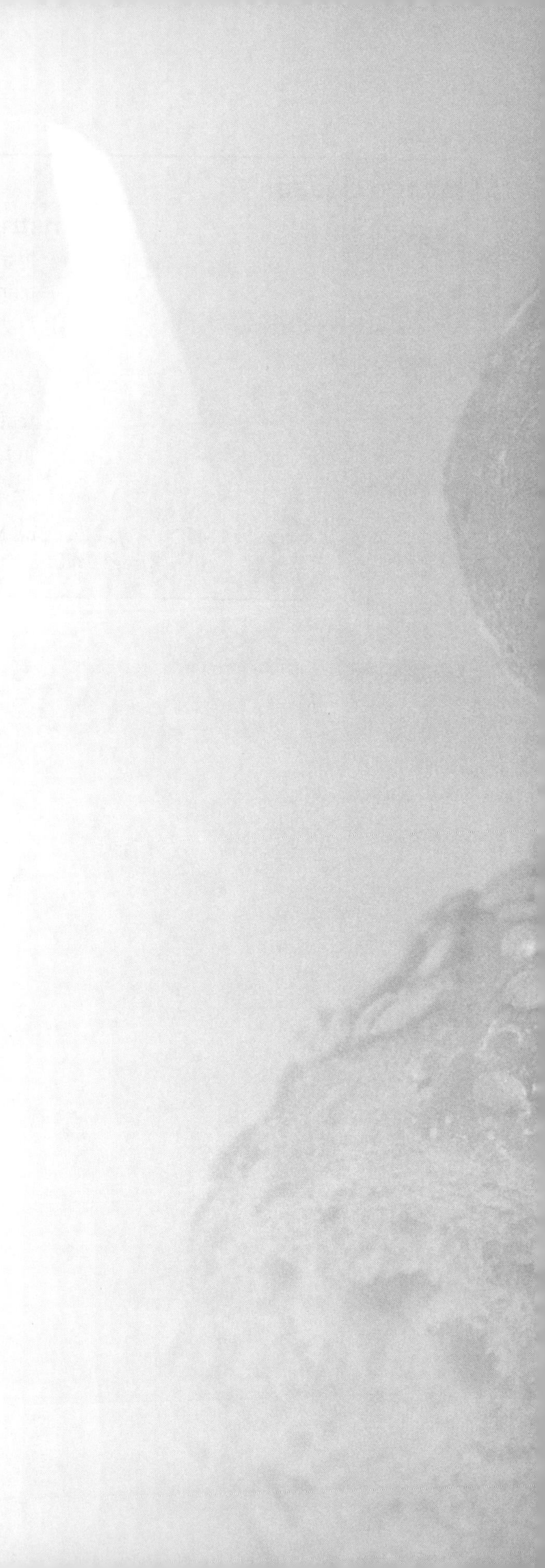

Grains, Beans, Nuts & Seeds

Chapter 16: Whole Wheat and Whole Grains

RECIPES IN THIS CHAPTER:

- Barley and Black-Eyed Pea Salad
- Aztecan Quinoa Salad
- Grilled Chicken Couscous Salad with Lemon-Yogurt Dressing
- Breakfast Bread with Carob and Carrots
- Lower-Fat French Toast
- Grits with Pecans and Brown Sugar
- Hearty Maple Wheat Bread
- Whole-Wheat Griddle Cakes with Cherry Sizzle
- Out-of-this-World Oatmeal Raisin Cookies
- Herbed Garlic Scented Bread

Wheat is the most cultivated plant in the world and foodstuffs made from the hearty, nutritious grain have an important place at dinner tables spanning the globe. In the Middle East, beloved tabouleh is made from **bulgur wheat**; in Turkey, wheat pilaf with yogurt and vegetables is a favourite, and Moroccan cuisine wouldn't be complete without **couscous**.

Unlike other grains, how wheat is processed determines its nutritional value. During processing or "polishing," the germ and the bran of grains (including many nutrients, such as vitamin B1) are removed, leaving only the endosperm, the least nutritious part of the grain. That's why, despite the fact that manufacturers "enrich" wheat products to replace some of the nutrients, it's best to stick to unprocessed or "whole" grains. When you see the term "whole," it means all three parts of the kernel remain.

Wheat is one of the most common grains and shows up in everything from pasta to cereal to crackers to bulgur, made from whole-wheat berries. But it's hardly the only grain available: **Oats**, **barley**, **corn**, **rye**, **quinoa**, **kasha**, **farro**, and **muesli** are all tasty alternatives to whole wheat.

NUTRITION AND HEALTH

Low in calories and fat, whole grains are a great source of complex carbohydrates, the primary fuel for our bodies. Whole grains also provide the bulk of the protein and soluble and non-soluble fiber in most of the world's cultures. Research shows that eating at least three servings of this powerful food each day can reduce your risk of diabetes and heart disease and help you maintain a healthy weight.

Whole wheat, a nutritionally dense food, is an important source of protein, fiber, B vitamins, and minerals such as iron, magnesium, and potassium.

Barley also provides B vitamins and iron, as well as the antioxidant selenium. Kasha (made from buckwheat groats) provides magnesium, which is key to bone growth, and copper, which helps red blood cells form. Oats are plentiful in iron, magnesium, selenium, zinc, and vitamin B1. The fiber in oats can help lower cholesterol. Corn has B vitamins, vitamin C, and iron, along with healthful fiber.

WHAT TO LOOK FOR

When buying bread and other wheat products, check the label. "Bleached," "enriched," or "refined" all mean that the grain has been processed. Be alert to labels that list "wheat flour." It sounds good, but wheat flour actually means it's 75 percent white flour and only 25 percent whole-wheat flour. As a rule of thumb, look for the "whole grain" label. If it doesn't say whole grain, then it probably isn't.

In addition, there are many products made from wheat berries, including bulgur, cracked wheat, and wheat germ. In many markets bulgur may be labeled cracked wheat and vice versa, but don't worry—they can be used interchangeably in many recipes. It comes in fine, medium, and coarse grinds. Fine or medium is most commonly used for tabouleh and coarse or medium are used for pilaf or stuffing. Cracked wheat is uncooked wheat berries that have been crushed. It comes in coarse and medium grinds and requires about 15 minutes of cooking. Wheat germ is made from the inner part of the wheat kernel.

Oats, barley, and couscous can be found in quick-cooking varieties. Quinoa has the whitest grains, about the size of mustard seeds. Cornmeal and grits (also called hominy) are ground and can be coarse, medium, or fine.

EASY STORAGE AND PREPARATION

Store all grains in a cool, dry cupboard, away from light. While they don't last forever, most will keep for up to a year under good conditions. Bulgur can go rancid, so it's best to buy it in smaller quantities or store it in the freezer.

Most whole grains should be washed before use, although soaking bulgur is another way to cook it. Before cooking quinoa, sauté it in a dry skillet for a few minutes for added flavor.

Wheat germ, tiny, crumb-like, pale-gold grains with a nutty taste, does not need to be cooked before using. But most grains need to be boiled or simmered in water.

BEST USES

- Grains' subtle flavors and interesting textures are a background for more dynamic culinary accents. They don't mind being a foil for more piquant foods such as wild mushrooms, chestnuts, and butternut squash or accents such as herbs, pine nuts, almonds, raisins, and currants.
- Whole-wheat bread is a great way to turn the average sandwich into a nutrition powerhouse.
- Wheat pasta is a good substitute for regular pasta—you will have the same great flavor and added nutrients. In addition to ordinary macaroni, look for Asian wheat noodles such as egg, udon, and somen noodles.
- Whole wheat works as cereal or in casseroles, salads, and stuffings. Wheat germ can simply be sprinkled over yogurt or hot cereal. Bulgur or cracked wheat make a tasty pilaf.
- Recently, many less familiar types of grains have become more available in the United States. Kasha, for instance, is whole buckwheat groats, much beloved by Russians and Ashkenazic Jews. It has a robust flavor and is dark tan in color. It usually comes in boxes at the market. Kasha is very hearty and filling, and is often mixed with noodles.
- Farro is an early variety of wheat. Cooked farro can be tossed with oil and vinegar to make a wonderful salad.

It's easy to incorporate the wide selection of nutritious grains into your everyday meals. They are perfect all year long, providing heartiness to winter dishes and delicate flavors to summer dishes. Here are some ways to add glorious grains to your meals, from grilled chicken salad to chewy cookies.

Barley and Black-Eyed Pea Salad

Recipe by FoodFit Chef John Ash, Fetzer Vineyard, Napa Valley, CA

ingredients

FOR THE SALAD:

1/3 cup pearl barley

1 1/3 cups vegetable stock

3/4 cup frozen black-eyed peas

3/4 large yellow bell pepper, charred, peeled, and diced

3/4 large tomato, seeds removed, and diced (about 3/4 cup)

3/4 cup green onions, sliced on the bias (about 1" pieces)

3/4 cup fresh sweet corn kernels

FOR THE DRESSING:

3 tablespoons fresh lime or lemon juice

1/2 teaspoon grated lime or lemon zest

1/2 teaspoon minced, blanched garlic

1/2 teaspoon ground cumin

1 1/2 teaspoons finely minced cilantro

1 1/2 tablespoons olive oil

honey

salt to taste

freshly ground black pepper

nutrition facts

Serving Size about 1/2 cup of salad

AMOUNT PER SERVING

Calories **135**

Total Fat **4 g**

Saturated Fat **1 g**

Cholesterol **0 mg**

Sodium **202 mg**

Total Carbohydrate **22 g**

Dietary Fiber **5 g**

Protein **4 g**

Percent Calories from Fat **26%**

Percent Calories from Protein **11%**

Percent Calories from Carbohydrate **63%**

Prep Time: **10 minutes**

Cooking Time: **45 minutes**

Serves **6**

cooking instructions

1. Place the barley in a dry saucepan over moderate heat and toast lightly (about 5 minutes). Stir regularly to prevent burning. Add the stock and bring to a boil. Reduce heat, cover, and simmer gently until liquid is absorbed, about 30 minutes. Remove from the heat, partially uncover, and allow the barley to cool before stirring.

2. While the barley is cooking, in a separate pot add the black-eyed peas to lightly salted water and cook until just tender but not mushy, 18 to 20 minutes. Drain, cool, and set aside.

3. Layer the barley, black-eyed peas, pepper, tomato, onions, and corn in a glass bowl.

4. In a separate small bowl, whisk together the lime (or lemon) juice, zest, garlic, cumin, cilantro, and oil, along with a few drops of honey, salt, and pepper to taste. Pour over the salad.

5. To serve, arrange greens on chilled plates and top with the salad mixture.

Aztecan Quinoa Salad

Recipe by FoodFit Chefs Mary Sue Milliken *and* Susan Feniger, *Border Grill, Santa Monica, CA*

ingredients

12 cups water

1 1/2 cups quinoa, rinsed

5 pickling cucumbers, peeled, ends trimmed and cut into 1/4" cubes

1 small red onion, cut into 1/4" cubes

1 medium tomato, cored, seeds removed, and diced

1 bunch (1/2 cup) Italian parsley leaves, chopped

1 bunch (1/2 cup) cilantro leaves, chopped

1/2 cup olive oil

1/4 cup red wine vinegar

juice of 1 lemon

1 1/2 teaspoons salt

1 teaspoon freshly ground black pepper

8 romaine lettuce leaves

nutrition facts

Serving Size about 3/4 cup salad

AMOUNT PER SERVING

Calories **276**

Total Fat **15 g**

Saturated Fat **2 g**

Cholesterol **0 mg**

Sodium **451 mg**

Total Carbohydrate **29 g**

Dietary Fiber **4 g**

Protein **6 g**

Percent Calories from Fat **49%**

Percent Calories from Protein **9%**

Percent Calories from Carbohydrate **42%**

Prep Time: **40 minutes**

Cooking Time: **15 minutes**

Serves **8**

cooking instructions

1. Bring water to a boil in a large saucepan. Add the quinoa, stir once, and return to boil. Cook uncovered, over medium heat for 12 minutes. Strain and rinse well with cold water, shaking the sieve well to remove all moisture.

2. When dry, transfer the quinoa to a large bowl. Add the cucumbers, onion, tomato, parsley, cilantro, olive oil, vinegar, lemon juice, salt, and pepper. Toss until well mixed.

3. Top each romaine leaf with about 3/4 cup of the salad and serve on chilled plates.

Grilled Chicken Couscous Salad with Lemon-Yogurt Dressing

ingredients

FOR THE DRESSING:

1 tablespoon fresh lemon juice
1/2 teaspoon salt
freshly ground black pepper
1 tablespoon sugar
2 cups plain, non-fat yogurt
1 tablespoon olive oil
1 teaspoon chopped fresh mint

FOR THE SALAD:

4 boneless, skinless chicken breasts, about 4 to 6 ounces each
1 cup cherry tomatoes, halved
1 medium cucumber, peeled, halved lengthwise, seeds removed, and sliced
1/2 cup chopped scallions
1 cup uncooked instant couscous
pinch of salt
1/4 cup halved, pitted black olives
1/2 cup crumbled feta cheese
4 fresh mint sprigs, for garnish

Prep Time:
20 minutes
Plus Marinating Time

Cooking Time:
15 minutes

Serves 4

cooking instructions

For the dressing:

1. In a small mixing bowl, whisk the lemon juice, salt, pepper, and sugar together. Whisk in the yogurt and olive oil and stir in the mint. (The dressing can be made in advance and stored in the refrigerator for several days.)

For the salad:

1. In a resealable bag or shallow container, marinate the chicken breast in 1 cup of the dressing. Refrigerate for 15 minutes (or can be marinated overnight).

2. In a large mixing bowl, combine the tomatoes, cucumber, scallions and the remaining dressing. Cover and refrigerate for 15 minutes (or can be marinated overnight).

3. Preheat the grill to medium.

4. Take the chicken out of the marinade and grill for about 6 minutes on each side, or until it is cooked through. Transfer the chicken to a cutting board, and when it is cool enough to handle, slice it into thin strips. Toss the chicken with the vegetable mixture and refrigerate.

Recipe continued on next page

Grilled Chicken Couscous Salad with Lemon-Yogurt Dressing (cont.)

5. Bring 1 1/2 cups of water to a boil. Stir in the couscous and a pinch of salt, cover, remove from heat, and let stand for 5 minutes. Fluff the couscous with a fork and transfer it to a large serving bowl. Stir in the vegetables and chicken and season with salt and pepper. (The salad can be made in advance and stored in the refrigerator for up to 2 days. It can be served chilled or at room temperature.)

6. Garnish the salad with olives, feta cheese, and mint sprigs.

nutrition facts
Serving Size 1 chicken breast with 1 cup couscous

AMOUNT PER SERVING
Calories **378**
Total Fat **11 g**
Saturated Fat **4 g**
Cholesterol **101 mg**
Sodium **740 mg**
Total Carbohydrate **27 g**
Dietary Fiber **2 g**
Protein **43 g**
Percent Calories from Fat **26%**
Percent Calories from Protein **46%**
Percent Calories from Carbohydrate **28%**

Breakfast Bread with Carob and Carrots

Recipe by FoodFit Chef Bill Wavrin, Miraval Resort and Spa, Catalina, AZ

ingredients

1 1/3 cups whole-grain wheat flour
3 tablespoons oat bran
1/2 teaspoon baking soda
1/2 teaspoon baking powder
1 1/8 teaspoons ground cinnamon
1/2 teaspoon ground ginger
3 tablespoons nonfat yogurt
1/2 cup apple juice
1 1/8 teaspoons vanilla extract
1/2 teaspoon canola oil
1 1/2 tablespoons honey
2 egg whites
3 tablespoons grated carrots
1 1/2 tablespoons carob chips
cooking spray

nutrition facts
Serving Size 2 slices of bread

AMOUNT PER SERVING
Calories **91**
Total Fat **1 g**
Saturated Fat **1 g**
Cholesterol **0 mg**
Sodium **90 mg**
Total Carbohydrate **18 g**
Dietary Fiber **3 g**
Protein **3 g**
Percent Calories from Fat **10%**
Percent Calories from Protein **14%**
Percent Calories from Carbohydrate **74%**

Prep Time:
15 minutes
Cooking Time:
45 minutes
Serves **10**
(2 loaves of bread)

cooking instructions

1. Preheat the oven to 350°F.

2. Sift together the wheat flour, oat bran, baking soda, baking powder, cinnamon, and ginger. Set aside. (This can be done the night before and kept covered at room temperature.)

3. In a separate bowl, mix the yogurt, apple juice, vanilla extract, oil, honey, egg whites, and carrots together.

4. Mix the dry ingredients into the wet ingredients.

5. Add the carob chips and fold together until blended. Do not overmix; this will toughen the bread.

6. Spray 2 small loaf pans with cooking spray and fill each pan 3/4 full with batter. Place on the center rack of the preheated oven and bake 45 minutes. The breads are done when a toothpick inserted into the center of a loaf comes out dry. Cool on a rack for 15 minutes. Slice each loaf into 10 slices.

Lower-Fat French Toast

ingredients

2 tablespoons egg substitute
3/4 cup skim milk
2 tablespoons sugar
1/4 teaspoon ground cinnamon
dash of nutmeg
1 teaspoon vanilla extract
peanut oil, as needed
4 slices whole-wheat bread, slightly stale

nutrition facts
Serving Size 2 slices of French toast

AMOUNT PER SERVING
Calories **241**
Total Fat **5 g**
Saturated Fat **1 g**
Cholesterol **2 mg**
Sodium **316 mg**
Total Carbohydrate **40 g**
Dietary Fiber **1 g**
Protein **11 g**
Percent Calories from Fat **18%**
Percent Calories from Protein **17%**
Percent Calories from Carbohydrate **63%**

Prep Time: **5 minutes**
Cooking Time: **10 minutes**
Serves **2**

cooking instructions

1. Whisk together the egg substitute, milk, sugar, cinnamon, nutmeg, and vanilla extract until thoroughly mixed. (This can be done ahead and refrigerated overnight.)
2. Heat a well-greased griddle or large frying pan with peanut oil until hot but not smoking.
3. Soak the bread slices in the egg mixture until moistened. Place the soaked slices on the griddle. Discard any excess egg mixture.
4. When the bottoms are golden brown, flip with a spatula, and brown the other side. Keep them in a warm oven until ready to serve.

Grits with Pecans and Brown Sugar

ingredients

2 cups water
2 cups skim milk
1 cup hominy
pinch of salt
2 teaspoons butter
2 tablespoons chopped pecans
1 tablespoon brown sugar

nutrition facts
Serving Size about 3/4 cup

AMOUNT PER SERVING
Calories **128**
Total Fat **4 g**
Saturated Fat **1 g**
Cholesterol **6 mg**
Sodium **169 mg**
Total Carbohydrate **19 g**
Dietary Fiber **3 g**
Protein **6 g**
Percent Calories from Fat **27%**
Percent Calories from Protein **17%**
Percent Calories from Carbohydrate **56%**

Prep Time: **10 minutes**
Cooking Time: **1 hour 10 minutes**
Serves **4**

cooking instructions

1. Bring the water and milk to a boil, then stir in the hominy, and add a pinch of salt. Cook over low heat, stirring constantly, until the grits thicken, about 5 minutes.

2. Cover and cook until the grits are tender, about 1 hour. (If the grits get too thick, add a little water to thin them.) Stir in the butter and pecans and sprinkle with brown sugar. Serve hot.

Hearty Maple Wheat Bread

ingredients

2 cups all-purpose flour
3/4 cup wheat germ
1 1/2 teaspoons baking powder
1/2 teaspoon baking soda
2 large eggs
1 cup 2% milk
2/3 cup maple syrup
1/4 cup canola oil

nutrition facts
Serving Size 1 slice

AMOUNT PER SERVING
Calories **211**
Total Fat **7 g**
Saturated Fat **1 g**
Cholesterol **37 mg**
Sodium **105 mg**
Total Carbohydrate **33 g**
Dietary Fiber **2 g**
Protein **6 g**
Percent Calories from Fat **28%**
Percent Calories from Protein **10%**
Percent Calories from Carbohydrate **61%**

Prep Time:
15 minutes
Cooking Time:
45 minutes
Makes 1 loaf

cooking instructions

1. Grease a 9 x 5" loaf pan. Preheat the oven to 350°F.
2. In a medium bowl, combine the flour, wheat germ, baking powder, and baking soda.
3. In a separate bowl, combine the eggs, milk, syrup, and oil.
4. Combine the dry and liquid ingredients, mixing well. Pour the batter into the prepared pan. Bake for 45 minutes or until a knife inserted in the center of the loaf comes out dry.

Whole-Wheat Griddle Cakes with Cherry Sizzle

ingredients

FOR THE CHERRY SIZZLE:

1 1/2 teaspoons butter
3 cups cherries, pitted and halved
3/4 cup maple syrup

FOR THE WHOLE-WHEAT GRIDDLE CAKES:

1/2 cup whole-wheat flour
1/2 cup all-purpose flour
2 teaspoons baking powder
1/2 teaspoon salt
2/3 cup skim milk
1 large egg
1 tablespoon canola oil
2 tablespoons honey

nutrition facts

Serving Size about 3 small cakes topped with 1/2 cup of cherry sizzle

AMOUNT PER SERVING
Calories **362**
Total Fat **6 g**
Saturated Fat **2 g**
Cholesterol **46 mg**
Sodium **362 mg**
Total Carbohydrate **74 g**
Dietary Fiber **4 g**
Protein **6 g**
Percent Calories from Fat **15%**
Percent Calories from Protein **7%**
Percent Calories from Carbohydrate **78%**

Prep Time:
15 minutes
Cooking Time:
25 minutes
Serves **5**

cooking instructions

For the cherry sizzle:

1. In a small skillet, melt the butter over medium heat. Add the cherries and cook until they begin to soften slightly, about 2 to 3 minutes.

2. Add the maple syrup and bring to a boil. Set aside and keep warm.

For the whole-wheat griddle cakes:

1. Mix the flours, baking powder, and salt in a bowl.

2. In a separate bowl, lightly beat the milk, egg, oil, and honey together.

3. Add the liquid ingredients all at once to the flour mixture. Stir with a wooden spoon until just moistened. Do not overmix; a few lumps are fine.

4. Warm a lightly greased griddle pan over medium heat. The pan is ready when a few drops of water sprinkled on the griddle form fast-moving bubbles.

5. Pour batter onto the griddle, 1/8 cup for small or 1/4 cup for large pancakes. When the tops of the pancakes are covered with holes and the bottoms are golden brown, flip to brown the other side.

6. Serve the griddle cakes topped with the warm cherry sizzle.

Out-of-this-World Oatmeal Raisin Cookies

ingredients

cooking spray
1 cup all-purpose flour
1 teaspoon baking powder
1/2 teaspoon baking soda
1/2 teaspoon salt
2 tablespoons butter
1/2 cup sugar
1/2 cup light brown sugar
1/4 cup unsweetened applesauce
1 large egg
1 teaspoon vanilla extract
1 1/3 cups rolled oats
1/2 cup raisins

nutrition facts
Serving Size 2 cookies

AMOUNT PER SERVING
Calories **186**
Total Fat **3 g**
Saturated Fat **1 g**
Cholesterol **11 mg**
Sodium **216 mg**
Total Carbohydrate **37 g**
Dietary Fiber **1 g**
Protein **3 g**
Percent Calories from Fat **14%**
Percent Calories from Protein **7%**
Percent Calories from Carbohydrate **79%**

Prep Time: **10 minutes**
Cooking Time: **12 minutes**
Serves **24**

cooking instructions

1. Preheat the oven to 375°F. Lightly spray two baking sheets with cooking spray.

2. In a large bowl, combine the flour, baking powder, baking soda, and salt.

3. In the bowl of an electric mixer, cream the butter and both sugars together. Beat until smooth, about 1 minute. Add the applesauce, egg, and vanilla extract and mix until blended, about 2 minutes. Add the flour to the applesauce mixture and mix well. Stir in the oats and raisins.

4. Drop rounded teaspoonfuls about two inches apart onto the prepared baking sheets.

5. Bake until slightly golden, about 10 to 12 minutes.

6. Remove the baking sheets from the oven and cool on wire racks for 5 minutes. Remove the cookies and cool completely. (These cookies can be made ahead and stored in an airtight container for up to two weeks.)

Herbed Garlic Scented Bread

Recipe by FoodFit Chef Bill Wavrin, *Miraval Resort and Spa, Catalina, AZ*

ingredients

2 1/2 cups warm water
2 tablespoons yeast
1 tablespoon salt
1 tablespoon honey
2 tablespoons olive oil
1 tablespoon chopped, fresh rosemary
1 tablespoon chopped, fresh oregano
2 tablespoons minced garlic
7 cups whole-grain wheat flour, more or less may be needed

nutrition facts
Serving Size about 1 slice of bread

AMOUNT PER SERVING
Calories **116**
Total Fat **1 g**
Saturated Fat **0 g**
Cholesterol **0 mg**
Sodium **235 mg**
Total Carbohydrate **24 g**
Dietary Fiber **4 g**
Protein **5 g**
Percent Calories from Fat **10%**
Percent Calories from Protein **13%**
Percent Calories from Carbohydrate **76%**

Prep Time:
1 hour

Cooking Time:
50 minutes

Makes **2** *loaves about* **15** *slices each*

cooking instructions

1. In a large mixing bowl add water, yeast, salt, and honey, and mix well. Then add the oil, herbs, and garlic. Allow 5 minutes for yeast to activate.

2. Add half of the whole-wheat flour to the yeast mixture. Mix by hand or with bread hook of a mixer. Continue to add a little flour at a time until all is incorporated into the dough. Continue kneading until the dough is no longer sticky, this should take about 7 to 8 minutes. The dough should be a little tacky but never sticky. (See Rule of Thumb below.)

3. Divide the dough in half. Massage to form two free-form loaves, or punch them into two 9" x 5" x 3" or equivalent loaf pans. Let rise to double in size, about 40 minutes.

4. Meanwhile, preheat the oven to 375°F.

5. Place the loaves in the center of your preheated oven and bake 40 to 50 minutes or until the bread is golden brown. Test by inserting a toothpick or skewer into the center of each loaf and, if it comes out clean, your bread is ready. Remove from the oven, take the bread out of the pans and set on a rack to cool before slicing. This bread will keep 3 to 4 days in an airtight container. When wrapped airtight with plastic film, it freezes well for 2 months.

   Rule of Thumb: "Insert thumb into dough and count to 5. If thumb comes out tacky with dough, add a little more flour and continue massaging until thumb comes out clean."

Chapter 17: Brown and Other Types of Rice

RECIPES IN THIS CHAPTER:

- Brown Rice and Crunchy Vegetable Salad
- Golden Rice Pilaf
- Wild Rice with Dried Cranberries and Walnuts
- Farro-Kale Risotto
- Asian Tofu Salad with Brown Rice
- Lemony Risotto with Asparagus and Shrimp
- Brown Rice Pilaf with Chicken and Dried Apricots
- Rice Pudding

Rice has been a mainstay in people's diets for thousands of years. It was first cultivated in Asia around 5,000 B.C., but was consumed long before that. There is a reference in the Koran to rice and barley as "the twin sons of heaven." Rice remains a global food staple because it is very filling, low in fat, affordable, and an excellent source of nutrients. Over 7,000 types of rice are grown around the world. Brown rice is simply white rice that has not been milled.

There are so many varieties of rice, you can have a different kind every night of the week. Besides **brown rice**, some of the more popular kinds of rice include **Arborio**, **basmati**, **black**, **Carolina**, **jasmine**, **Louisiana pecan/wild pecan**, **sticky**, **sushi**, **texmati**, **risotto**, and **wild rice**. Both brown and white rice come in short, medium, and long-grain varieties.

NUTRITION AND HEALTH

Different types of rice provide different vitamins and minerals, but all are a good source of fiber, which can help prevent heart disease, cancer, and diabetes. Just 1 cup of brown rice contains 3 1/2 grams of fiber. All rice is low in fat and calories, and rich in carbohydrates, but white rice is not quite as wholesome as brown.

Long-grain brown rice is a good source of fiber, iron, phosphorus, and three B vitamins. It is also very rich in magnesium, which aids nerve and muscle function and bone growth. In the United States, white rice is often fortified with B vitamins, including folate, and iron to make it more nutritious.

Wild rice, which is really a seed, is particularly high in protein.

WHAT TO LOOK FOR

Long-grain brown rice is a whole, unpolished grain. Medium-grain rice has a short, plump kernel. Short-grain is more dense and sticky when cooked.

Because brown rice contains natural oils, it can turn rancid on the shelf. Choose a store that has high turnover, and check for usability dates on packages. You should also look for whole, unbroken kernels.

Basmati, available in white or brown, is an aromatic long-grain rice from India and Pakistan that has slender, fragrant grains and a nutty flavor.

Instant rice is a great option for busy cooks. Both brown and white rice are available in instant forms. Look for packages marked "instant" or "quick-cooking." Instant rice shortens the cooking time to about 5 minutes, and is almost as nutritious as its longer-cooking counterpart.

EASY STORAGE AND PREPARATION

Most rice can be stored in the pantry in sealed containers for extensive periods of time, but brown rice should be stored in the refrigerator or freezer.

Most rice should be rinsed before cooking. To cook rice, bring 1 part rice and 2 parts water or stock or broth to a boil. Brown rice takes about 45 minutes to cook, at a simmer, while white rice cooks in about 18 minutes.

Using a rice cooker is an easy way to cook rice. Depending on the brand and capacity, a rice cooker will cut the cooking time for brown rice to about 20 minutes, while the cooking time for white rice stays about the same.

BEST USES

- Long-grain brown rice is delicious with curried vegetables or in a stuffing for pork chops. It also makes an excellent pilaf, side dish, or salad. Medium-grain brown rice is an all-purpose rice used in soups, side dishes, and salads.
- Short-grain brown rice can be used instead of white rice in sushi. Most Chinese restaurants also offer brown rice. Ask for it on your next visit to your favorite sushi bar or Chinese restaurant.
- To make a classic risotto, use short-grain Arborio rice. Use the rice as a base and add whatever vegetables are in the market, such as Swiss chard, asparagus, mushrooms, and tomatoes.
- Wild rice adds an earthy flavor to every dish, as well as a distinctive color. Hot or cold, wild rice makes a tasty rice salad. Toss some toasted nuts in it for an added crunch.

Rice, a staple in many of the world's cuisines, can play a part as a side dish, entrée, and even dessert, and offers a number of varieties to please any palate. These recipes span the globe from Asia to Italy, and are sure to spark a love affair with this versatile grain.

ABOUT HERBS AND SPICES

Curry powder is a blend of herbs and spices. Turmeric, cinnamon, ginger, pepper, coriander, and cumin are common components. Look for ground powder. Curry is widely used in Indian cooking to make savory meat, fish, or vegetables dishes. There is no one specific blend.

Brown Rice and Crunchy Vegetable Salad

ingredients

1 cup short-grain brown rice
2 medium zucchini, diced
4 stalks celery, diced
2 carrots, diced
2 yellow bell peppers, diced
4 tablespoons fresh lemon juice
1/2 cup low-sodium chicken or vegetable broth
2 tablespoons coarse-grained prepared mustard
2 tablespoons olive oil
salt to taste
freshly ground black pepper
1 bunch arugula, chopped
8 scallions, chopped

nutrition facts
Serving Size about 1 cup of salad

AMOUNT PER SERVING
Calories **156**
Total Fat **5 g**
Saturated Fat **1 g**
Cholesterol **0 mg**
Sodium **64 mg**
Total Carbohydrate **25 g**
Dietary Fiber **3 g**
Protein **4 g**
Percent Calories from Fat **28%**
Percent Calories from Protein **10%**
Percent Calories from Carbohydrate **63%**

Prep Time:
20 minutes
Cooking Time:
25 minutes
Serves **8**

cooking instructions

1. Fill a 4-quart saucepan with salted water and bring to a boil. Add the rice and boil, uncovered, stirring occasionally, until al dente, about 25 minutes. Drain the rice in a colander and rinse under cold water until cool. Drain rice well.

2. To blanch the vegetables, prepare an ice bath and bring another pot of salted water to a boil. Cook the zucchini, celery, carrots, and bell peppers for 1 minute. Drain in a colander and plunge into the ice bath. Drain the vegetables well.

4. In a large bowl, whisk together the lemon juice, broth, mustard, oil, salt, and pepper. Add the rice, blanched vegetables, arugula, and scallions, and toss well to combine. Adjust the salt and pepper to taste and serve at room temperature.

Golden Rice Pilaf

ingredients

1 1/2 teaspoons butter, unsalted
2/3 cup finely chopped onion
2 sprigs fresh thyme
4 threads of saffron
1 1/3 cups converted rice
2 cups vegetable broth or water
salt to taste
freshly ground black pepper
2/3 cup golden raisins

nutrition facts
Serving Size 2/3 cup

AMOUNT PER SERVING
Calories **165**
Total Fat **1 g**
Saturated Fat **0 g**
Cholesterol **2 mg**
Sodium **102 mg**
Total Carbohydrate **37 g**
Dietary Fiber **1 g**
Protein **3 g**
Percent Calories from Fat **5%**
Percent Calories from Protein **7%**
Percent Calories from Carbohydrate **88%**

Prep Time:
10 minutes
Cooking Time:
20 minutes
Serves **8**

cooking instructions

1. Preheat the oven to 350°F.
2. In a small ovenproof pot, melt the butter over medium-low heat. Add the onion and thyme and cook for 3 to 4 minutes, until the onions become translucent but not brown. Add the saffron threads and stir.
3. Add the rice and stir to coat evenly with butter. Cook for 3 to 4 minutes.
4. Add the broth and bring to a boil over high heat.
5. As soon as the broth comes to a boil, cover the pot, place it in the oven, and bake for 18 minutes.
6. Remove from the oven and add the salt and pepper to taste along with the golden raisins, and fluff with a fork.

Wild Rice with Dried Cranberries and Walnuts

ingredients

1 cup wild rice
1/2 onion, quartered
1 carrot, peeled and quartered
1 stalk celery, quartered
salt to taste
freshly ground black pepper
2 tablespoons olive oil
2 teaspoons red wine vinegar
4 teaspoons finely chopped shallots
2 1/2 tablespoons dried cranberries
2 apples, peeled and diced
2 1/2 tablespoons chopped walnuts, toasted
2 teaspoons finely chopped parsley
4 teaspoons finely chopped scallions

nutrition facts
Serving Size about 1/2 cup

AMOUNT PER SERVING
Calories **167**
Total Fat **5 g**
Saturated Fat **1 g**
Cholesterol **0 mg**
Sodium **158 mg**
Total Carbohydrate **37 g**
Dietary Fiber **3 g**
Protein **4 g**
Percent Calories from Fat **28%**
Percent Calories from Protein **9%**
Percent Calories from Carbohydrate **63%**

Prep Time: **15 minutes**
Cooking Time: **55 minutes**
Serves **8**

cooking instructions

1. Wash the rice in a strainer under running water until water is clear.

2. Place the rice, onion, carrot, and celery in a saucepan. Season with salt and pepper and cover with water.

3. Bring to boil, reduce heat, and simmer until the rice is tender and fully fluffed, about 45 to 60 minutes.

4. Drain the rice and remove the onion, carrot, and celery pieces.

5. Combine the rice in a bowl with the remaining ingredients. Adjust seasoning.

6. Serve warm or at room temperature.

Farro-Kale Risotto

Recipe by FoodFit Chef Kathy Cary, *Lilly's, Louisville, KY*

ingredients

1 medium onion, chopped
3 cloves garlic, chopped
2 tablespoons olive oil
2 tablespoons butter
8 ounces farro
1/2 cup white wine
1 bay leaf
5 cups beef stock, heated
3/4 pound kale, trimmed and chopped
1/2 teaspoon salt
1/4 teaspoon black pepper
1/4 pound Manchego cheese, shaved (optional)

nutrition facts

Serving Size about 3/4 cup

AMOUNT PER SERVING

Calories **279**
Total Fat **11 g**
Saturated Fat **3 g**
Cholesterol **10 mg**
Sodium **363 mg**
Total Carbohydrate **67 g**
Dietary Fiber **2 g**
Protein **10 g**
Percent Calories from Fat **32%**
Percent Calories from Protein **14%**
Percent Calories from Carbohydrate **49%**

Prep Time: **10 minutes**

Cooking Time: **1 hour**

Serves **6**

cooking instructions

1. Sauté the onion and garlic in olive oil until softened. Add the butter and farro and stir until well coated. Add the wine and bay leaf, and continue to cook, reducing the liquid by half, stirring occasionally.

2. Add 1 cup of the hot beef stock and stir. With the heat on low, stir occasionally and add beef stock by the cupful as needed while the farro absorbs the liquid. Continue until the farro is tender and approximately all 5 cups are used. This will take approximately one hour.

3. Ten minutes before serving, stir in the chopped kale and leave on very low heat for about 10 minutes. The "risotto" is then ready to serve. Season with salt and pepper. If desired, top with the shaved Manchego cheese.

Asian Tofu Salad with Brown Rice

ingredients

1 1/2 cups cooked, short-grain brown rice
1/2 small red pepper, diced
1 stalk celery, diced
2 scallions, white and green part, thinly sliced
1/2 cup dried currants
1 cup tofu cubed
1 1/2 tablespoons low-sodium soy sauce
2 teaspoons canola oil
1 tablespoon chopped parsley
salt to taste
freshly ground black pepper

nutrition facts
Serving Size 1/2 cups

AMOUNT PER SERVING
Calories **404**
Total Fat **11 g**
Saturated Fat **1 g**
Cholesterol **0 mg**
Sodium **905 mg**
Total Carbohydrate **68 g**
Dietary Fiber **7 g**
Protein **14 g**
Percent Calories from Fat **22%**
Percent Calories from Protein **13%**
Percent Calories from Carbohydrate **64%**

Prep Time:
20 minutes

Serves **2**

instructions

1. Combine the rice, red pepper, celery, scallions, currants, and tofu in a medium bowl. Set aside.

2. In a large bowl, whisk the soy sauce, canola oil, parsley, and fresh pepper together. Stir in the tofu-and-rice mixture. Season with salt and pepper.

Lemony Risotto with Asparagus and Shrimp

ingredients

1 cup asparagus, trimmed and cut into 2" lengths
4 cups low-sodium chicken broth
salt to taste
freshly ground black pepper
2 teaspoons olive oil
1/3 cup diced onions
1 pound medium shrimp, peeled and deveined
1 clove garlic, minced
1/2 teaspoon finely grated lemon zest
1 cup Arborio rice
1/2 cup freshly grated Parmesan cheese

nutrition facts

Serving Size 1 bowl

AMOUNT PER SERVING

Calories	**456**
Total Fat	**9 g**
Saturated Fat	**4 g**
Cholesterol	**185 mg**
Sodium	**602 mg**
Total Carbohydrate	**53 g**
Dietary Fiber	**2 g**
Protein	**36 g**
Percent Calories from Fat	**19%**
Percent Calories from Protein	**33%**
Percent Calories from Carbohydrate	**48%**

Prep Time: **20 minutes**
Cooking Time: **40 minutes**
Serves 4

cooking instructions

1. Cook the asparagus in a pot of well-salted boiling water until it is crisp-tender, about 3 minutes. Drain. Transfer the asparagus to a bowl of ice water. When the asparagus is cool, drain and refrigerate. (This can be done ahead and stored in the refrigerator for 1 day.)

2. Heat the chicken broth in a saucepan, season well with salt and pepper, and keep hot over low heat.

3. Heat the olive oil over medium heat in a separate medium-size pot. Add the onion, season lightly with salt and pepper, and cook until it turns translucent, about 5 minutes.

4. Turn the heat to high, add the shrimp, garlic, and lemon zest, and season with salt and pepper. Cook the shrimp until they are just opaque, about 2 minutes. Transfer the shrimp to a plate and set aside.

5. Add the rice to the onions in the pot, stir, and turn the heat to low. Add about 1 cup of the hot broth to the rice mixture and stir slowly until the broth is absorbed. Continue to add the broth 1 cup at a time, stirring slowly, letting the rice absorb the broth before adding more.

6. The risotto is cooked when it is creamy on the outside and slightly firm (al dente) in the center, about 20 to 25 minutes total. Stir in the shrimp, half of the Parmesan cheese, and half of the asparagus. Season with salt and pepper to taste. If the risotto is too thick, add a little more broth until it becomes creamy.

7. Divide the risotto into warm serving dishes and sprinkle with the remaining cheese and asparagus.

Brown Rice Pilaf with Chicken and Dried Apricots

ingredients

2 1/2 cups water
pinch of salt
1 cup long-grain brown rice
4 cooked chicken breasts, grilled, poached, or baked
1/4 cup red wine vinegar
3 tablespoons extra virgin olive oil
salt
freshly ground black pepper
1 cup dried apricots, chopped
2 cups baby spinach leaves
2 tablespoons fresh goat cheese
1/4 cup chopped, toasted walnuts

nutrition facts
Serving Size 1 cup of rice with chicken

AMOUNT PER SERVING
Calories **572**
Total Fat **21 g**
Saturated Fat **5 g**
Cholesterol **93 mg**
Sodium **307 mg**
Total Carbohydrate **60 g**
Dietary Fiber **5 g**
Protein **35 g**
Percent Calories from Fat **33%**
Percent Calories from Protein **25%**
Percent Calories from Carbohydrate **42%**

Prep Time:
15 minutes
Cooking Time:
40 minutes
Serves **4**

cooking instructions

1. Place the water in a medium saucepan with a pinch of salt and bring it to a boil. Add the rice, adjust the heat so that the water is simmering, and cover. Cook until the rice is tender and the water is absorbed, about 30 to 40 minutes. Let cool.

2. Meanwhile, slice the chicken and set aside.

3. In a large bowl, whisk the vinegar, olive oil, salt, and pepper together. Add the cooked rice and toss to combine. Add the chicken, half of the apricots, and spinach, and toss again. Taste and adjust the seasoning. (This can be made in advance and stored in the refrigerator for up to 2 days. You may want to refresh it with a drizzle of oil and vinegar.)

4. Transfer the rice mixture to a serving platter or individual plates and garnish with the remaining apricots, goat cheese, and walnuts. Serve at room temperature.

Rice Pudding

ingredients

1/2 cup short-grain white rice
3 cups skim milk, heated
1/2 teaspoon salt
1 teaspoon vanilla extract
1 teaspoon sugar
1/4 cup raisins

Prep Time: **5 minutes**
Cooking Time: **1 hour**
Serves **6**

cooking instructions

1. Combine the rice, milk, and salt in the top of a double boiler. Cover and allow the mixture to steam for about 1 hour, stirring frequently.

2. When the rice is tender, allow it to cool slightly and stir in the vanilla, sugar, and raisins.

nutrition facts
Serving Size about 3/4 cup

AMOUNT PER SERVING
Calories **136**
Total Fat **1 g**
Saturated Fat **1 g**
Cholesterol **5 mg**
Sodium **260 mg**
Total Carbohydrate **25 g**
Dietary Fiber **1 g**
Protein **5 g**
Percent Calories from Fat **9%**
Percent Calories from Protein **16%**
Percent Calories from Carbohydrate **74%**

Jasmine Rice

ingredients

1 cup long-grain jasmine rice
1 1/2 cups water

cooking instructions

1. Place the rice in a large, deep saucepan and cover with water. Drain and repeat until the water rinses clear. Lift the rice with your fingers several times to fluff the kernels.
2. Place the rice and water in a heavy saucepan with a lid. Heat uncovered until the water boils.
3. Lower the heat, cover, and simmer for about 18 to 20 minutes, or until the water has evaporated and the rice kernels are just tender.
4. Remove from the heat and fluff lightly with a fork to separate the grains.
5. Serve the rice immediately while hot, or let the rice cool on a baking sheet. Cover with plastic and store in the refrigerator.

Prep Time: **5 minutes**
Cooking Time: **35 minutes**
Serves **5**

nutrition facts
Serving Size about 1/2 cup

AMOUNT PER SERVING
Calories **170**
Total Fat **0 g**
Saturated Fat **0 g**
Cholesterol **0 mg**
Sodium **0 mg**
Total Carbohydrate **38 g**
Dietary Fiber **1 g**
Protein **3 g**
Percent Calories from Fat **0%**
Percent Calories from Protein **7%**
Percent Calories from Carbohydrate **93%**

Chapter 18: Soy and Other Beans

Although soy has been used in other cultures for centuries as a food source and for medicinal purposes, it is just now catching on in the United States. With the rise in popularity, tofu is no longer the only option: rich in protein and isoflavones, soybeans are eaten mostly when processed into tempeh, soy nut butter, soy dairy products like soymilk, and, of course, soy sauce.

Soybeans, grown in northern China as early as the 11th century BC, were among the first crops grown by man. By the 17th century, European visitors became aware of this unfamiliar bean, and soybeans were being grown in Europe and North America by the 18th century. Today, the United States grows almost three million bushels of soybeans.

Like other beans, soy beans are legumes, seeds that grow within pods. Legumes are an excellent source of protein. Adding beans to your diet is easy—there are many other varieties to choose from! **Kidney beans**, **pinto beans**, **black beans**, **white beans**, **lentils**, **split peas**, and **chickpeas** (also called garbanzo beans) are among the most popular.

NUTRITION AND HEALTH

Soy and other beans are low in calories and fat, and high in fiber. Fiber is crucial to lowering blood sugar levels, as well as preventing constipation. Many beans, such as soy, are also a good source of protein. In 1999, the U.S. Food and Drug Administration gave the green light to food companies to make health claims about the role of soy protein in reducing cholesterol and the risk of heart disease. To earn the claim, a food must contain at least 6.25 grams of soy protein per serving.

RECIPES IN THIS CHAPTER:

- South-of-the-Border Soup
- Split Pea Soup
- White Bean Minestrone
- Asian Snow Pea Salad with Sesame-Soy Dressing
- Greek Chickpea Salad
- Tuna and White Bean Salad
- Spiced Pineapple Lentils
- Cranberry Beans with Rice and Cabbage
- Sesame Tofu with Stir-Fried Vegetables
- Breakfast Burritos
- Asian Tofu Sandwich with Grilled Vegetables

Soybeans also have a lot of folate, which helps reduce the risk of birth defects, and iron. Soy also contains phytochemicals, including isoflavones, weak estrogen-like substances that many scientists suspect are key weapons in our disease-fighting arsenal.

Beans are a hearty and healthy protein source for vegetarians. Many beans, such as the Great Northern beans, lentils, and chickpeas, are also plentiful in fiber, folate, and iron.

WHAT TO LOOK FOR

Soybeans are a medium-size oval, yellowish bean with a very bland flavor and firm texture. Soybeans are processed to make tofu and soy nut butter, among other foods, and soy milk, which comes in full fat or low-fat varieties.

Dried beans vary in size, color, and texture, but generally you will want to watch out for discolored or shrivelled beans and pebbles! Dried beans are usually a better bet than canned for 2 reasons. First, dried beans are lower in sodium than canned beans, and second, they have a better texture and flavor.

EASY STORAGE AND PREPARATION

Dried beans can be stored in air-tight containers almost indefinitely, but they lose moisture as they sit.

Beans must be soaked before cooking because it allows them to absorb moisture slowly and therefore cook evenly. In addition, soaked beans cook faster and retain more nutrients. Long soaking (at least six hours) also reduces the gas-producing properties of beans. Cooking time varies for different types of beans, but most need to be soaked overnight. Lentils are an exception to this rule. They require no soaking and can cook in as little as 10 minutes.

To soak, cover soybeans in a bowl with 2 to 3 inches of cold water. Let soak at least 12 hours or overnight in the refrigerator. For a quicker soak, cover the beans in a saucepan with 2 to 3 inches of cold water, bring to a boil for 2 minutes, remove from heat, cover, and let stand for 1 to 2 hours. Drain and cook, according to your recipe.

BEST USES

- Fresh or frozen soybeans, otherwise known as edamame, are a good substitute for green peas or as a snack straight from the pod. Or, mix shelled fresh or frozen soybeans with other flavorful ingredients.
- Baked tofu is sold seasoned and ready to eat. Chop it up and add it to a salad or a burrito. Tofu is also excellent in stir-fries and soups.
- Soymilk is delicious in a smoothie or latte or poured over a bowl of granola and fruit.

- Other beans are equally versatile. They make a great base for soups, add protein to salads, and can be mashed into dips.
- Most people recognize chickpeas from the popular Middle Eastern dish hummus, but they are also wonderful in green salads or simply mixed with sliced onions and a splash of olive oil.
- Black bean soup is easy to prepare and makes a delectable meal. Black beans are also a great addition to your favorite chili recipe.

Soy and other beans add flavor and texture to familiar dishes in addition to providing healthful benefits. They can be paired with almost any vegetable or meat with tasty results. Become a globetrotter by experimenting with these bean recipes from around the world.

South-of-the-Border Soup

ingredients

1 1/2 cups dried pinto beans (soaked)
1 15-ounce can diced tomatoes, undrained
1 small onion, quartered
2 cloves garlic
1 tablespoon olive oil
4 ounces angel hair pasta, broken into 1" pieces
1/2 pound pork tenderloin, trimmed of fat and cut into 1/2" pieces
6 cups low-sodium chicken broth
salt to taste
freshly ground black pepper
chopped fresh cilantro, for garnish

nutrition facts
Serving Size about 1 1/2 cups

AMOUNT PER SERVING
Calories **299**
Total Fat **6 g**
Saturated Fat **2 g**
Cholesterol **28 mg**
Sodium **254 mg**
Total Carbohydrate **40 g**
Dietary Fiber **14 g**
Protein **23 g**
Percent Calories from Fat **17%**
Percent Calories from Protein **30%**
Percent Calories from Carbohydrate **53%**

Prep Time: **10 minutes**
Cooking Time: **15 minutes**
Serves **6**

cooking instructions

1. Drain the beans. Place them in a large pot and cover them with fresh water. Cover the pot, and simmer very slowly for 30 minutes. Add a pinch of salt and then simmer for about 1 hour, until the beans are soft. If the mixture appears dry, add enough water during the cooking to keep the beans covered.

2. In a food processor, combine the tomatoes, onion, and garlic. Process until smooth.

3. In a heavy soup pot, heat the oil over medium heat. Add the pasta and pork and cook, stirring occasionally, until the pasta starts to turn golden, about 5 to 7 minutes. Add the beans, tomato mixture, and the chicken stock. Increase the heat to medium-high and bring to a boil. Cook, uncovered, until the pasta is al dente, about 5 minutes. Season with salt and pepper.

4. Ladle the soup into 6 bowls and garnish with the cilantro. Serve immediately.

Split Pea Soup

ingredients

4 teaspoons olive oil
1/2 cup chopped carrot
1/2 cup finely chopped celery
1/2 cup finely chopped onion
2 sprigs fresh or 1/2 teaspoon dried thyme
freshly ground black pepper
2 quarts low-sodium chicken broth
2 2/3 cups dried split peas
salt to taste

nutrition facts

Serving Size about 1 cup

AMOUNT PER SERVING

Calories **282**
Total Fat **5 g**
Saturated Fat **1 g**
Cholesterol **4 mg**
Sodium **223 mg**
Total Carbohydrate **43 g**
Dietary Fiber **17 g**
Protein **19 g**
Percent Calories from Fat **14%**
Percent Calories from Protein **27%**
Percent Calories from Carbohydrate **59%**

Prep Time:
10 minutes

Cooking Time:
1 hour

Serves **8**

cooking instructions

1. Heat the oil in a saucepan over low heat. Add the carrot, celery, onion, and thyme, season lightly with pepper and cook for 10 minutes.
2. Add the broth and split peas and bring to a boil quickly over high heat.
3. Lower the heat and simmer until the peas are tender, about 1 hour.
4. Puree 2/3 of the soup in a blender and stir it into the remaining 1/3.
5. If the soup is too thick, thin it by adding a little more broth.
6. Add salt and additional pepper to taste.

NOTE: Do not add salt until the peas are fully cooked because salt will prevent the peas from becoming tender.

White Bean Minestrone

Recipe by FoodFit Chef Roberto Donna, *Galileo, Washington DC*

ingredients

3/4 cup dried white beans
1/4 cup diced onion
1/4 cup diced carrot
1/3 cup diced celery
2 medium russet potatoes, peeled and cubed
1 bay leaf
4 cups water
1/3 cup barley
salt to taste
freshly ground black pepper

nutrition facts

Serving Size 1 bowl

AMOUNT PER SERVING
Calories **164**
Total Fat **1 g**
Saturated Fat **0 g**
Cholesterol **0 mg**
Sodium **321 mg**
Total Carbohydrate **34 g**
Dietary Fiber **9 g**
Protein **8 g**
Percent Calories from Fat **3%**
Percent Calories from Protein **19%**
Percent Calories from Carbohydrate **78%**

Prep Time:
15 minutes

Cooking Time:
60 minutes

Serves **6**

cooking instructions

1. Bring a large soup pot of water to a boil. Add the beans, turn off the heat, cover, and let stand for 1 hour.

2. Drain the beans. Put them back in the soup pot along with the onion, carrot, celery, potatoes, bay leaf, and 4 cups of water. Simmer until the beans are tender, about 1 hour.

3. Meanwhile, in a small saucepan, bring 1 cup salted water to a boil. Add the barley, reduce the heat to low, and cook until the barley is tender, about 45 minutes. Set aside.

4. Remove the bay leaf. Using a blender, puree 1/3 of the beans and vegetables, and pour back into the soup pot.

5. Add the barley to the bean soup. Season with salt and pepper. Heat thoroughly and serve.

Asian Snow Pea Salad with Sesame-Soy Dressing

ingredients

2 pounds fresh snow peas, trimmed
2 tablespoons rice vinegar
1 tablespoon low-sodium soy sauce
1/8 teaspoon red chili flakes
2 tablespoon sliced scallions
1 1/2 tablespoons sesame oil
1 red bell pepper, diced
1 teaspoon sesame seeds

nutrition facts

Serving Size 3/4 cup of salad with vinaigrette

AMOUNT PER SERVING
Calories **103**
Total Fat **4 g**
Saturated Fat **1 g**
Cholesterol **0 mg**
Sodium **108 mg**
Total Carbohydrate **13 g**
Dietary Fiber **5 g**
Protein **5 g**
Percent Calories from Fat **33%**
Percent Calories from Protein **17%**
Percent Calories from Carbohydrate **49%**

Prep Time: **10 minutes**
Cooking Time: **5 minutes**
Serves **6**

cooking instructions

1. Put about 2 inches of water in a large pot, insert a rack or steamer basket into the pot, and bring the water to a boil. Steam the snow peas in the basket for about 2 minutes, or until the snow peas turn bright green. Remove the basket and run the peas under cold water to stop the cooking process. Set aside.

2. Meanwhile, in a small bowl, whisk the rice vinegar and soy sauce together. Add the red chili flakes and the scallions and slowly whisk in the sesame oil. (This dressing can be made in advance and stored in the refrigerator for up to 5 days.)

3. Gently toss the snow peas and red bell pepper in the dressing. Sprinkle with sesame seeds. This dish can be served at room temperature or chilled.

Greek Chickpea Salad

ingredients

2 16-ounce cans chickpeas (garbanzo beans), rinsed and drained
3 plum tomatoes, diced
3 celery stalks, finely diced
3 scallions, sliced thinly
1/2 cup Kalamata olives, pitted and chopped
8 basil leaves, chiffonade (shredded)
1 tablespoon olive oil
juice of 3 lemons
salt to taste
freshly ground black pepper

nutrition facts

Serving Size 3/4 cup

AMOUNT PER SERVING
Calories **162**
Total Fat **6 g**
Saturated Fat **0 g**
Cholesterol **0 mg**
Sodium **452 mg**
Total Carbohydrate **25 g**
Dietary Fiber **9 g**
Protein **5 g**
Percent Calories from Fat **30%**
Percent Calories from Protein **13%**
Percent Calories from Carbohydrate **57%**

Prep Time:
20 minutes
Serves **8**

instructions

1. Combine the chickpeas, tomatoes, celery, scallions, olives, basil, olive oil, lemon juice, salt, and pepper in a large bowl. Toss well and taste for seasoning.

2. Serve at room temperature or chilled. (This recipe can be made in advance and stored in the refrigerator for up to 3 days.)

Hummus

ingredients

8 ounces canned chickpeas (garbanzo beans)
1 tablespoon tahini
1 tablespoon lemon juice
1 teaspoon finely chopped garlic
3 tablespoons olive oil
salt to taste
freshly ground black pepper

Prep Time:
15 minutes
Serves **8**

instructions

1. Drain and rinse the chickpeas.
2. Puree the chickpeas in a blender or food processor with the tahini, lemon juice, and garlic.
3. With the machine running, add the olive oil slowly, until the hummus becomes thick and creamy.
4. Add salt and pepper to taste.
5. Serve with pita bread.

nutrition facts

Serving Size about 2 tablespoons

AMOUNT PER SERVING
Calories **141**
Total Fat **5 g**
Saturated Fat **1 g**
Cholesterol **0 mg**
Sodium **104 mg**
Total Carbohydrate **18 g**
Dietary Fiber **4 g**
Protein **6 g**
Percent Calories from Fat **33%**
Percent Calories from Protein **17%**
Percent Calories from Carbohydrate **49%**

Tuna and White Bean Salad

ingredients

1 12-ounce can solid white tuna packed in water, drained

juice of 1 lemon

1/3 cup chopped red onion

3 tablespoons chopped fresh parsley

2 cups cooked cannellini beans (white kidney beans)

1/2 cup Roasted Shallot Vinaigrette (see page 67)

2 large bunches arugula, washed

12 black olives

1 pint cherry tomatoes

nutrition facts
Serving Size about 1 1/2 cups salad

AMOUNT PER SERVING
Calories **318**
Total Fat **10 g**
Saturated Fat **1 g**
Cholesterol **36 mg**
Sodium **660 mg**
Total Carbohydrate **31 g**
Dietary Fiber **2 g**
Protein **27 g**
Percent Calories from Fat **28%**
Percent Calories from Protein **34%**
Percent Calories from Carbohydrate **38%**

Prep Time: **10 minutes**

Serves **4**

cooking instructions

1. Place the tuna in a medium-sized bowl and squeeze the juice from the lemon all over the tuna.

2. Add the onion, parsley, beans, and the Roasted Shallot Vinaigrette to the tuna and gently mix.

3. Divide the arugula evenly among 4 chilled plates and place the tuna mixture on top. Garnish with the olives and cherry tomatoes.

Spiced Pineapple Lentils

Recipe by FoodFit Chefs Mary Sue Milliken and Susan Feniger, *Border Grill, Santa Monica, CA*

ingredients

6 tablespoons vegetable oil
4 onions, diced
2 teaspoons salt
2 teaspoons freshly ground black pepper
6 cloves garlic, crushed
4 cups lentils, washed and picked over
6 cups water
1 cup canned crushed pineapple

nutrition facts

Serving Size about 3/4 cup

AMOUNT PER SERVING
Calories **305**
Total Fat **7 g**
Saturated Fat **1 g**
Cholesterol **0 mg**
Sodium **400 mg**
Total Carbohydrate **43 g**
Dietary Fiber **21 g**
Protein **19 g**
Percent Calories from Fat **21%**
Percent Calories from Protein **24%**
Percent Calories from Carbohydrate **55%**

Prep Time:
10 minutes
Cooking Time:
1 hour
Serves **8**

cooking instructions

1. Heat the oil in a medium pot over moderate heat. Sauté the onions with the salt and pepper and cook until golden, about 10 minutes.

2. Stir in the garlic and lentils and cook for 2 minutes, stirring frequently. Pour in the water, bring to a boil, and reduce to a simmer. Cook, covered, for 45 minutes.

3. Stir in the pineapple, remove from the heat, and serve.

Cranberry Beans with Rice and Cabbage

ingredients

salt to taste
4 cups dried cranberry beans
2 tablespoons olive oil
1 cup chopped onions
1 head green cabbage, thinly shredded
3 1/2 cups low-sodium chicken broth
2 cups medium-grain Arborio rice
freshly ground black pepper

nutrition facts

Serving Size about 1 1/2 cup

AMOUNT PER SERVING
Calories **412**
Total Fat **4 g**
Saturated Fat **1 g**
Cholesterol **0 mg**
Sodium **493 mg**
Total Carbohydrate **74 g**
Dietary Fiber **13 g**
Protein **17 g**
Percent Calories from Fat **8%**
Percent Calories from Protein **17%**
Percent Calories from Carbohydrate **74%**

Prep Time: **15 minutes**

Cooking Time: **1 hour**

Serves **8**

cooking instructions

1. Rinse the beans well and soak them overnight in about 3 times their volume of water. Drain the soaked beans, rinse, and, in a large saucepan, cover generously in fresh water; simmer over medium-low heat until tender. Add a pinch of salt toward the end of the cooking process.

2. In a large saucepan, heat the olive oil over low heat. Add the chopped onions and cook, stirring occasionally, until they are translucent, about 5 minutes.

3. Stir in the shredded cabbage, 1 cup of the broth, and a pinch of salt. Cover the saucepan and cook over medium-low heat for about 20 minutes.

4. Stir in the beans and the remaining 2 1/2 cups of the stock and bring to a simmer. Add the rice and salt to taste. Reduce the heat to low, cover and cook until the rice is tender and most of the stock has been absorbed, about 15 to 20 minutes. (Add a little more water or stock if needed.) Sprinkle with pepper and serve.

Sesame Tofu with Stir-Fried Vegetables

ingredients

1/4 cup low-sodium tamari
1 tablespoon rice vinegar
2 tablespoons sesame oil
2 tablespoons freshly grated ginger root
2 cloves garlic, minced
1 package (14 ounces) firm tofu
2 cups broccoli florets
3 cups julienned carrots
2 cups sliced shiitake mushrooms
1 red pepper, seeds removed, and cut into strips
2 cups julienned bok choy
1 tablespoon toasted sesame seeds

nutrition facts
Serving Size about 2 cups

AMOUNT PER SERVING	
Calories	**213**
Total Fat	**11 g**
Saturated Fat	**2 g**
Cholesterol	**0 mg**
Sodium	**636 mg**
Total Carbohydrate	**19 g**
Dietary Fiber	**6 g**
Protein	**13 g**
Percent Calories from Fat	**24%**
Percent Calories from Protein	**27%**
Percent Calories from Carbohydrate	**49%**

Prep Time:
20 minutes
Plus Marinating Time

Cooking Time:
15 minutes

Serves **4**

cooking instructions

1. In a mixing bowl, combine the tamari, vinegar, 1 tablespoon of the sesame oil, 1 tablespoon of the ginger root, and 1 tablespoon of the garlic.

2. Cut the tofu into cubes, add it to the tamari mixture, and marinate the tofu in the refrigerator for 1 hour.

3. In a nonstick pan, steam the broccoli and carrots in 2 cups of water for 2 minutes. Drain and set aside.

4. Wipe out the pan with a paper towel. Heat 1 teaspoon of the remaining sesame oil in the pan over high heat. With a slotted spoon, lift the tofu out of the marinade (reserve the marinade), add the tofu to the pan, and brown it on all sides. Transfer the tofu to a plate.

5. Heat the remaining 2 teaspoons of sesame oil in the pan, add the mushrooms, and cook for 2 minutes. Add the red pepper and bok choy and cook for 5 minutes more. Add the broccoli, carrots, the remaining ginger, and the remaining garlic and cook for 2 minutes. Add the reserved marinade, simmer for a minute or two, and add the browned tofu.

6. Divide the tofu, vegetables, and sauce among 4 serving plates and garnish with sesame seeds.

Breakfast Burritos

Recipe by FoodFit Chef Anne Rosenzweig, *Inside, New York, NY*

ingredients

FOR THE RELISH:

1 tomato, finely diced
1/2 small red onion, minced
1 hot, fresh chili pepper, seeded and minced
1/2 cup chopped, fresh parsley
1/2 cup chopped, fresh cilantro
1 tablespoon fresh lemon or lime juice
salt to taste

FOR THE BURRITOS:

8 small corn tortillas
3/4 cup cooked black beans, red beans, or refried beans
4 large eggs
4 large egg whites
salt to taste
freshly ground black pepper
1 tablespoon canola oil

nutrition facts

Serving Size 2 burritos

AMOUNT PER SERVING
Calories **296**
Total Fat **14 g**
Saturated Fat **3 g**
Cholesterol **213 mg**
Sodium **241 mg**
Total Carbohydrate **32 g**
Dietary Fiber **6 g**
Protein **13 g**
Percent Calories from Fat **42%**
Percent Calories from Protein **17%**
Percent Calories from Carbohydrate **42%**

Prep Time: **45 minutes**
Cooking Time: **10 minutes**
Serves **4**

cooking instructions

For the relish:

1. Mix all the ingredients together and chill. This can be made ahead and refrigerated overnight.

For the burritos:

1. Preheat the oven to 350°F. Wrap the tortillas in aluminum foil and warm in the oven.

2. Heat the beans in a small pan or in the microwave until very warm.

3. Break the eggs into a bowl. Add the egg whites and salt and pepper to taste and mix well with a fork.

4. Heat the oil in a large skillet over medium-high heat. Pour the eggs into the pan and scramble until the eggs are just cooked, about 1 1/2 to 2 minutes.

5. To put it together: Place a spoonful of beans in the center of each tortilla. Divide the scrambled eggs among the tortillas, spooning them over the beans. Spoon a teaspoon of relish on top of the eggs. Roll up the tortillas and place 2 burritos, seam side down, on each plate. Top with more relish and serve immediately.

Asian Tofu Sandwich with Grilled Vegetables

Recipe by FoodFit Chef Bill Wavrin, Miraval Resort and Spa, Catalina, AZ

ingredients

FOR THE ASIAN TOFU:

1/4 pound firm tofu, sliced about 1/4" thick

2 tablespoons Asian Marinade (see page 206)

1/2 red bell pepper, seeds removed, and julienned

1/2 red onion, sliced 1/4" thick

1/2 yellow, summer squash, sliced 1/4" thick

1 scallion

1/4 lime

1/2 teaspoon low-sodium soy sauce

FOR THE SANDWICH:

1 slice Herbed Garlic Scented Bread (see page 181)

lettuce leaf

1 tomato, sliced

nutrition facts

Serving Size 1 sandwich

AMOUNT PER SERVING
Calories **240**
Total Fat **6 g**
Saturated Fat **1 g**
Cholesterol **0 mg**
Sodium **61 mg**
Total Carbohydrate **11 g**
Dietary Fiber **3 g**
Protein **9 g**
Percent Calories from Fat **33%**
Percent Calories from Protein **30%**
Percent Calories from Carbohydrate **37%**

Prep Time:
2 minutes
Plus Marinating Time

Cooking Time:
25 minutes

Serves 1

cooking instructions

For the Asian tofu:

1. Drain the tofu in a colander over a bowl in the refrigerator.

2. Remove the tofu from the colander and place it in a bowl with the marinade. Marinate for at least 2 to 3 hours for the tofu to absorb the marinade flavor.

3. Remove the tofu from the marinade. Reserve the marinade to use with the vegetables.

4. Preheat the grill to medium.

5. When the grill is hot, toss the vegetables in the marinade for about 5 seconds. Place the vegetables (except the scallion) on a grill-pan and toss for about 3 minutes until the vegetables begin to wilt and brown.

6. Place the tofu slices on the grill and cook each side for about 3 minutes or until the tofu is golden brown. Set aside to cool.

7. While the tofu is cooling, grill the scallion until golden. Place the scallion on a plate and squeeze the lime and soy sauce over it.

For the sandwich:

1. To assemble the open-faced sandwich, toast the bread and top with a lettuce leaf and slice of tomato. Place the tofu and scallion and the grilled vegetables on top.

Asian Marinade

ingredients

1/4 cup rice wine vinegar
3 tablespoons low-sodium soy sauce
2 tablespoons balsamic vinegar
1 teaspoon finely minced, fresh ginger root
2 cloves garlic, finely minced
pinch of red chili flakes
1/2 teaspoon finely chopped, fresh rosemary
1/2 teaspoon sesame oil
1/4 teaspoon freshly cracked black pepper

cooking instructions

1. Place all the ingredients together in a bowl. Keep covered in the refrigerator until ready to use. The marinade will keep stored in the refrigerator for a week or two.

Note: Use to marinate vegetables, tofu, fish, or chicken. Do not reuse marinade. The possibility of bacteria buildup is present.

nutrition facts

Serving Size about 2 tablespoons

AMOUNT PER SERVING
Calories **17**
Total Fat **0 g**
Saturated Fat **0 g**
Cholesterol **0 mg**
Sodium **271 mg**
Total Carbohydrate **3 g**
Dietary Fiber **0 g**
Protein **0 g**
Percent Calories from Fat **15%**
Percent Calories from Protein **9%**
Percent Calories from Carbohydrate **76%**

Prep Time: **10 minutes**

Serves **8**

Recipe by FoodFit Chef Bill Wavrin, Miraval Resort and Spa, Catalina, AZ

Chapter 19: Walnuts and Other Nuts and Seeds

Many Americans think of walnuts as a crunchy addition in their favorite cookies and cakes. However, walnuts are wonderful in savory dishes, too: They add flavor and texture to salads, stews, pasta dishes, and sauces.

Walnuts are believed to have originated in Asia. Today, they are especially prized in Mediterranean countries, including Greece, Turkey, France, and parts of Italy. The famous pesto of Liguria is often made with walnuts instead of pine nuts. Walnuts are also popular in the Middle East; a classic Persian dish, fesenjan, braises duck in a fragrant sauce of walnuts and pomegranate, but the sauce is also excellent with chicken.

Some other loved—and equally versatile—members of the nut family are **almonds**, **hazelnuts**, **pecans**, **pistachios**, **pine nuts**, and **peanuts**. Many nuts—pecans, pine nuts, and walnuts, to name a few—are considered aphrodisiacs. Similarly, toasted seeds—especially **sesame**, **pumpkin**, and **squash**—add texture and flavor to many dishes.

RECIPES IN THIS CHAPTER:

- Polenta-Stuffed Mushrooms with Walnuts
- Belgian Endive, Mâche, Beets, and Apple with Walnuts and Sherry Vinaigrette
- Zucchini Sauté with Oregano and Walnuts
- Sautéed Snow Peas with Sesame Seeds
- Fettuccine with Basil-Walnut Pesto
- Sautéed Spinach with Pine Nuts
- Apple-Pecan Stuffing
- Cranberry Nut Muffins
- Lemon-Pistachio Biscotti

NUTRITION AND HEALTH

Tree nuts and peanuts are rich in polyunsaturated fats and monounsaturated fats. These fats are healthy because they help to decrease "bad" LDL cholesterol levels, without affecting the HDL or "good" cholesterol levels. Walnuts are high in omega-3 fatty acids, which also help lower cholesterol and can calm inflammation. They are also high in fiber.

Plus, nuts offer calcium, magnesium, zinc, potassium, and vitamin E, among other nutrients. Granted, nuts are not low in calories, but a small serving (nutritionists usually suggest about 1/4 cup) goes a long way. And a few tablespoons are all that it takes to make a dish more interesting and fun to eat. There is also new research that nuts can help you lose weight when you're counting calories.

Seeds offer a good amount of iron and phosphorous. Like nuts, seeds can be used to enhance cooked dishes and salads.

WHAT TO LOOK FOR

When purchasing shelled walnuts, look for walnut halves. The larger the pieces, the better control you will have over their use in a recipe. Coarsely chopped walnut pieces are often too small to pick up with a fork, an important consideration when adding them to salads. Nuts also come whole, with or without shells, salted and unsalted, and in flour and paste form.

Don't buy nuts if they look like they've been on the shelf for a long period of time. Because they're full of oil, nuts go rancid easily. It's easy to tell if they're rancid: they have a faint, fishy odor.

Nut butters are another way to enjoy nuts' nutritional benefits. Peanut butter is always a favorite, but almond butter and cashew butter are also available. Watch your portions, though: 1 tablespoon of peanut butter has 95 calories, about 8 grams of fat, and 4 grams of protein. (Surprisingly, the reduced fat version contains the same number of calories, but a bit more sugar.) The protein and the fat combine to satisfy and "stick to the ribs" longer than a snack with carbohydrates alone. Before purchasing, check the label for sugar content; some nut butters, especially peanut butters, can be high in sugar.

EASY STORAGE AND PREPARATION

One way to be sure nuts and seeds don't go bad is to store them in the freezer. They will remain fresh for up to a year. They may also be kept in the refrigerator. Seeds will keep at room temperature for up to three months.

Before using walnuts in a recipe, especially if they have been frozen or refrigerated, spread them on a baking sheet and toast them in a 350°F oven for about 10 minutes, until you can smell them. The toasting revitalizes the dormant nut oils, releases the nuts' wonderful aroma and gives them extra crunch.

As with nuts, seeds taste best when toasted. You can toast them for a few minutes in the oven or on the stove in a skillet or saucepan; just watch them carefully so they don't burn!

ABOUT HERBS AND SPICES

Bay leaf is an herb with dark green leaves and a pungent aroma. Look for fresh or whole dried leaves. Bay leaves are superb in beef stews, tomato sauces, and other long-cooking dishes. Remove the leaves before serving. They're inedible.

Cloves are the dried bud from a tropical evergreen tree. Cloves have a strong, sweet, aromatic taste. Look for whole dried buds or ground powder. Cloves are a versatile spice in baked goods and sauces. Cloves' strong flavor pairs well with pork, ham, and stews. They can also be used in chutneys and in stewed fruit dishes.

BEST USES

- Toasted nuts add texture to ordinary salads. Try adding cashews to plain chicken salad or toss a handful of sunflower seeds over a garden salad for extra crunch.
- For a variation on the classic pesto, substitute fresh cilantro for the basil and use walnuts instead of pine nuts. This version has a zesty, fresh flavor and is delicious over chicken and turkey, or with your favorite pasta.
- If you like to snack on nuts, mix them with dried fruit. It's a delicious combination and will prevent you from overindulging on nuts.
- If you're in the mood for the classic peanut butter and jelly sandwich, try using almond or cashew butter instead. You'll get the same nutrients but a unique flavor. Or try nut butters smeared on a piece of celery for a light snack.

Need to liven up a meal? Nuts and seeds are a great bet. The collection of dishes here spans from muffins to fettuccine and allows you to experiment with walnuts, pistachios, and more. The recipes contain just enough nuts to add flavor and texture, but not too much fat.

Polenta-Stuffed Mushrooms with Walnuts

ingredients

FOR THE POLENTA:

1 teaspoon olive oil
1 clove garlic, minced
1 cup skim milk
1 sprig thyme
1/2 bay leaf
1 pinch cayenne pepper
1/4 cup cornmeal
1/4 cup freshly grated Parmesan cheese
salt to taste
freshly ground black pepper

FOR THE MUSHROOMS:

48 small white (or button) mushrooms
1 tablespoon olive oil
24 walnut halves

Prep Time:
30 minutes
Cooking Time:
15 minutes
Serves 12

cooking instructions

For the polenta:

1. Heat the olive oil in a pot over low heat. Add the garlic and cook for 1 minute, keeping the heat low so the garlic doesn't burn.

2. Add the milk, thyme, bay leaf, and cayenne pepper. Increase the heat and bring to a boil.

3. Slowly whisk the cornmeal into the hot milk. After all the cornmeal has been added, cook 3 to 4 minutes more, stirring constantly.

4. Remove the pot from the heat and slowly stir in the grated cheese. Generously season the polenta with salt and pepper to taste.

For the mushrooms:

1. Preheat the oven to 350°F.

2. Carefully remove the stems from the mushrooms. Arrange the mushroom caps on a nonstick baking sheet with the tops up. (Reserve the stems for another use.) Brush the top of the mushroom caps with olive oil and sprinkle them with salt.

3. Cook the mushrooms in the oven until they are thoroughly cooked, about 10 to 15 minutes for small mushrooms.

Polenta-Stuffed Mushrooms with Walnuts (cont.)

4. Turn the mushrooms over and season the insides with salt and pepper. Fill the caps with polenta. Break each walnut half into two pieces and place a walnut piece on top of each stuffed mushroom. (This can be made ahead of time and stored in the refrigerator for up to 2 days.)

5. Heat the stuffed mushrooms in the oven for 8 to 10 minutes before serving, longer if the stuffed mushrooms are cold from the refrigerator.

6. Serve warm on small plates.

nutrition facts
Serving Size 4 mushrooms

AMOUNT PER SERVING
Calories **81**
Total Fat **4 g**
Saturated Fat **1 g**
Cholesterol **2 mg**
Sodium **131 mg**
Total Carbohydrate **8 g**
Dietary Fiber **1 g**
Protein **4 g**
Percent Calories from Fat **50%**
Percent Calories from Protein **20%**
Percent Calories from Carbohydrate **37%**

Belgian Endive, Mâche, Beets, and Apple with Walnuts and Sherry Vinaigrette

Recipe by FoodFit Chef Nora Pouillon, *Restaurant Nora, Washington, DC*

ingredients

16 small beets (about 1 pound), washed and trimmed

1/2 cup English walnut halves

8 heads of Belgian endive

4 to 6 ounces mâche (or watercress), washed and spun dry

FOR THE VINAIGRETTE:

2 tablespoons sherry vinegar

6 tablespoons extra virgin olive oil

sea salt

freshly ground black pepper

nutrition facts

Serving Size about 1 salad

AMOUNT PER SERVING

Calories **279**

Total Fat **15 g**

Saturated Fat **2 g**

Cholesterol **0 mg**

Sodium **172 mg**

Total Carbohydrate **33 g**

Dietary Fiber **19 g**

Protein **9 g**

Percent Calories from Fat **45%**

Percent Calories from Protein **12%**

Percent Calories from Carbohydrate **43%**

Prep Time: **10 minutes**

Cooking Time: **25 minutes**

Serves **8**

cooking instructions

1. Preheat the oven to 350°F.
2. Steam the beets for 12 to 15 minutes in a covered saucepan using a collapsible steamer. Set the beets aside to cool.
3. Place the walnuts on a baking sheet and bake them in the oven for 8 to 10 minutes or until fragrant and toasted.
4. Peel and quarter the cooked beets.
5. Wipe the outside of the endive with a damp cloth, trim the base, and separate the leaves.
6. To make the vinaigrette, mix the vinegar, olive oil, salt, and pepper together in a small bowl.
7. Just before serving, toss the endive and mâche (or watercress) with some of the sherry vinaigrette.
8. Divide the endive and mâche among the 8 dinner plates. Arrange the quartered beets and walnuts on top of the greens.

Zucchini Sauté with Oregano and Walnuts

ingredients

2 teaspoons olive oil
1 teaspoon crushed garlic
4 cups zucchini, sliced in 1/2" circles
salt to taste
freshly ground black pepper
1 tablespoon freshly chopped oregano
2 teaspoons chopped, toasted walnuts

nutrition facts

Serving Size about 1 cup

AMOUNT PER SERVING
Calories **47**
Total Fat **3 g**
Saturated Fat **0 g**
Cholesterol **0 mg**
Sodium **86 mg**
Total Carbohydrate **5 g**
Dietary Fiber **2 g**
Protein **2 g**
Percent Calories from Fat **51%**
Percent Calories from Protein **14%**
Percent Calories from Carbohydrate **35%**

Prep Time: **5 minutes**
Cooking Time: **5 minutes**
Serves **4**

cooking instructions

1. Heat the olive oil in a 10" skillet over medium-low heat.

2. Add the garlic and cook for 1 minute.

3. Add the zucchini slices, salt, pepper, and oregano, and sauté until the zucchini turns bright green and becomes tender, about 3 to 5 minutes. Remove from the skillet, sprinkle with toasted walnuts, and serve.

Sautéed Snow Peas with Sesame Seeds

ingredients

2 teaspoons peanut oil
1 teaspoon crushed garlic
4 cups snow peas, washed and trimmed
1 tablespoon low-sodium soy sauce
freshly ground black pepper
2 teaspoons sesame seeds

nutrition facts

Serving Size about 1 cup

AMOUNT PER SERVING
Calories **54**
Total Fat **3 g**
Saturated Fat **0 g**
Cholesterol **0 mg**
Sodium **85 mg**
Total Carbohydrate **6 g**
Dietary Fiber **2 g**
Protein **2 g**
Percent Calories from Fat **43%**
Percent Calories from Protein **15%**
Percent Calories from Carbohydrate **41%**

Prep Time:
5 minutes
Cooking Time:
5 minutes
Serves **4**

cooking instructions

1. Heat the peanut oil in a 10" skillet over medium-low heat.

2. Add the garlic and cook for 1 minute.

3. Add the snow peas, soy sauce, and pepper, and sauté until the snow peas turn bright green and are tender, about 3 to 4 minutes. Remove from the skillet, sprinkle with the sesame seeds, and serve.

Fettuccine with Basil-Walnut Pesto

ingredients

2 teaspoons walnuts, toasted

1 medium garlic clove

1 1/4 cups fresh basil leaves (about 3 bunches)

1 1/4 tablespoons freshly grated Parmesan cheese

1/2 splash lemon juice

1 tablespoon extra virgin olive oil

1/3 cup low-fat ricotta cheese

1/3 pound fettuccine

nutrition facts

Serving Size 1 bowl (about 2 cups)

AMOUNT PER SERVING

Calories **435**

Total Fat **15 g**

Saturated Fat **4 g**

Cholesterol **16 mg**

Sodium **134 mg**

Total Carbohydrate **59 g**

Dietary Fiber **4 g**

Protein **18 g**

Percent Calories from Fat **30%**

Percent Calories from Protein **16%**

Percent Calories from Carbohydrate **54%**

Prep Time: **5 minutes**

Cooking Time: **10 minutes**

Serves **2**

cooking instructions

1. Bring a large pot of salted water to a boil.

2. Meanwhile, drop the walnuts and garlic through the food chute of a food processor while it is running. Add the basil, Parmesan cheese, and lemon juice, and process until the mixture is finely minced.

3. With the motor still running, slowly pour the oil through food chute and process until well blended.

4. Transfer the basil mixture to a large pasta bowl and stir in the ricotta cheese.

5. Add the fettuccine to the boiling water and cook until it is al dente, about 8 to 10 minutes. Drain.

6. Toss the hot fettuccine with the basil and ricotta mixture and serve immediately.

Sautéed Spinach with Pine Nuts

ingredients

1/4 cup raisins or currants
1 teaspoon olive oil
2 pounds spinach, washed and stems removed
2 tablespoons toasted pine nuts
1 tablespoon balsamic vinegar
salt to taste
freshly ground black pepper

nutrition facts
Serving Size about 3/4 cup

AMOUNT PER SERVING
Calories **118**
Total Fat **4 g**
Saturated Fat **1 g**
Cholesterol **0 mg**
Sodium **328 mg**
Total Carbohydrate **17 g**
Dietary Fiber **7 g**
Protein **8 g**
Percent Calories from Fat **27%**
Percent Calories from Protein **23%**
Percent Calories from Carbohydrate **50%**

Prep Time:
10 minutes
Cooking Time:
5 minutes
Serves **4**

cooking instructions

1. Place the raisins in a small bowl and add 1/2 cup hot water. Let sit until the raisins plump, about 5 minutes. Drain and pat dry.

2. In a large skillet, heat the oil over medium heat.

3. Add the spinach, drained raisins, and pine nuts, and toss quickly until the greens are just wilted. Sprinkle the balsamic vinegar over the greens and stir until warmed, about 30 seconds. Adjust the salt and pepper to taste.

4. Divide evenly on 4 warmed plates.

Apple-Pecan Stuffing

ingredients

2 tablespoons butter

2 medium onions, finely chopped

4 stalks celery, finely chopped

4 tart apples (such as Granny Smith), cores removed, and diced

4 sprigs fresh thyme or 1 teaspoon dried thyme

2 teaspoons chopped, fresh sage

5 cups cubed bread, preferably 2 or 3 days old

1 cup chopped, toasted pecans

1/2 cup chopped, fresh parsley

salt to taste

freshly ground black pepper

1/2 cup low-sodium chicken broth

nutrition facts

Serving Size about 1 cup

AMOUNT PER SERVING

Calories **321**

Total Fat **11 g**

Saturated Fat **2 g**

Cholesterol **5 mg**

Sodium **453 mg**

Total Carbohydrate **54 g**

Dietary Fiber **12 g**

Protein **10 g**

Percent Calories from Fat **28%**

Percent Calories from Protein **11%**

Percent Calories from Carbohydrate **61%**

Prep Time: **15 minutes**

Cooking Time: **35 minutes**

Serves **12**

cooking instructions

1. Melt the butter in a large nonstick skillet over medium heat. Add the onions and celery, and cook until the vegetables are soft, about 10 minutes.

2. Add the apples, thyme, and sage, and continue cooking until the apples soften, but still hold their shape, about 5 more minutes.

3. Transfer the apple mixture to a large bowl. Stir in the bread, pecans, and parsley. Add just enough chicken broth to moisten the stuffing, and season to taste with salt and pepper. (This can be made up to 2 days in advance and kept covered in the refrigerator.)

4. Preheat the oven to 350°F.

5. Bake the stuffing, covered with foil, for 30 minutes. Remove the foil and bake until the stuffing is golden brown on the edges, about 5 more minutes.

Cranberry Nut Muffins

ingredients

cooking spray
2 cups flour
1 cup sugar
2 teaspoons baking powder
1/4 teaspoon salt
1 large egg, at room temperature
1 cup milk, at room temperature
4 tablespoons unsalted butter, melted
1/2 cup chopped, dried cranberries
1/2 cup finely chopped pecans

nutrition facts
Serving Size about 1 muffin

AMOUNT PER SERVING
Calories **81**
Total Fat **3 g**
Saturated Fat **1 g**
Cholesterol **10 mg**
Sodium **35 mg**
Total Carbohydrate **13 g**
Dietary Fiber **0 g**
Protein **1 g**
Percent Calories from Fat **31%**
Percent Calories from Protein **6%**
Percent Calories from Carbohydrate **62%**

Prep Time: **15 minutes**
Cooking Time: **15 minutes**
Serves **36**

cooking instructions

1. Preheat the oven to 400°F. Coat a muffin pan with cooking spray.
2. Sift the flour, sugar, baking powder, and salt together. (This can be done the night before and kept covered on the counter.)
3. Whisk together the egg, milk, and melted butter. (If the egg and milk are cold, the butter may solidify.)
4. Make a well in the center of the dry ingredients and add the liquid all at once. Stir with a wooden spoon until the dry ingredients are just moistened. Fold in the cranberries and pecans. The batter will be a little lumpy, but do not overmix.
5. Fill the pans 2/3 full, being careful not to drip batter on the edge of the tins where it will burn and cause sticking.
6. Bake until golden brown and set in the center, approximately 12 to 15 minutes. The muffins are done when a small knife inserted in the center of a muffin comes out dry. Cool for 5 minutes before removing from the pan.

Lemon-Pistachio Biscotti

ingredients

2 1/2 cups flour
1 cup sugar
1/2 teaspoon baking powder
1/2 teaspoon baking soda
1/4 teaspoon freshly ground black pepper
1 pinch salt
3 lemons
3 large eggs
1 cup crushed pistachio nuts
powdered sugar, for rolling

nutrition facts
Serving Size 3 biscotti

AMOUNT PER SERVING
Calories **120**
Total Fat **3 g**
Saturated Fat **0 g**
Cholesterol **24 mg**
Sodium **63 mg**
Total Carbohydrate **21 g**
Dietary Fiber **0 g**
Protein **3 g**
Percent Calories from Fat **24%**
Percent Calories from Protein **10%**
Percent Calories from Carbohydrate **66%**

Prep Time: **15 minutes**
Cooking Time: **30 minutes**
Serves 72

cooking instructions

1. Preheat the oven to 350°F and line two cookie sheets with parchment paper.

2. In a mixing bowl, combine the flour, sugar, baking powder, baking soda, pepper, and salt.

3. Finely grate 1 tablespoon of zest from the lemons and set aside. Squeeze 4 tablespoons of juice through a strainer and reserve.

4. In a separate bowl, whisk the eggs, lemon zest, and juice together. Add this to the flour mixture along with the pistachios and stir until a stiff dough forms.

5. Place the dough onto a lightly sugared work surface and divide it into 4 pieces. Roll each piece with the palms of your hands into a log slightly shorter than the length of your cookie sheet.

6. Place two logs on each cookie sheet, several inches apart (the logs will double in width). Bake for 15 minutes, until the logs feel set or firm to the touch. Set the cookie sheets on racks and let cool. Reset the oven to 300°F.

7. When cool to the touch, place the logs on a cutting board. With a serrated knife, slice them into 1/2-inch diagonal slices.

8. Lay the biscotti out on the cookie sheets lined with fresh parchment in a single layer and bake for an additional 10 to 15 minutes, until they are dry and lightly toasted. Cool completely.

9. Store in an airtight tin or plastic container at room temperature for up to 2 weeks.

PART V

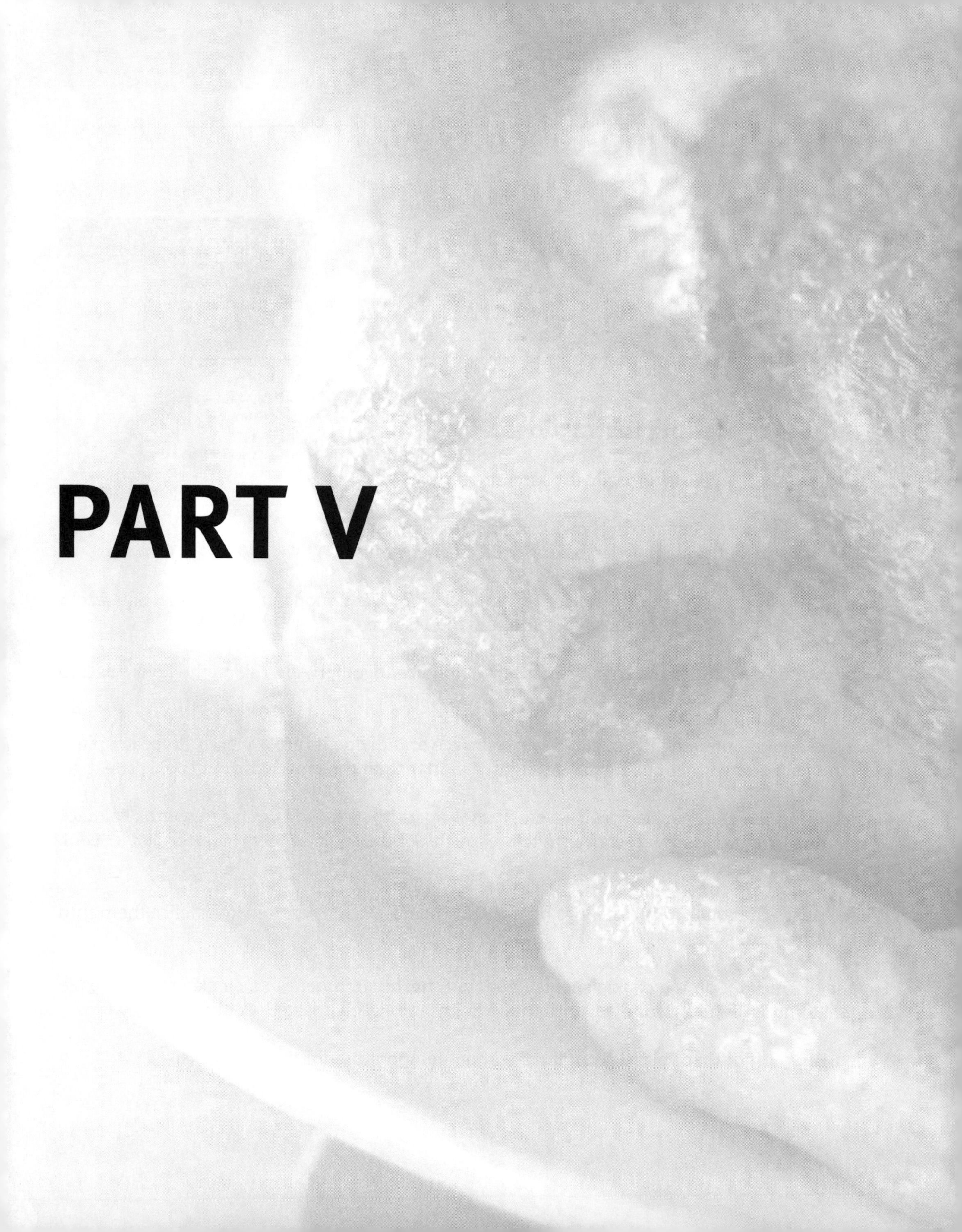

Poultry, Fish, Meat & Dairy

Chapter 20: Turkey and Poultry

RECIPES IN THIS CHAPTER:

- Chicken and Corn Chowder
- Roast Turkey, Sun-Dried Tomato, and Basil Wraps
- Easy Barbecue Turkey Burgers
- Quick Chicken Parmesan
- Herb Roasted Cornish Hens
- Grilled Chicken Marinated in Yogurt and Herbs in a Tomato Chutney

Turkey—the quintessential American bird—isn't just for Thanksgiving dinner. It is high in protein and full of nutrients and its mild flavor makes it a great base for so many recipes.

The turkeys we know today are actually descendants of wild turkeys that were domesticated by the Aztecs and brought to Europe by the Spanish. Almost all of the turkeys that end up on our dinner tables are bred to be plumper and to maximize their white meat.

Other types of poultry include **chicken**, **duck**, **goose**, and **pheasant**. Chicken surpasses turkey in popularity and is widely used in cuisines around the globe. People love chicken because it is great-tasting and remarkably versatile. It lends itself to a host of low-fat cooking methods like roasting, grilling, and broiling. The skinless chicken breasts available in markets nowadays are the busy home chef's dream come true: They are nutritious, easy-to-prepare, quick-to-cook, and delicious.

NUTRITION AND HEALTH

Turkey and other poultry, particularly with the skin removed, is relatively low in calories and fat, especially when compared to other meats. Turkey is a rich source of high-quality protein, one of the mighty macronutrients. Skip the skin with the fat layer, however; it contributes a lot of unneccessary fat and calories.

Skinless turkey breast is the leanest of all meats with just 119 calories and less than half a gram of fat in a 3-ounce serving. Dark meat is higher in fat than white meat, but it is still relatively lean (with 138 calories and 4 grams of fat) if you eat it without the skin. Turkey also delivers B vitamins, iron, selenium, and zinc, a mineral that is essential for normal growth, development, and immunity.

Chicken is just as nutritious: A 3-ounce skinless chicken breast has 140 calories and is high in B vitamins, iron, zinc, and selenium. Duck breast is high in vitamin B, iron, and selenium.

WHAT TO LOOK FOR

Chicken and turkey are available fresh or frozen, whole, or in parts. (Some types of poultry, such as guinea hens, are only available whole.) When purchasing poultry, look for cream-colored to yellow-colored skin, free of bruises and tears. Avoid poultry that has an off odor. Frozen turkeys should be rock hard; be sure the package is tightly sealed and the turkey is free of freezer burn. Avoid packages that have a lot of frozen liquid in them; the fluid indicates that the turkey was defrosted and refrozen.

Whole ducks are most often available frozen, although your butcher may be able to order fresh. Duck breasts are commonly available in the meat section of your supermarket.

In general, the leanest cut of turkey and chicken is the all-white meat breast, which comes in whole or half form, with the bone in or boneless. Cutlets and wings are another source of white meat. Thighs and drumsticks are dark meat.

EASY STORAGE AND PREPARATION

Raw poultry can be stored for up to 2 days in the refrigerator; otherwise, freeze it for up to 2 months. Cooked poultry can be kept in the refrigerator for up to 4 days.

Check the sell-by date on poultry before purchasing. Defrost frozen poultry in the refrigerator. (You can use a microwave to defrost poultry that you are going to cook immediately.)

Salmonella, a food-borne bacteria that causes food poisoning, is a risk when handling poultry. To prevent cross-contamination, store all poultry in its original wrapping. Be sure that the poultry is not leaking juices on other foods in the refrigerator. Washing the countertop, any utensils, and your hands with soap and hot water after handling raw poultry are other ways you can protect yourself.

BEST USES

- The best methods for cooking poultry are baking, grilling, roasting, braising, and stewing. The best way to ensure poultry is well-cooked is to use a meat thermometer.
- Turkey and poultry leftovers make great salads: Add a dash of low-fat mayonnaise, curry, and celery for a quick lunch, or wrap up leftover turkey or chicken

and a spoonful of mango chutney in a tortilla for an easy and tasty wrap. And who can forget the classic turkey and cranberry sauce sandwich?

- When roasting a stuffed turkey, make sure to check the internal temperature of the stuffing with a meat thermometer. Properly cooked stuffing should be 165°F.
- Be sure to save the bones from fresh turkey or chicken to make a homemade stock.
- Ground turkey can be a great alternative to ground beef in dishes such as chili, burgers, and meatloaf. Just remember that unlike ground beef, turkey meat tends to dry out and needs added moisture during cooking. Egg whites added to ground white meat turkey provide a low-fat source of moisture.
- Cook boneless chicken and turkey to 170°F and bone-in chicken and turkey to 180°F. Whether you're preparing a whole bird or just the parts, cooking the meat with the skin helps keep the meat moist—just be sure to remove the skin before eating for a healthier meal.

Chicken and turkey offer endless recipe options. They taste wonderful grilled, baked, stewed, sautéed, shredded, or broiled. You can easily enhance their flavor with fresh herbs or spice rubs. Try these simple, savory recipes for poultry, from juicy turkey burgers to elegant Cornish hens.

ABOUT HERBS AND SPICES

Sage is an herb with an intense musty-mint flavor and aroma. Look for fresh leaves, whole dried and crumbled leaves, or ground leaves. Sage is wonderful with pork and in poultry stuffing, sausages, dried bean soups, and stews. Dried sage is more powerful than fresh and should be used sparingly.

Thyme is an herb with tiny, light green leaves and a minty, lemony aroma and flavor. Look for fresh whole leaves or dried whole and crumbled leaves. Thyme is wonderful in poultry, fish, and vegetable dishes and in slow-cooked stews and soups. Its flavor blends well with many other herbs. Chopped fresh leaves are much more pungent than dried.

Chicken and Corn Chowder

ingredients

2 large ears of corn, shucked
1 slice uncooked bacon, diced
1/2 cup chopped onion
1/2 cup chopped celery
1 sprig fresh thyme
1 bay leaf
6 small red potatoes
1 1/2 cups low-sodium chicken or vegetable broth
2 cups reduced-fat (2%) milk
1 red bell pepper, diced
1 pound boneless, skinless chicken breasts, uncooked, cut into 1/2" pieces
1 teaspoon chopped, fresh dill
salt to taste
freshly ground black pepper

nutrition facts
Serving Size 1 cup

AMOUNT PER SERVING
Calories **291**
Total Fat **4 g**
Saturated Fat **2 g**
Cholesterol **51 mg**
Sodium **312 mg**
Total Carbohydrate **42 g**
Dietary Fiber **5 g**
Protein **28 g**
Percent Calories from Fat **12%**
Percent Calories from Protein **35%**
Percent Calories from Carbohydrate **53%**

Prep Time: **10 minutes**
Cooking Time: **25 minutes**
Serves **6**

cooking instructions

1. Preheat the grill or broiler to high.
2. Grill or broil the corn until it turns golden brown. Set aside to cool.
3. Put the bacon in a soup pot and heat over low heat. Add the onion, celery, thyme, and bay leaf, turn the heat up to medium, and cook until the vegetables are soft, about 10 minutes.
4. Meanwhile, slice the corn kernels from the cob.
5. Dice the potatoes and add them to the soup pot, along with the chicken broth. Simmer until the potatoes are just tender, about 10 minutes. Add the milk, bell pepper, chicken, and dill, and cook until the chicken is just cooked through, approximately 5 minutes. Remove the thyme and bay leaf. Add salt and pepper to taste and serve.

Roast Turkey, Sun-Dried Tomato, and Basil Wraps

ingredients

1/4 cup low-fat, whipped cream cheese
3 sun-dried tomatoes, rehydrated and chopped
5 basil leaves, chopped
2 large flour tortillas
6 ounces sliced smoked turkey breast
2 lettuce leaves, green leaf, Bibb, or romaine, shredded

nutrition facts
Serving Size about 1 wrap

AMOUNT PER SERVING
Calories **356**
Total Fat **10 g**
Saturated Fat **3 g**
Cholesterol **61 mg**
Sodium **316 mg**
Total Carbohydrate **33 g**
Dietary Fiber **2 g**
Protein **31 g**
Percent Calories from Fat **27%**
Percent Calories from Protein **36%**
Percent Calories from Carbohydrate **38%**

Prep Time:
15 minutes

Serves **2**

instructions

1. In a small mixing bowl, combine the cream cheese, sun-dried tomatoes, and basil.

2. Lay the tortillas out and spread 1 tablespoon of the cream cheese mixture on each of them. Divide the turkey among the tortillas and spread the remaining cream cheese mixture on top of the turkey. Divide the shredded lettuce among the tortillas and tightly roll each tortilla into a cylinder, ending with the seam side down.

3. Cut the wraps in half on the diagonal and serve.

Easy Barbecue Turkey Burgers

ingredients

2 tablespoons fat-free mayonnaise
2 tablespoons barbecue sauce
1 pound lean ground turkey
salt to taste
freshly ground black pepper
4 slices tomato
4 rolls

nutrition facts

Serving Size 1 burger

AMOUNT PER SERVING
Calories **406**
Total Fat **14 g**
Saturated Fat **5 g**
Cholesterol **91 mg**
Sodium **777 mg**
Total Carbohydrate **41 g**
Dietary Fiber **2 g**
Protein **29 g**
Percent Calories from Fat **31%**
Percent Calories from Protein **29%**
Percent Calories from Carbohydrate **40%**

Prep Time:
15 minutes
Cooking Time:
10 minutes
Serves 4

cooking instructions

1. In a small bowl, stir the mayonnaise and barbecue sauce together.
2. Preheat the grill to medium-high.
3. Shape the turkey into 4 patties, about 1/2" thick. Season with salt and pepper.
4. Grill the burgers on both sides until they are cooked through, about 6 minutes per side.
5. Toast the rolls on the grill.
6. Top the burgers with the mayonnaise sauce and sliced tomatoes and serve them on the toasted rolls.

Quick Chicken Parmesan

ingredients

2 boneless chicken cutlets, about 4 ounces each
2 teaspoons olive oil
salt to taste
freshly ground black pepper
1/4 teaspoon dried oregano
flour for dredging
1 cup tomato sauce
2 tablespoons low-fat shredded mozzarella cheese
2 tablespoons freshly grated Parmesan cheese

nutrition facts

Serving Size 1 cutlet

AMOUNT PER SERVING
Calories **292**
Total Fat **10 g**
Saturated Fat **3 g**
Cholesterol **75 mg**
Sodium **210 mg**
Total Carbohydrate **17 g**
Dietary Fiber **2 g**
Protein **33 g**
Percent Calories from Fat **31%**
Percent Calories from Protein **46%**
Percent Calories from Carbohydrate **24%**

Prep Time: **10 minutes**
Cooking Time: **20 minutes**
Serves **2**

cooking instructions

1. Preheat the oven to 375°F.
2. Lay the chicken cutlets between two pieces of waxed paper. Pound each cutlet with the flat end of a mallet until thin.
3. Heat the olive oil in a large, nonstick skillet. While the oil is heating, season the chicken with salt, pepper, and oregano, and dredge it in flour.
4. Sauté the chicken over medium-high heat until golden brown, about 2 minutes on each side. Transfer the chicken to a shallow baking dish. Pour the tomato sauce over the chicken and sprinkle with both cheeses.
5. Bake for 15 to 20 minutes until the sauce is bubbling and the cheese is melted and lightly golden. Let stand for 5 minutes before serving.

Herb Roasted Cornish Hens

ingredients

4 Cornish hens
salt to taste
freshly ground black pepper
4 cloves garlic, sliced
4 teaspoons minced, fresh rosemary leaves
4 teaspoons minced, fresh thyme
2 bay leaves
4 shallots, roughly chopped
3 carrots, roughly chopped into 1-inch pieces
3 stalks celery, roughly chopped into 1" pieces
2 lemons

nutrition facts
Serving Size 1/2 cornish hen

AMOUNT PER SERVING
Calories **163**
Total Fat **4 g**
Saturated Fat **1 g**
Cholesterol **109 mg**
Sodium **345 mg**
Total Carbohydrate **6 g**
Dietary Fiber **1 g**
Protein **25 g**
Percent Calories from Fat **24%**
Percent Calories from Protein **62%**
Percent Calories from Carbohydrate **14%**

Prep Time: **15 minutes**
Cooking Time: **45 minutes**
Serves **8**

cooking instructions

1. Preheat the oven to 375°F.
2. Rinse the Cornish hens with cold water and pat dry. Season with salt and pepper inside and out.
3. Stuff the insides of the hens with garlic, rosemary, thyme, and 1/2 bay leaf each. Place a few pieces of shallots, carrots, and celery in the cavity.
4. Squeeze juice from the lemons all over the hens and place 1/2 lemon in each hen cavity. Roast in the oven until the the hens are golden brown and crisp and the juices run clear when the thigh is pierced with a sharp knife, about 45 minutes.
5. Transfer the hens to a carving board and let rest for about 5 minutes. Remove the skin from the hens, cut each one in half, and serve.

Grilled Chicken Marinated in Yogurt and Herbs in a Tomato Chutney

Recipe by FoodFit Chef Todd English, *Olives, Boston, MA*

ingredients

FOR THE CHICKEN:

1 cup low-fat or non-fat plain yogurt
zest of 1 lemon, grated
1 tablespoon curry powder
2 cloves garlic, minced
2 tablespoons honey
1/4 cup minced red onion
2 tablespoons chopped, fresh mint
4 boneless, skinless chicken breasts, about 4 to 6 ounces each
salt to taste
freshly ground black pepper

FOR THE CHUTNEY:

2 teaspoons olive oil
1 cup diced white onions
4 large tomatoes, diced
3/4 cup dried currants
1/4 cup cider vinegar
1 cup orange juice
1/2 cup tomato juice
1 jalapeño pepper, seeds removed and diced
1 teaspoon kosher salt

FOR THE GARNISH:

2 tablespoons chopped, fresh mint
2 tablespoons chopped, fresh cilantro
2 tablespoons chopped scallions

Prep Time:
20 minutes
Plus Marinating Time

Cooking Time:
40 minutes

Serves 4

cooking instructions

To marinate the chicken:

1. Mix all the yogurt, lemon zest, curry powder, garlic, honey, red onion, and mint in a large bowl.

2. Add the chicken to the mixture and coat evenly.

3. Cover the bowl and refrigerate overnight.

For the chutney:

1. Heat the oil in a small saucepan over medium heat. Add the onion and tomatoes and cook until soft, about 3 to 4 minutes.

2. Add the currants, vinegar, and juices, and cook until reduced by one-third, about 12 to 15 minutes.

3. Add the jalapeño pepper and cook 5 more minutes.

4. Add the salt and set aside.

Grilled Chicken Marinated in Yogurt and Herbs in a Tomato Chutney (cont.)

To cook the chicken:

1. Preheat the grill to medium-high.

2. Remove the chicken from the marinade and discard the marinade. (This protects against cross-contamination.) Sprinkle the chicken with salt and pepper.

3. Place the chicken on the hot grill and cook until the juices run clear, 6 to 8 minutes per side.

4. Garnish the chicken with the mint, cilantro, and scallions. Serve with rice and chutney on the side.

nutrition facts
Serving Size 1 chicken breast with about 1/2 cup of chutney

AMOUNT PER SERVING
Calories **483**
Total Fat **9 g**
Saturated Fat **2 g**
Cholesterol **122 mg**
Sodium **743 mg**
Total Carbohydrate **55 g**
Dietary Fiber **6 g**
Protein **51 g**
Percent Calories from Fat **15%**
Percent Calories from Protein **41%**
Percent Calories from Carbohydrate **44%**

Chapter 21: Salmon and Seafood

Salmon is a supermarket staple these days. Between fresh and frozen salmon, you can enjoy this flavorful, heart-healthy fish all year round. Salmon lovers get a special treat in the spring and summer when wild Pacific varieties are in season. The flavor and texture of the fresh, free-range fish will truly wow you.

Health experts recommend eating at least two servings of fish each week. Wild salmon is a top choice, but other good fresh fish to consider are **dolphinfish** (**mahi mahi**); farmed **tilapia**, **catfish**, and **rainbow trout**; **yellowfin**, **bigeye**, and **albacore tuna**; **Pacific cod**, **flounder** and **sole**; **Alaskan halibut**; and **striped bass**. Dig into the shellfish family to incorporate more seafood into your diet. **Crawfish**, **Dungeness crab**, **shrimp**, **Maine lobster**, and farmed **mussels**, **oysters**, and **clams** are tasty choices that can be prepared quickly.

Some people are intimidated by the idea of cooking fish. But fish fillets are just as simple to prepare as chicken breasts, and they offer a much greater range of tastes.

RECIPES IN THIS CHAPTER:

- Mom's Crab Dip
- Grilled Salmon Salsa Wraps with Lime Sour Cream
- Salmon Burgers with Dill Mustard
- Grilled Fish Tacos with Mango-Avocado Salsa
- Pan-Seared Halibut Steaks with Lemon Zest
- Grilled Salmon with Lemon-Fennel Slaw
- Lemon-Pepper Fettuccine with Asparagus and Shrimp
- Roasted Cod and Tomatoes with Basil and White Wine
- Cod with Tomato-Orange Relish

NUTRITION AND HEALTH

Most fish are high in protein, vitamins, and minerals and low in artery-clogging saturated fat. They also contain polyunsaturated omega-3 fatty acids, a fat that can promote heart health. As far as fish is concerned, this is a rare instance where the more fat the better! Fish that contain more than 5 percent of fat are considered fatty fish. White, flaky fish are usually lower in fat than darker-colored fish.

Salmon, which has 7 to 11 grams of fat in a 3-ounce serving, is particularly popular because it tastes so pleasing and is incredibly versatile. Wild salmon gets extra points for flavor and may contain lower levels of cancer-causing PCBs and other pollutants than farm-raised salmon.

Some large fish found in deeper waters, like shark, swordfish, king mackerel, and tilefish, contain high levels of methylmercury, which can be harmful. The U.S. Food and Drug Administration advises women who are pregnant or may become pregnant, nursing mothers, and young children not to consume these fish. Another commonly eaten fish, albacore white tuna, has more mercury than canned light tuna, so FDA recommends eating no more than 6 ounces of albacore tuna each week. Fish with low mercury levels include shrimp, canned light tuna, salmon, pollock, and catfish.

Shellfish can contribute to a healthy diet. It is a source of high-quality protein and, depending on how it is prepared, is low in saturated fat and calories. (Three ounces of boiled or steamed shrimp contain only 84 calories.) Although cholesterol can be a concern with shellfish, many types of shellfish are lower in cholesterol than beef or chicken. Steamed, boiled, or sautéed scallops, mussels, clams, and oysters are good choices.

WHAT TO LOOK FOR

There is no mandatory federal program for inspecting fish, so be sure to purchase your fish from a fishmonger (seller) you trust. The fish counter should be bright and clean, and fish should be displayed on ice or stored in a refrigerator. The catch of the day should smell sweet and clean, not fishy or, worse still, like ammonia. The fillets, steaks, or whole fish you select should be moist-looking and without any bruises or odd-colored spots.

It is important to consider that when certain types of fish become very popular, their numbers may suffer drastically. For example, Chilean sea bass and Atlantic swordfish stocks have been depleted in recent years. To be sure that you are making an ocean-friendly choice when purchasing fish, first consult a website devoted to seafood conservation.

Wild salmon is usually labeled as such or called Alaskan or Pacific, while farm-raised salmon is often referred to as Atlantic or Icelandic. Because salmon feed from the sea, their diet affects their appearance. The sockeye salmon, for example, has intensely red flesh due to the large amount of crustaceans that it eats.

EASY STORAGE AND PREPARATION

At home, be careful to store your seafood tightly wrapped in a well-chilled refrigerator. Before cooking, rinse the fish with cold water and pat dry with a paper towel. Cook it within a day or two days at most. PCBs accumulate in the skin and the fat of salmon, so experts recommend trimming your fish before cooking.

Because shellfish is extremely perishable, be sure to refrigerate it immediately after you get home from the store. You should cook raw shellfish within a day of purchasing it, although live shellfish such as oysters and clams can be stored in the refrigerator for 4 to 7 days. Ask your fishmonger for specific instructions on how to store shellfish, as they vary according to the type.

BEST USES

- Jazz up salmon and other fish with a rub or a marinade. One delicious and easy rub for fish is equal parts salt, pepper, and chopped fresh or dried oregano, parsley, and rosemary. Sprinkle the mixture on the fish steak or fillet and rub it in with your fingers. Let its flavors absorb for 15 minutes before cooking.
- Shrimp is a natural on the grill. Try shrimp kebabs with basil leaves. Another nice cooking technique is to use a rosemary sprig (simply strip the leaves off with your fingers ahead of time) or other herb stalk as the skewers.

Americans are ordering more seafood than ever in restaurants today, but it's surprisingly simple to create fish dishes at home. These quick recipes enable you to enjoy the heart-healthy benefits of the fresh fish and shellfish you find in the market, from salmon to crab to rainbow trout.

ABOUT HERBS AND SPICES

Fennel is an herb with a slight licorice flavor. Look for fresh stalks and whole dried seeds. Fresh chopped leaves are good in stuffing, sauces, soups, vegetables and seafood salads. Seeds are a unique addition to breads, sausages, spicy meat mixtures, and curries.

Lemongrass is an herb with a sour lemon taste and fragrance. Look for fresh and dried stalks. An important herb in Thai and Indonesian cooking, lemongrass adds a wonderful accent to seafood, soups, and vinaigrettes. Use fresh stalks whole or chopped. Bruise the stem to release flavor and make sure to discard the upper fibrous part. Soak dried stalks in hot water before use.

Mom's Crab Dip

Recipe by FoodFit Chef Tom Douglas, *Dahlia Lounge, Seattle, WA*

ingredients

3 tablespoons tomato paste
1 tablespoon honey
3/4 cup fat-free mayonnaise
2 tablespoons thinly sliced chives
1 tablespoon fresh lemon juice
1 tablespoon sweet red cherry peppers (marinated in jar of vinegar), seeds removed and minced
2 teaspoons grated lemon zest
1 teaspoon prepared horseradish
1/4 teaspoon Tabasco sauce
1 hard-boiled egg, finely chopped
3/4 pound fresh Dungeness crabmeat, picked over for bits of shell and cartilage with claw meat and large pieces of crab left whole
salt to taste
freshly ground black pepper
juice of 1/2 lemon
chips, crackers, or pita wedges for dipping

nutrition facts

Serving Size 1/4 cup

AMOUNT PER SERVING
Calories **81**
Total Fat **1 g**
Saturated Fat **0 g**
Cholesterol **57 mg**
Sodium **361 mg**
Total Carbohydrate **8 g**
Dietary Fiber **1 g**
Protein **10 g**
Percent Calories from Fat **13%**
Percent Calories from Protein **49%**
Percent Calories from Carbohydrate **37%**

Prep Time:
15 minutes
Serves **8**

instructions

1. In a large bowl, whisk the tomato paste and the honey together until smooth.

2. Whisk in the mayonnaise, chives, lemon juice, cherry peppers, lemon zest, horseradish, and Tabasco.

3. Using a rubber spatula, gently fold in the egg. (You can make the dressing a day ahead and store it, covered with plastic wrap, in the refrigerator. When you're ready to serve, mix the dressing with the crabmeat.)

4. Add the crabmeat to the bowl and toss it with the dressing.

5. Season to taste with salt and pepper and a squeeze of lemon.

6. To serve, set a bowl of crab dip on a large platter and surround it with chips, crackers, or pita wedges for dipping.

Grilled Salmon Salsa Wraps with Lime Sour Cream

Recipe by FoodFit Chef Andy Husbands, Tremont 647, Boston, MA

ingredients

FOR THE LIME SOUR CREAM:

1/2 cup low-fat sour cream

juice of 1 lime (2 tablespoons)

1/2 teaspoon cumin seeds, toasted and ground

1 dried chipotle pepper, rehydrated and minced (or squeezed of extra liquid if canned)

salt to taste

freshly ground pepper

FOR THE SALSA:

1 large ripe tomato, core removed, and diced (about 1 cup)

1/2 red onion, peeled and diced (1 cup)

1/2 red bell pepper, seeds removed, and diced (about 3/4 cup)

1/2 green bell pepper, seeds removed, and diced (about 3/4 cup)

2 tablespoons chopped cilantro

juice of 1 lime (2 tablespoons)

FOR THE SALMON WRAPS:

1/2 pound boneless salmon fillet

1 tablespoon canola oil

salt to taste

freshly ground black pepper

4 6" flour tortillas

nutrition facts
Serving Size 1/2 a filled tortilla

AMOUNT PER SERVING

Calories **246**
Total Fat **7 g**
Saturated Fat **2 g**
Cholesterol **20 mg**
Sodium **247 mg**
Total Carbohydrate **34 g**
Dietary Fiber **3 g**
Protein **12 g**
Percent Calories from Fat **27%**
Percent Calories from Protein **19%**
Percent Calories from Carbohydrate **55%**

Prep Time: **10 minutes**

Cooking Time: **5 minutes**

Serves **8**

cooking instructions

For the lime sour cream:

1. Combine all ingredients in a small mixing bowl and stir thoroughly. (The lime sour cream will keep in an airtight container in the refrigerator for about a week.)

For the salsa:

1. Combine the tomato, onion, peppers, cilantro, and lime juice in a bowl and mix well.

For the salmon wraps:

1. Preheat the grill to high. Lightly coat salmon with oil and season generously with salt and pepper.
2. Grill the fish, skin side up on the hot grill until well-seared on bottom, about 2 to 3 minutes. Turn and grill until fish is cooked through, 2 to 3 minutes longer. Remove skin and cool slightly, 2 to 3 minutes.
3. Working over the bowl of salsa, use your fingers to break the fish into chunks. Using a spatula, gently fold the fish into the salsa.
4. Adjust seasoning with salt, pepper, and lime juice.
5. Grill each tortilla, flipping until warm and ever-so-slightly browned.
6. Spoon 1/4 cup salmon salsa and 1 tablespoon lime sour cream down the center of 1 tortilla.
7. Fold one end in and roll up tightly. Cut in half and serve immediately.

Salmon Burgers with Dill Mustard

ingredients

FOR THE DILL MUSTARD:

1/4 cup sugar
2 cups fresh dill sprigs
2 tablespoons Dijon mustard
2 teaspoons fresh lemon juice
2 tablespoons white wine vinegar
1/4 cup olive oil

FOR THE SALMON BURGERS:

3/4 pound boneless, skinless salmon fillet
1 egg
1 cup bread crumbs
2 tablespoons chopped, fresh dill
2 tablespoons chopped shallots
1 teaspoon chopped capers
salt to taste
freshly ground black pepper
4 hamburger buns
lettuce leaves
1 large tomato, sliced

nutrition facts
Serving Size 1 salmon burger

AMOUNT PER SERVING
Calories **500**
Total Fat **15 g**
Saturated Fat **4 g**
Cholesterol **100 mg**
Sodium **841 mg**
Total Carbohydrate **61 g**
Dietary Fiber **3 g**
Protein **30 g**
Percent Calories from Fat **27%**
Percent Calories from Protein **24%**
Percent Calories from Carbohydrate **49%**

Prep Time: **15 minutes**
Cooking Time: **10 minutes**
Serves **4**

cooking instructions

For the dill mustard:

1. Place the sugar and dill in a small food processor fitted with the blade attachment and process for 1 minute.

2. Add the mustard, lemon juice, and vinegar, and process until smooth.

3. With the processor running, add the olive oil slowly through the feed tube. (This makes about 1 1/2 cups. Extra sauce can be stored in the refrigerator for up to 5 days and served with fish and shellfish.)

For the salmon burgers:

1. Cut the salmon into 1" pieces. Place the salmon in the food processor, fitted with the blade attachment. Coarsely grind the salmon.

2. In a small bowl, stir the egg, bread crumbs, dill, shallots, and capers together with a sprinkling of salt and pepper. Add the ground salmon and stir to combine. Form the salmon mixture into 4 patties, about 1/2" thick.

3. Over medium heat, heat a nonstick skillet sprayed with cooking spray. Cook the burgers on both sides until they are golden brown and just cooked through, about 3 minutes per side.

4. Meanwhile, toast the hamburger buns.

5. Serve the salmon burgers on the toasted buns with the dill mustard sauce, lettuce, and tomato.

Grilled Fish Tacos with Mango-Avocado Salsa

ingredients

FOR THE MANGO-AVOCADO SALSA:

1 ripe avocado
1/4 cup fresh lime juice
1 cup diced mango
1/4 cup diced red pepper
1/4 cup chopped scallions

FOR THE FISH:

2 fish fillets, such as sea bass, red snapper or salmon, 8 ounces each
2 teaspoons canola oil
salt to taste
freshly ground black pepper

FOR THE TACOS:

8 corn tortillas
1 cup shredded lettuce
2 plum tomatoes, diced
lime wedges, for garnish

nutrition facts

Serving Size 2 tacos with salsa

AMOUNT PER SERVING
Calories **331**
Total Fat **13 g**
Saturated Fat **2 g**
Cholesterol **60 mg**
Sodium **292 mg**
Total Carbohydrate **39 g**
Dietary Fiber **7 g**
Protein **18 g**
Percent Calories from Fat **34%**
Percent Calories from Protein **21%**
Percent Calories from Carbohydrate **45%**

Prep Time: **15 minutes**
Cooking Time: **8 minutes**
Serves **4**

cooking instructions

For the salsa:

1. Remove and discard the pit and skin from the avocado and brush the flesh of the avocado with some of the lime juice to prevent it from discoloring.

2. Chop the avocado and toss it with the remaining lime juice, mango, red pepper, and scallions. (This can be made in advance and stored in the refrigerator for up to 1 day.)

For the fish:

1. Preheat the grill to medium-high.

2. Brush the fillets with oil and season generously with salt and pepper.

3. Grill the fillets on both sides until just cooked through, about 5 minutes per side. (Thin fillets take less time; thicker fillets take more.) Cool slightly and cut into 1" pieces.

4. Meanwhile, separate the tortillas into 2 stacks, wrap them in foil, and warm them on the grill while the salmon is cooking.

5. To serve the tacos, fill the tortillas with fish, lettuce, tomatoes, and mango-avocado salsa. Serve 2 tacos per person with lime wedges on the side.

Pan-Seared Halibut Steaks with Lemon Zest

ingredients

4 halibut steaks, about 5 ounces each
salt to taste
freshly ground black pepper
1 teaspoon lemon zest
1 1/2 tablespoons olive oil

nutrition facts

Serving Size 1 steak

AMOUNT PER SERVING
Calories **200**
Total Fat **6 g**
Saturated Fat **1 g**
Cholesterol **63 mg**
Sodium **579 mg**
Total Carbohydrate **0 g**
Dietary Fiber **0 g**
Protein **35 g**
Percent Calories from Fat **27%**
Percent Calories from Protein **73%**
Percent Calories from Carbohydrate **0%**

Prep Time:
5 minutes
Cooking Time:
5 minutes
Serves **4**

cooking instructions

1. Season the halibut steaks with salt, pepper, and lemon zest and then drizzle with olive oil.

2. Preheat the oven to 350°F.

3. Place an ovenproof sauté pan large enough to accommodate all the steaks over medium-high heat. Add the halibut and lower the heat to medium. Sear the steaks about 3 minutes per side and then place in the hot oven to finish cooking for about 5 to 6 minutes depending on the thickness of the fish.

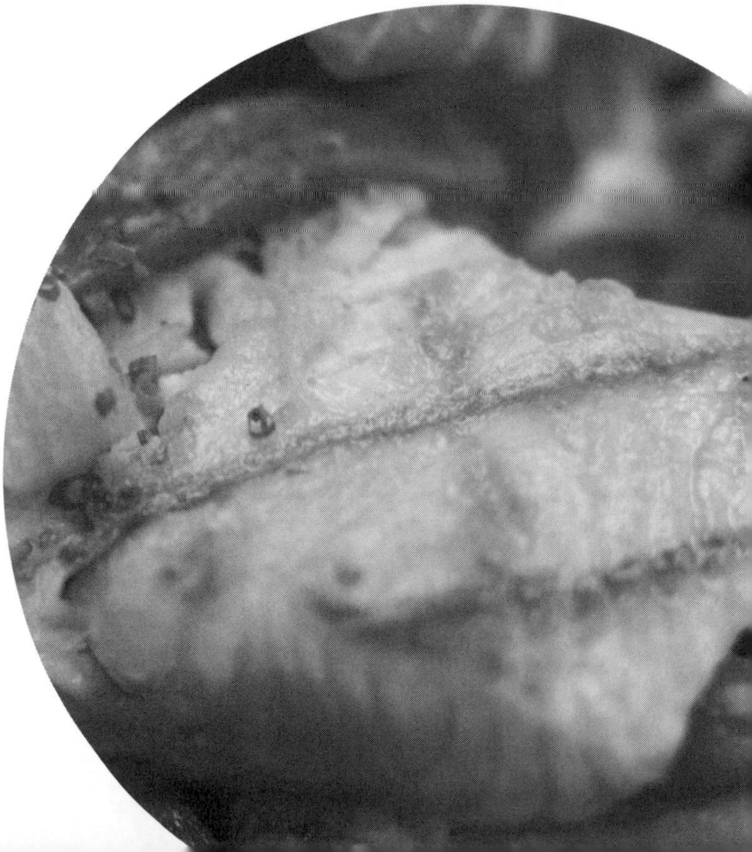

Grilled Salmon with Lemon-Fennel Slaw

ingredients

FOR THE LEMON-FENNEL SLAW:

2 small fennel bulbs, quartered and cored
1/2 small red onion
juice of 2 lemons
2 tablespoons extra virgin olive oil
salt to taste
freshly ground black pepper
1 teaspoon chopped, fresh dill

FOR THE GRILLED SALMON:

4 salmon fillets, about 4 to 6 ounces each
salt to taste
freshly ground black pepper
cooking spray

nutrition facts
Serving Size 1 salmon fillet with slaw

AMOUNT PER SERVING
Calories **250**
Total Fat **11 g**
Saturated Fat **2 g**
Cholesterol **59 mg**
Sodium **610 mg**
Total Carbohydrate **16 g**
Dietary Fiber **7 g**
Protein **25 g**
Percent Calories from Fat **38%**
Percent Calories from Protein **37%**
Percent Calories from Carbohydrate **25%**

Prep Time:
15 minutes
Cooking Time:
10 minutes
Serves **4**

cooking instructions

For the lemon-fennel slaw:

1. Slice the fennel and onion as thinly as possible using a mandolin or a sharp knife.

2. Toss the fennel and onion with the lemon juice, olive oil, and a sprinkling of salt and pepper. Sprinkle with chopped dill. (This can be made in advance and stored in the refrigerator for up to 3 days.)

For the grilled salmon:

1. Generously season the salmon fillets with salt and pepper.

2. Spray a grill with cooking spray and preheat the grill to medium-high.

3. Place the salmon on the grill and cook for 3 to 4 minutes on each side. Thicker fillets may need to be finished in a 350°F oven for about 5 minutes. Serve with the lemon-fennel slaw on the side.

Lemon-Pepper Fettuccine with Asparagus and Shrimp

ingredients

1 pound asparagus, cut into 2" lengths
1 pound fettuccine
3 tablespoons extra virgin olive oil
30 large shrimp (about 2 pounds), peeled and deveined
2 cloves garlic, minced
salt to taste
freshly ground black pepper
1/2 cup freshly grated Parmesan cheese
2 tablespoons chopped fresh parsley
zest of 2 lemons, finely grated

nutrition facts
Serving Size 5 shrimp with pasta

AMOUNT PER SERVING
Calories **453**
Total Fat **13 g**
Saturated Fat **3 g**
Cholesterol **179 mg**
Sodium **618 mg**
Total Carbohydrate **51 g**
Dietary Fiber **6 g**
Protein **36 g**
Percent Calories from Fat **26%**
Percent Calories from Protein **31%**
Percent Calories from Carbohydrate **44%**

Prep Time: **20 minutes**
Cooking Time: **15 minutes**
Serves **6**

cooking instructions

1. Bring a pot of salted water to a boil, drop in the asparagus and cook until al dente. Remove the asparagus with a colander or slotted spoon and plunge it into a bowl of ice water.

2. Bring the water back to a boil, drop in the fettuccine, and cook until al dente. Drain the pasta, reserving 1/2 cup of the cooking liquid.

3. Meanwhile, heat 1 tablespoon of the olive oil in a large nonstick skillet over high heat. Add the shrimp and garlic, season with salt and pepper and cook for 1 minute. Add the asparagus and cook until the shrimp are cooked through and the asparagus is warmed through, about 2 minutes more.

4. Return the pasta to the pot and toss it with half of the Parmesan, half of the parsley, lemon zest, remaining olive oil, and reserved cooking liquid. Season with salt and a generous sprinkling of coarsely ground fresh pepper.

5. Divide the pasta among 6 warm bowls. Arrange the shrimp and asparagus on top and sprinkle with the remaining Parmesan cheese and parsley. Serve immediately.

Roasted Cod and Tomatoes with Basil and White Wine Sauce

ingredients

2 cups cherry tomatoes
1 tablespoon olive oil
salt to taste
freshly ground black pepper
2 cloves garlic, minced
1 tablespoon chopped fresh basil
4 thick cod fillets, about 4 to 6 ounces each
1/2 cup dry white wine, such as Sauvignon Blanc

nutrition facts
Serving Size 1 fillet

AMOUNT PER SERVING
Calories **207**
Total Fat **5 g**
Saturated Fat **1 g**
Cholesterol **73 mg**
Sodium **749 mg**
Total Carbohydrate **4 g**
Dietary Fiber **1 g**
Protein **31 g**
Percent Calories from Fat **21%**
Percent Calories from Protein **59%**
Percent Calories from Carbohydrate **8%**

Prep Time:
10 minutes

Cooking Time:
30 minutes

Serves 4

cooking instructions

1. Preheat the oven to 400°F.

2. Place the tomatoes in a large baking dish (large enough to eventually accommodate the cod fillets in a single layer). Drizzle the tomatoes with half of the olive oil, and sprinkle with salt. Roast the tomatoes in the oven until they are very soft, about 15 to 20 minutes.

3. Remove the tomatoes from the oven and turn the oven down to 350° F. Transfer the tomatoes to a small bowl, add the garlic and basil, toss to combine and set aside.

4. Season the cod fillets with salt and pepper, drizzle them with the remaining olive oil, and place them in the baking dish. Pour the tomato mixture and wine over the fish. Cover the dish with foil and place it in the oven. Cook until the fish is just cooked through, about 12 to 15 minutes, depending on the thickness of the fish.

Cod with Tomato-Orange Relish

ingredients

FOR THE RELISH:

1 cup grape tomatoes, halved
2 teaspoons finely grated orange zest
2 teaspoons finely diced shallot
1 tablespoon chopped fresh basil leaves
1/4 cup fresh orange juice
salt to taste
freshly ground black pepper

FOR THE COD:

2 cod fillets, about 4 to 6 ounces each
1/4 cup white wine
salt to taste
freshly ground black pepper
1 tablespoon olive oil
2 tablespoons fresh lemon juice

nutrition facts
Serving Size 1 fillet with relish

AMOUNT PER SERVING
Calories **242**
Total Fat **8 g**
Saturated Fat **1 g**
Cholesterol **61 mg**
Sodium **403 mg**
Total Carbohydrate **11 g**
Dietary Fiber **2 g**
Protein **27 g**
Percent Calories from Fat **29%**
Percent Calories from Protein **43%**
Percent Calories from Carbohydrate **18%**

Prep Time: **15 minutes**
Cooking Time: **15 minutes**
Serves **2**

cooking instructions

1. In a mixing bowl, combine the tomatoes, orange zest, shallot, basil, and orange juice. Season to taste with salt and pepper. (This can be made in advance and stored in the refrigerator for 3 days.)

2. Preheat the oven to 350°F.

3. In a shallow baking dish, arrange the cod fillets in a single layer. Pour the wine over the fillets and season them with salt and pepper.

4. Bake the cod for 8 to 12 minutes, until it is cooked through. Remove it from the oven and sprinkle olive oil and lemon juice over it.

5. Serve the cod with a large spoonful of the relish and a drizzle of the relish liquid.

Chapter 22: Lean Beef and Other Meat

RECIPES IN THIS CHAPTER:

- Steak Salad with Tomatoes, Peppers, Sweet Onions, and Balsamic Vinaigrette
- Beef and Black Bean Tortillas with Fresh Salsa
- Apple-Horseradish Flank Steak
- Pepper-Crusted Beef Tederloin with Roasted Vegetables
- Asian Grilled Pork Chops
- Roasted Pork with Potatoes, Spring Greens, and Pear Vinaigrette
- Jambalaya
- Lamb with White Beans and Arugula
- Mediterranean Lamb with Minted Cucumber Sauce

Lean beef and other lean meats earn their place among the Fit Foods because they are full of flavor and full of nourishment. The key is to be moderate—always choose lean cuts, eat small portions, and trim the fat before cooking.

Steaks and burgers may be quintessential American fare, but ironically enough beef is actually a European import. The early European settlers brought the animals with them to the New World, but beef didn't become popular until the late 1800's when a boom in cattle ranching, coupled with the introduction of railway cattle cars and refrigerated cars, made beef widely available. Nowadays, Americans eat about 60 pounds of beef a year.

Other lean meats include lean cuts of **pork**, which is popular in cuisines circling the globe. **Veal**, the meat from very young calves, is a favorite in Europe, but pricier than most meats. **Lamb**, a staple of the Middle East and North Africa, is another lean meat, which has a distinctive taste.

NUTRITION AND HEALTH

Beef is an excellent source of protein, as well as important micronutrients, including iron, zinc, and B vitamins. Interestingly, the iron found in beef is more easily absorbed than the iron in plant food. This vital mineral helps carry oxygen to the cells, aids in brain development, and supports the immune system. Unfortunately, beef can also be a source of saturated fat. For that reason, it is important to choose and cook the leanest cuts. Your butcher can help you make healthful selections.

Pork provides high-quality protein, as well as B vitamins, and the minerals iron, selenium, and zinc.

For variety, choose a piece of lamb. It has a nutritional profile similar to beef.

WHAT TO LOOK FOR

Shop for perishable beef and other meat last at the grocery store and put plastic-wrapped packages of raw meat in disposable plastic bags whenever possible to prevent cross contamination with other foods in your grocery cart if the packages should leak.

Choose lean beef with the longest "sell by" date, and look at the color of the fat—it should be white, not yellow. There are hundreds of names for retail cuts of lean beef, but an easy way to select lean cuts is to look for the words "round" or "loin" in the name, such as sirloin or top round. Flank steak is another good choice. Beef is graded by the USDA, according to the fat marbling. There are three grades: Prime, Choice, and Select. Stick with the "Select" grade—it has the least amount of marbling and the least amount of fat. It is also the most economically priced.

When you are buying pork, opt for blade loins, center loins, sirloins, loin chops, loin cutlets, and whole tenderloins. They are the leanest and most tender cuts. Crown roasts and country-style ribs also come from the loin. Fresh pork should be pink in color with creamy white fat, although pork tenderloin is deep red. (There is no grading system for pork because fresh pork is uniform in quality, but the USDA does inspect pork for wholesomeness, which ensures that the animal is disease-free.)

Fresh veal is available in various cuts, including breast, leg, roasts, cutlets, and scallops. It is also available ground. Veal should be light pink in color with little marbling.

The hind shank is the one of the leanest cuts of lamb, along with leg of lamb and lamb fore shank. Leg of lamb is the most commonly available cut. Fresh lamb should be pink in color.

EASY STORAGE AND PREPARATION

Lean, fresh beef, veal, lamb, and pork will keep for 3 to 5 days in the refrigerator. All 4 types of meat can also be frozen. (Ground meat will last for up to 4 months in the freezer, while other cuts can last for up to a year.)

There are countless ways to cook lean beef: grilling, broiling, stewing, and braising to name a few. No matter what method you use, trim off all visible fat from the meat before cooking. The color of the meat is not always a reliable way to tell when it is done. Always use a food thermometer; it's the most accurate method. Ground beef should reach an internal temperature of 160°F, while steaks and roasts should have an internal temperature of 145°F for medium-rare and 160°F for medium.

Lean cuts of pork can be braised, stewed, grilled, or roasted. As with beef, trim off any visible fat before cooking. Pork should be cooked to an internal temperature of 160°F for medium and 170°F for well-done. Depending on the cut, lamb can be grilled, broiled, or roasted. Once again, be sure to trim off any visible fat from the meat before cooking. Not only is the fat unhealthy, it can impart an off flavor to the meat.

BEST USES

- Grilling is an easy, high-flavor, low-fat cooking method for beef and other meat.
- Spice rubs and marinades are terrific ways to add flavor to lean beef and other meat. Rubs can be done minutes before cooking. Marinating meat not only adds flavor, it enhances texture. Try marinating your meat in olive oil, garlic, vinegar, red wine, soy sauce, or fresh ginger. For flavor, marinate your meat from 15 minutes up to 2 hours; to tenderize, marinate from 6 hours up to 24 hours.
- Dress up plain hamburgers by livening up the condiments that accompany them. Top your burgers with a spoonful of salsa; use yellow or other heirloom tomatoes; or try different types of cheese, such as pepper jack or Emmenthal.
- Lean cuts of pork are easily overcooked, so check the meat often during cooking. The meat should be just slightly pink in the middle. Try roasting pork tenderloin with garlic and herbs for a delicious main course. Use ground pork to prepare healthy meatballs for pasta or soups.
- Veal scallop is the leanest cut and should be sautéed or braised, while the shoulder and leg cuts are best braised, stewed, or roasted.
- Lamb paired with rosemary and garlic is a culinary match made in heaven. This meat is also great in kebabs. Keep in mind that lean cuts of lamb may need to be tenderized in a marinade before cooking.

Lean meat is so tasty and versatile it can be eaten simply grilled or star in dishes ranging from salad to jambalaya. What's more, it is a good co-star. Lean meat complements many other foods, from apricots to potatoes. Whether you serve it as a stand-alone or as part of a dish, you will be filling your body with important nutrients. Here are some recipe ideas that show off lean beef and other lean meats in all their glory.

ABOUT HERBS AND SPICES

Parsley is an herb with a fresh, slightly peppery flavor. Two common varieties are Italian flat leaf and curly leaf. Look for fresh leaves and dried leaves. Parsley is good in salads, dressings, soups, and goes well with poultry, meats, fish, and seafood. Flat leaf parsley is best for cooking, because it is more flavorful and stands up better to heat. Curly leaf parsley is less flavorful but makes an ideal garnish.

Rosemary is an herb with a piney, lemony flavor and aroma. Look for fresh needlelike leaves and dried leaves. Rosemary is delicious with lamb, pork, veal, and beef, and with roasted potatoes and mushrooms. To release the flavor of dried leaves, crush them just before using. Use whole sprigs to infuse long-cooking dishes with flavor; remove before serving.

Steak Salad with Tomatoes, Peppers, Sweet Onions, and Balsamic Vinaigrette

ingredients

FOR THE VINAIGRETTE:

1 tablespoon finely chopped shallots
3 tablespoons balsamic vinegar
1 1/2 tablespoons olive oil
salt to taste
freshly ground black pepper

FOR THE STEAK:

2 top sirloin steaks, about 8 ounces each
salt to taste
freshly ground black pepper

FOR THE SALAD:

2 cups cherry tomatoes, rinsed
1 green bell pepper, stems and seeds removed and diced
1/2 cup thinly sliced Vidalia onion
8 cups romaine lettuce, washed and torn into bite-size pieces
4 small crusty rolls

nutrition facts

Serving Size about 3 ounces of cooked steak with 2 cups of salad

AMOUNT PER SERVING
Calories **283**
Total Fat **11 g**
Saturated Fat **3 g**
Cholesterol **60 mg**
Sodium **230 mg**
Total Carbohydrate **19 g**
Dietary Fiber **3 g**
Protein **29 g**
Percent Calories from Fat **34%**
Percent Calories from Protein **40%**
Percent Calories from Carbohydrate **26%**

Prep Time:
20 minutes
Cooking Time:
15 minutes
Serves **4**

cooking instructions

For the vinaigrette:

1. Place the shallots and vinegar in a small mixing bowl and whisk to combine. Continue whisking and slowly add the olive oil. Season to taste with salt and pepper. (This can be made in advance and stored in the refrigerator for up to 3 days.)

For the steak:

1. Preheat the grill to medium-high.
2. Season the steaks with salt and pepper.
3. Grill the steaks on both sides until they are cooked through, about 6 minutes per side, depending on the thickness. Transfer the steaks to a cutting board. (The steak can be grilled in advance and stored in the refrigerator for up to 3 days.)

For the salad:

1. Slice the steaks into strips and place them in a mixing bowl. Add the tomatoes, bell pepper, and onion slices and half of the balsamic vinaigrette.
2. Place the romaine lettuce in a separate salad bowl and toss it with the remaining vinaigrette. Arrange the steak, tomato, bell pepper, and onion mixture on top. Serve with a crusty roll.

Beef and Black Bean Tortillas with Fresh Salsa

ingredients

FOR THE SALSA:

1 small onion, chopped
1 15-ounce can diced tomatoes, drained
4 dried chipotle peppers, stems and seeds removed
4 cloves garlic, peeled
1/4 cup chopped fresh oregano, or
1 teaspoon dried oregano
2 cups water
1/2 teaspoon salt
1/4 teaspoon freshly ground black pepper
a pinch of sugar

FOR THE TORTILLAS:

1 pound ground beef sirloin
salt to taste
freshly ground black pepper
12 corn tortillas
1 1/2 cups cooked black beans
1 1/2 cups cooked rice
3/4 cup non-fat sour cream
1/3 cup fresh cilantro leaves

nutrition facts

Serving Size 2 tortillas

AMOUNT PER SERVING
Calories **496**
Total Fat **15 g**
Saturated Fat **5 g**
Cholesterol **64 mg**
Sodium **369 mg**
Total Carbohydrate **60 g**
Dietary Fiber **9 g**
Protein **31 g**
Percent Calories from Fat **27%**
Percent Calories from Protein **25%**
Percent Calories from Carbohydrate **48%**

Prep Time: **20 minutes**
Cooking Time: **20 minutes**
Serves **6**

cooking instructions

For the salsa:

1. Combine all of the salsa ingredients in a small saucepan. Bring to a boil, adjust the heat so that the mixture simmers and cook until half the liquid evaporates, about 15 minutes. Turn off the heat and let cool.

2. Pour the mixture into a blender and puree. Chill. (This can be made in advance and stored in the refrigerator for up to 1 week.)

For the tortillas:

1. Preheat the oven to 350°F.

2. Place the ground sirloin in a skillet over a medium high heat and cook until browned and cooked through. Use a spatula to break apart the ground sirloin into small chunks while cooking. Season to taste with salt and pepper.

3. Wrap the tortillas in foil and place them in the hot oven.

4. Reheat the beans and rice separately in a microwave.

5. Everyone can create their own tortillas with rice, beans, beef, and salsa. Garnish the tortillas with extra salsa, sour cream, and cilantro leaves if desired.

Apple-Horseradish Flank Steak

Recipe by FoodFit Chef Ann Cooper, Ann Cooper Culinary Consulting, East Hampton, NY

ingredients

1 1/2 pounds flank steak
1/2 cup apple cider concentrate
1/2 cup horseradish, freshly grated
freshly cracked black pepper

nutrition facts
Serving Size 3 to 4 slices

AMOUNT PER SERVING
Calories **212**
Total Fat **8 g**
Saturated Fat **4 g**
Cholesterol **55 mg**
Sodium **83 mg**
Total Carbohydrate **12 g**
Dietary Fiber **0 g**
Protein **24 g**
Percent Calories from Fat **34%**
Percent Calories from Protein **44%**
Percent Calories from Carbohydrate **22%**

Prep Time: **10 minutes**
Cooking Time: **12 minutes**
Serves **6**

cooking instructions

1. Brush the flank steak with the cider concentrate and rub it with horseradish. Sprinkle with black pepper and marinate 30 minutes or overnight.
2. Preheat the grill to medium-high.
3. Grill the steak on each side until medium-rare, about 6 minutes per side.
4. Thinly slice the steak on the bias (that is, at an angle).

Pepper-Crusted Beef Tenderloin with Roasted Vegetables

ingredients

4 small red-skinned potatoes, halved
2 carrots, peeled and cut into 3/4" pieces
2 parsnips, peeled and cut into 3/4" pieces
2 tablespoons olive oil
1 tablespoon chopped fresh rosemary leaves, or 1 teaspoon dried rosemary
salt to taste
freshly ground black pepper
1 pound beef tenderloin

nutrition facts
Serving Size 2 to 3 slices of beef with vegetables

AMOUNT PER SERVING
Calories **455**
Total Fat **14 g**
Saturated Fat **6 g**
Cholesterol **98 mg**
Sodium **96 mg**
Total Carbohydrate **47 g**
Dietary Fiber **6 g**
Protein **35 g**
Percent Calories from Fat **28%**
Percent Calories from Protein **31%**
Percent Calories from Carbohydrate **41%**

Prep Time:
15 minutes
Cooking Time:
45 minutes
Serves **4**

cooking instructions

1. Preheat the oven to 425°F.

2. In a mixing bowl, toss the potatoes, carrots, and parsnips together with the olive oil, rosemary, salt, and pepper. Transfer the vegetables to a shallow roasting pan and roast them in the oven for 10 minutes.

3. Season the beef with salt and a generous amount of pepper. Remove the vegetables from the oven and place the beef on top of them in the roasting pan. Return the pan to the oven and roast the vegetables and beef for 15 minutes.

4. Turn the temperature down to 350°F and continue roasting for an additional 15 minutes or until the vegetables are tender and the beef is cooked to the desired doneness. (To check for doneness, insert a meat thermometer into the thickest part of the roast. It should read 135°F for medium-rare.)

5. Let the tenderloin rest for 10 minutes before slicing. Serve a few slices of the beef with a large spoonful of the vegetables for each person.

Asian Grilled Pork Chops

ingredients

2 1/2 tablespoons olive oil
2 teaspoons soy sauce
1 clove garlic, crushed
2 teaspoons minced ginger
2 teaspoons Dijon mustard
salt to taste
freshly ground black pepper
4 center-cut pork loin chops, about 1/2" thick

nutrition facts
Serving Size 1 chop

AMOUNT PER SERVING
Calories **150**
Total Fat **6 g**
Saturated Fat **2 g**
Cholesterol **62 mg**
Sodium **142 mg**
Total Carbohydrate **0 g**
Dietary Fiber **0 g**
Protein **22 g**
Percent Calories from Fat **38%**
Percent Calories from Protein **60%**
Percent Calories from Carbohydrate **1%**

Prep Time: **5 minutes**
Cooking Time: **20 minutes**
Serves 4

cooking instructions

1. Mix the oil, soy sauce, garlic, ginger, mustard, salt, and pepper together, and brush on the pork chops. Refrigerate for at least 30 minutes or overnight.
2. Preheat the grill to medium-high.
3. Grill the chops for 5 to 8 minutes on each side, depending on the thickness. Let the chops rest on a plate for 1 or 2 minutes before serving.

Roasted Pork with Potatoes, Spring Greens, and Pear Vinaigrette

ingredients

FOR THE PORK:

1 tablespoon olive oil
2 pork tenderloins, about 12 ounces each
salt to taste
freshly ground black pepper
12 small red potatoes, boiled

FOR THE VINAIGRETTE:

1 pear
2 teaspoons Dijon mustard
1 tablespoon sherry vinegar
2 teaspoons honey
1 tablespoon extra virgin olive oil
salt to taste
freshly ground black pepper

FOR THE SALAD:

12 cups mixed baby greens
1/4 cup crumbled goat cheese
2 tablespoons chopped hazelnuts, toasted

nutrition facts

Serving Size 3 slices of pork, 2 potatoes, and 2 cups of salad

AMOUNT PER SERVING
Calories **424**
Total Fat **16 g**
Saturated Fat **5 g**
Cholesterol **77 mg**
Sodium **298 mg**
Total Carbohydrate **38 g**
Dietary Fiber **5 g**
Protein **32 g**
Percent Calories from Fat **34%**
Percent Calories from Protein **30%**
Percent Calories from Carbohydrate **36%**

Prep Time: **10 minutes**
Cooking Time: **15 minutes**
Serves **6**

cooking instructions

For the pork:

1. Preheat the oven to 350°F.

2. Heat the olive oil in a large nonstick skillet over high heat. Season the pork with salt and pepper. Brown the pork tenderloins on all sides.

3. Place the pork in the oven and cook until the pork is cooked through, about 10 minutes. Remove the pork from the oven and let it rest for about 5 minutes before slicing.

For the vinaigrette:

1. In a small food processor, puree the pear with the mustard, vinegar, and honey. Add the olive oil and puree. Season to taste with salt and pepper.

For the salad:

1. Toss the greens with the dressing and divide among 6 plates. Garnish each salad with goat cheese and hazelnuts.

2. Serve 3 to 4 slices of pork and 2 potatoes alongside the salad.

Jambalaya

Recipe by FoodFit Chef Susan Spicer, Bayona, New Orleans, LA

ingredients

3/4 pound Andouille or smoked sausage, cut into 1/2" pieces
1 tablespoon peanut oil
3/4 pound boneless chicken breast or thighs, cut into 1/2" strips
1 large white onion, chopped
3 stalks celery, chopped
1 green or red pepper, chopped
1 1/2 tablespoons chopped garlic
2 2/3 cups raw rice
1 1/3 cups diced, fresh or canned tomatoes, drained
3 1/3 cups low-sodium chicken broth
1/2 teaspoon dried thyme
2 bay leaves
2/3 teaspoon salt
Tabasco or other hot sauce to taste
2 1/2 teaspoons Worcestershire sauce
3/4 pound shrimp, peeled and deveined
5 scallions, chopped

nutrition facts
Serving Size 2 cups

AMOUNT PER SERVING
Calories **415**
Total Fat **17 g**
Saturated Fat **6 g**
Cholesterol **116 mg**
Sodium **972 mg**
Total Carbohydrate **33 g**
Dietary Fiber **2 g**
Protein **30 g**
Percent Calories from Fat **38%**
Percent Calories from Protein **30%**
Percent Calories from Carbohydrate **33%**

Prep Time: **20 minutes**
Cooking Time: **40 minutes**
Serves **8**

cooking instructions

1. In a deep skillet or sauté pan, brown the sausage pieces over medium-high heat for 1 to 2 minutes on each side. Remove them to a plate. Drain off the fat from the pan, add the peanut oil, and return the pan to medium-high heat. Brown the chicken pieces for 2 to 3 minutes on each side, then remove them to the same plate as the sausage.

2. Return the pan to medium heat. Cook the onion, celery, and pepper for 5 minutes. Stir in the garlic, rice, and tomatoes.

3. Add the sausage and chicken. Add the broth, thyme, bay leaves, salt, hot sauce, Worcestershire sauce, and shrimp. Bring to a boil, then lower to a simmer. Cover and cook for 20 minutes. Add more broth if it gets too dry.

4. Adjust the salt, hot sauce, and Worcestershire sauce to taste. Stir in half of the scallions. Remove to a warm platter and garnish with the remaining scallions.

Lamb with White Beans and Arugula

ingredients

FOR THE WHITE BEANS AND ARUGULA:

2/3 cup dried cannellini beans
2 cups low-sodium chicken broth
1 carrot, cut into 1" pieces
1 stalk celery, cut into 1" pieces
2 teaspoons olive oil
2 cloves garlic, chopped
salt to taste
freshly ground black pepper
2 cups arugula, washed and stems removed

FOR THE LAMB:

8 loin lamb chops, about 2 to 3 ounces each
salt to taste
freshly ground black pepper

Prep Time: **15 minutes**
Cooking Time: **45 minutes**
Serves **4**

cooking instructions

1. Soak the cannellini beans in water overnight in the refrigerator.

2. Drain the beans, place them in a pot, and add the chicken broth, carrot, celery, and enough water to cover the beans by an inch or so.

3. Bring to a simmer uncovered over medium-high heat. Do not boil. Skim off any foam that comes to the surface. (Do not add salt because it will prevent the beans from becoming tender.)

4. When the beans are tender, after about 1 hour, remove from heat. Drain and discard the carrot and celery. Set the beans aside. (The beans can be cooked ahead of time, covered, and refrigerated up to 3 days.)

5. In a large skillet, heat the olive oil over medium heat, add the garlic, and cook for 1 minute.

6. Add the beans, season with salt and pepper, and heat thoroughly.

7. Turn off the heat and gently fold in the arugula leaves.

8. Preheat the broiler.

9. Season the lamb chops with salt and pepper.

Lamb with White Beans and Arugula (cont.)

10. Place the lamb chops on a broiler pan and broil 3 inches from the heat for 4 to 5 minutes. Turn and broil for an additional 3 minutes for medium-rare, or 5 minutes for medium.

11. Place 2 lamb chops on each plate and serve with the white beans and arugula.

NOTE: To soak the beans quickly, place them in a pot of water, bring to a boil and turn off the heat. Let them stand for 1 hour and proceed with Step 2.

nutrition facts
Serving Size 2 lamb chops with 3/4 cup white beans

AMOUNT PER SERVING
Calories **243**
Total Fat **10 g**
Saturated Fat **3 g**
Cholesterol **77 mg**
Sodium **302 mg**
Total Carbohydrate **10 g**
Dietary Fiber **2 g**
Protein **27 g**
Percent Calories from Fat **38%**
Percent Calories from Protein **46%**
Percent Calories from Carbohydrate **16%**

Mediterranean Lamb with Minted Cucumber Sauce

ingredients

1/4 cup fresh lemon juice
2 cloves garlic, chopped
1 teaspoon dried oregano
1 tablespoon olive oil
8 lamb chops, about 2 to 3 ounces each
1 medium cucumber, peeled and seeds removed
1 cup plain, non-fat yogurt
1 tablespoon fresh, finely chopped mint
2 pinches of sugar
pinch of salt
freshly ground black pepper

nutrition facts

Serving Size 2 lamb chops with minted cucumber sauce

AMOUNT PER SERVING
Calories **234**
Total Fat **10 g**
Saturated Fat **4 g**
Cholesterol **83 mg**
Sodium **253 mg**
Total Carbohydrate **7 g**
Dietary Fiber **1 g**
Protein **27 g**
Percent Calories from Fat **41%**
Percent Calories from Protein **46%**
Percent Calories from Carbohydrate **13%**

Prep Time: **45 minutes**

Cooking Time: **10 minutes**

Serves **4**

cooking instructions

1. Mix together the lemon juice, chopped garlic, oregano, and olive oil. Marinate the lamb chops in this mixture for about 30 minutes.

2. While the lamb is marinating, make the cucumber sauce. Puree the cucumber in a blender until chunky but not liquefied. Transfer the cucumber to a bowl and stir in the yogurt, mint, and a pinch of sugar.

3. Remove the lamb from the marinade. Season with salt, pepper, and a pinch of sugar.

4. Place the lamb chops on a broiler pan and broil 3 inches from the heat for 4 to 5 minutes. Turn and broil for an additional 3 minutes for medium-rare, or 5 minutes for medium.

5. Serve 2 lamb chops per person topped with minted cucumber sauce.

Chapter 23: Yogurt, Dairy, and Eggs

Yogurt has been a food staple in the Middle East and Eastern Europe for thousands of years, but its popularity in the United States is a relatively new phenomenon. Today, many Americans enjoy the tangy, creamy taste of yogurt and reap its health benefits.

Yogurt is a form of curdled milk usually made from cow, buffalo, or goat milk. It is believed yogurt was invented by nomadic Balkan tribes, who accidentally curdled milk during their travels. Yogurt making is bit more complicated today: It is prepared in controlled environments where two live, active cultures are added to milk. You can find yogurt in an array of flavors, sweetened or unsweetened, low-fat, or full fat.

Highly nutritious milk products like yogurt should be a regular part of your diet. The 2005 Dietary Guidelines recommend 3 cups a day. In addition to yogurt, today's dairy case is complete with **cottage cheese**, **cream cheese**, **regular cheese**, and a variety of dairy and non-dairy **milk**. Most dairy foods are available in low-fat or fat-free varieties that are healthful and tasty.

Eggs are another important food in the dairy section. Now that we have new knowledge about cholesterol, eggs are back on the menu for healthy eaters.

RECIPES IN THIS CHAPTER:

- Bean and Cheese Nachos
- Endive and Roquefort Salad
- Cucumber Soup
- Three-Cheese Mashed Potatoes
- Smoked Salmon Crepes with Cream Cheese
- Greek Frittata with Spinach, Oregano, and Feta Cheese
- Honey Vanilla Frozen Yogurt
- Peppermint Ice-Cream Sandwiches

NUTRITION AND HEALTH

Yogurt, milk, and cheese are awesome sources of calcium, a mighty mineral essential for building and maintaining healthy bones and teeth. Calcium needs vary depending on your age. It may come as a surprise, but children and teens need more calcium than seniors because their bones are still growing. Older people are a close second. They need calcium to help minimize bone loss that occurs naturally with age and to keep osteoporosis at bay. A cup of yogurt supplies over one-third of your daily calcium needs. It is also full of protein and B vitamins, plus zinc and selenium. Plain or vanilla-flavored varieties are good choices because they are low in or free of added sugars. Milk is also a wonderful source of calcium.

There is a common misconception that skim or fat-free milk products are skimmed of vitamins and protein. The truth is, the only difference between them and whole milk products is the calorie and fat count.

Dieters take note—there is a growing body of research that suggests that drinking milk can help you trim down. A recent study showed that dieters who drank at least 3 8-ounce glasses of fat-free milk each day lost more weight than dieters who drank little or no milk.

Eggs are a source of high-quality protein, as well as some B vitamins and the mineral selenium, which scientists believe may protect against some cancers. Egg yolks are high in cholesterol and fat, so it's best to consume whole eggs in moderation. But egg whites are a different story: They are almost pure protein, so you can enjoy them as often as you like.

EASY STORAGE AND PREPARATION

When you're shopping for yogurt, double-check the date stamp on the carton and observe the "sell by" dates. Yogurt often comes in large containers; be sure to keep them tightly sealed and refrigerated. Yogurt tends to separate out a cloudy watery liquid. If it is still within its dated life, you can either pour off the liquid or stir it back in.

Check the date stamp for milk products and always keep them cold. Buy cheese in packages that are tightly sealed and free of any mold. Wrap cheese well and store it away from other foods in the refrigerator. Do not freeze any dairy products except butter. Wrapped sticks of butter can last up to one month in the freezer.

Eggs should be kept in the refrigerator in their original carton. Fresh eggs will keep for at least 4 to 5 weeks, but their consistency does change. Be sure to check the date stamp on the carton. As with raw poultry, raw eggs do carry the risk of salmonella. Be sure to cook your eggs thoroughly, and use egg substitutes (available in the refrigerated section of your grocery store) in recipes that call for raw eggs, such as Caesar salad. Egg substitutes, such as liquid egg whites and Egg Beaters™ (egg whites with additional nutrients added), are pasteurized egg products that can be substituted for eggs in any recipe.

WHAT TO LOOK FOR

Look for yogurt brands containing active cultures. In addition, try products that include inulin, a naturally occurring, fiber-like carbohydrate that's found in fruits and vegetables. Inulin is now being used in yogurt and other dairy items because it's been found to increase the activity of live cultures and prevent the growth of harmful bacteria in the digestive tract. Inulin's biggest bonus is that it aids in the absorption of calcium.

Fresh milk is available whole, reduced-fat, low-fat, skim, and organic. Powdered, evaporated, sweetened, and condensed forms of milk are also on the grocer's shelves.

Everyone loves cheese, but, as health-conscious consumers know, certain kinds are high in fat. When eaten in moderation, cheese livens up dishes and offers nutritional benefits. Fresh cottage cheese, cream cheese, and mozzarella, semisoft Havarti and provolone, soft-ripened Brie, firm Cheddar, hard Parmesan, and blue-veined Roquefort and Stilton, in addition to goat's and sheep's milk cheeses, are just some of the delicious varieties you'll find in the market.

Eggs are categorized according to their grade and size. The USDA grades of AA, A, and B indicate the quality of the egg and the size indicates their weight. The color of the egg has no bearing on the nutritional level or quality of the egg; it merely indicates the breed of hen. Purchase Grade AA or A eggs; they are essentially the same. Check that the carton contains eggs with no cracks or marks on them.

BEST USES

- Try yogurt in savory dishes like curries. Or use plain non-fat (or low-fat) yogurt instead of mayonnaise or sour cream when making salad dressings or dipping sauces.
- Add skim or low-fat milk to a fruit smoothie, or use a cup of skim or low-fat milk in place of water to make your morning oatmeal.
- Cheese has the fullest flavor when it is served at room temperature. The possibilities are endless: String cheese is a fortifying snack any time, grated cheese can jazz up a salad, and who doesn't love cheese and crackers? Explore the cheese section in your favorite local market. There are so many kinds to try.
- Eggs can be prepared in oodles of ways: fried, scrambled, poached, boiled, shirred, and baked. Omelets are a great breakfast (or dinner!); you can stuff them with any veggie you like, as well as low-fat cheese.

It's a treat to add bone-building dairy to your diet when you enjoy these recipes. Get a delicious dose of calcium with these tasty, dairy-rich dishes, featuring yogurt, milk, and cheese. You can even enjoy slimmed-down versions of comfort foods like ice-cream sandwiches and mashed potatoes.

ABOUT HERBS AND SPICES

Fines herbes are a traditional French blend of four herbs: parsley, chive, chervil, and tarragon. Look for crumbled dry leaves or fresh leaves. Sprinkle on fish, poultry, eggs, and cheese for wonderful flavor.

Bean and Cheese Nachos

Recipe by FoodFit Chefs Mary Sue Milliken *and* Susan Feniger, *Border Grill, Santa Monica, CA*

ingredients

1 16-ounce can fat-free refried pinto or black beans

4 tablespoons grated Monterey Jack or Cheddar cheese

1/2 cup favorite tomato salsa

1 bag baked tortilla chips

nutrition facts

Serving Size 1/4 of the plate

AMOUNT PER SERVING

Calories **298**
Total Fat **5 g**
Saturated Fat **2 g**
Cholesterol **17 mg**
Sodium **561 mg**
Total Carbohydrate **52 g**
Dietary Fiber **10 g**
Protein **13 g**
Percent Calories from Fat **16%**
Percent Calories from Protein **17%**
Percent Calories from Carbohydrate **67%**

Prep Time: **5 minutes**

Cooking Time: **10 minutes**

Serves **4**

cooking instructions

1. With a dull knife or spatula spread the refried beans in an even layer on a microwave-proof platter.

2. Sprinkle the cheese and salsa over the beans.

3. Cover loosely with plastic.

4. Place in microwave and cook on high about 2 minutes. Let cool before removing plastic.

5. Stand tortilla chips in the beans or serve chips alongside for dipping.

Endive and Roquefort Salad

ingredients

1 bunch frisée lettuce (curly endive)

1 Belgian endive

1/2 cup crumbled Roquefort cheese (or other blue cheese)

4 tablespoons chopped chives

1/4 cup low-fat dressing, such as Roasted Shallot Vinagrette (see page 67)

Prep Time:
10 minutes

Serves **4**

nutrition facts
Serving Size 1 cup

AMOUNT PER SERVING

Calories **86**

Total Fat **5 g**

Saturated Fat **3 g**

Cholesterol **15 mg**

Sodium **335 mg**

Total Carbohydrate **5 g**

Dietary Fiber **4 g**

Protein **5 g**

Percent Calories from Fat **54%**

Percent Calories from Protein **24%**

Percent Calories from Carbohydrate **22%**

cooking instructions

1. Wash and dry the frisée and tear the leaves into bite-size pieces.

2. Slice through the end of the Belgian endive stalk and pull off any dried outer leaves. Divide the remaining leaves attractively onto four chilled plates.

3. Place the frisée on top of the endive, sprinkle with the Roquefort and garnish each plate with the chives.

4. Serve with Roasted Shallot Vinaigrette or other low-fat salad dressing.

Cucumber Soup

ingredients

3 cups plain, nonfat yogurt
1 large cucumber, peeled, halved, seeds removed, and coarsely grated
2 cloves garlic, minced
1 tablespoon extra virgin olive oil
1 1/2 tablespoons chopped, fresh mint
2 1/2 tablespoons chopped, fresh dill
2 cups milk
3 tablespoons white wine vinegar or fresh lemon juice
salt to taste
freshly ground black pepper
thin slices of cucumber
fresh dill sprigs

nutrition facts
Serving Size about 1 cup

AMOUNT PER SERVING
Calories **98**
Total Fat **4 g**
Saturated Fat **2 g**
Cholesterol **10 mg**
Sodium **155 mg**
Total Carbohydrate **11 g**
Dietary Fiber **0 g**
Protein **6 g**
Percent Calories from Fat **33%**
Percent Calories from Protein **24%**
Percent Calories from Carbohydrate **44%**

Prep Time:
10 minutes
Plus Draining Time
Serves 4

instructions

1. Drain the yogurt overnight in a fine sieve or a colander lined with cheesecloth and discard the liquid. Add the grated cucumber, garlic, olive oil, mint, dill, and milk. Mix well.

2. Stir in the vinegar or lemon juice. Cover and chill. Season with salt and pepper to taste and garnish with thinly sliced cucumber and dill.

Three-Cheese Mashed Potatoes

ingredients

1 1/2 large potatoes (Idaho or russet)
about 1/3 cup low-sodium chicken broth
1 tablespoon finely diced Vidalia onion
1 tablespoon shredded Cheddar cheese
1 tablespoon freshly grated Parmesan cheese
1 tablespoon freshly grated, Gouda cheese (or smoked Gouda)
salt to taste
freshly ground black pepper

nutrition facts
Serving Size about 1/2 cup

AMOUNT PER SERVING
Calories **118**
Total Fat **3 g**
Saturated Fat **2 g**
Cholesterol **9 mg**
Sodium **187 mg**
Total Carbohydrate **21 g**
Dietary Fiber **2 g**
Protein **7 g**
Percent Calories from Fat **18%**
Percent Calories from Protein **21%**
Percent Calories from Carbohydrate **62%**

Prep Time:
10 minutes

Cooking Time:
30 minutes

Serves **2**

cooking instructions

1. Peel the potatoes and cut them in half. Place them in a pot and cover with cold water. Bring to a boil over high heat and simmer until the potatoes are tender when pricked with a fork, about 30 minutes depending on the size of the potatoes. Drain.

2. Bring the broth to a boil and then lower to a simmer.

3. Mash the potatoes with a potato masher or fork, or use a food mill. Slowly add the broth until the desired consistency is reached.

4. Fold in the onion and cheeses. Adjust the salt and pepper to taste.

Smoked Salmon Crêpes with Cream Cheese

Recipe by FoodFit Chef Rick Tramonto, *Tru, Chicago, IL*

ingredients

FOR THE CRÊPES:

3/4 cup all-purpose flour
3 teaspoons sugar
pinch of salt
1 1/4 cups 1% milk
3 large eggs
1 tablespoon melted butter

FOR THE FILLING:

2 ounces low-fat cream cheese, softened
1 tablespoon fresh lemon juice
salt to taste
freshly ground black pepper
1/2 pound thinly sliced smoked salmon

Prep Time: **5 minutes**

Cooking Time: **12 minutes**

Serves **6**

cooking instructions

For the crêpes:

1. Whisk together the flour, sugar, and salt in a medium-sized bowl.
2. Make a well in the center of the mixture and pour in the milk. Whisk the milk into the flour mixture until the batter is smooth and well blended.
3. Whisk in the eggs until blended.
4. Strain the batter through a sieve into another medium-size bowl. Cover with plastic wrap and refrigerate for at least 2 hours to give the batter time to rest.
5. Heat an 8" nonstick skillet or crêpe pan over medium heat. Lightly brush the pan with melted butter.
6. Ladle about 1/4 cup of the batter into the skillet and tilt the pan in all directions to evenly coat the bottom.
7. Cook the crêpes for about 30 seconds or until the bottom is lightly brown. Loosen the edges with a spatula and flip the crêpe over.
8. Cook the underside for 10 to 15 seconds or until it is set, dry, and browned in spots.
9. Slide the crêpe onto a flat plate and cover with a piece of wax paper.

Smoked Salmon Crêpes with Cream Cheese (cont.)

10. Repeat with the remaining batter, brushing the pan with more butter as needed, and stacking the crêpes between wax paper. The crêpes may be made up to 3 days ahead; cover with plastic wrap and refrigerate. Bring to room temperature before using.

For the filling:

1. Place the cream cheese in a small bowl with 2 teaspoons of the lemon juice. Mix well and season with salt and pepper to taste.

2. Using a 3-inch round cookie cutter, stamp out 4 rounds of the smoked salmon and 5 rounds of crêpes.

3. Place 1 crêpe on a work surface and top with a salmon round. Spread about 1 tablespoon of the cream cheese over the salmon.

4. Continue the layering, ending with a plain crêpe on top.

5. Cut the stack of salmon crêpes into 6 wedges and serve.

nutrition facts
Serving Size 1 crêpe wedge

AMOUNT PER SERVING
Calories **207**
Total Fat **8 g**
Saturated Fat **4 g**
Cholesterol **127 mg**
Sodium **479 mg**
Total Carbohydrate **18 g**
Dietary Fiber **0 g**
Protein **14 g**
Percent Calories from Fat **37%**
Percent Calories from Protein **28%**
Percent Calories from Carbohydrate **35%**

Greek Frittata with Spinach, Oregano, and Feta Cheese

ingredients

3 teaspoons olive oil
2 cups fresh spinach, washed, tough stems removed
salt to taste
freshly ground black pepper
4 large eggs
6 large egg whites
1 cup finely crumbled feta cheese
2 teaspoons fresh, chopped oregano
1/2 cup chopped onion
6 small potatoes, cooked and halved

nutrition facts
Serving Size 1 slice

AMOUNT PER SERVING
Calories **224**
Total Fat **8 g**
Saturated Fat **3 g**
Cholesterol **153 mg**
Sodium **320 mg**
Total Carbohydrate **25 g**
Dietary Fiber **3 g**
Protein **12 g**
Percent Calories from Fat **34%**
Percent Calories from Protein **22%**
Percent Calories from Carbohydrate **45%**

Prep Time: **15 minutes**
Cooking Time: **20 minutes**
Serves **6**

cooking instructions

1. Heat 2 teaspoons of olive oil in a skillet over medium-high heat. Add the spinach and season with salt and pepper to taste. Toss quickly until leaves are barely wilted, about 30 seconds. Remove from heat, drain, and set aside.
2. Whisk the eggs, egg whites, cheese, oregano, salt, and pepper (to taste) together until thoroughly combined.
3. In an 8" or 10" ovenproof, nonstick skillet, heat the remaining teaspoon of olive oil over medium heat. Add the onion and cook until soft and translucent, about 5 minutes.
4. Turn the heat to low, and add the spinach and halved potatoes (cut side down).
5. Add the egg mixture (do not stir) and cook over low heat until the eggs are set, about 15 to 20 minutes. Meanwhile, preheat the broiler.
6. Place the skillet under the broiler for 30 to 45 seconds to finish cooking the top of the frittata.

Honey Vanilla Frozen Yogurt

Recipe by FoodFit Chef Susan Goss, *Zinfandel Restaurant, Chicago, IL*

ingredients

3 cups plain low-fat yogurt, about 1 1/2 pounds

1 cup clover honey

1 large vanilla bean, split

nutrition facts
Serving Size about 1/2 cup

AMOUNT PER SERVING
Calories **179**
Total Fat **1 g**
Saturated Fat **1 g**
Cholesterol **7 mg**
Sodium **58 mg**
Total Carbohydrate **41 g**
Dietary Fiber **0 g**
Protein **4 g**
Percent Calories from Fat **5%**
Percent Calories from Protein **9%**
Percent Calories from Carbohydrate **85%**

Prep Time: **25 minutes**

Cooking Time: **15 minutes**

Serves **8**

cooking instructions

1. Place the yogurt in a large bowl.

2. Combine the honey and vanilla bean in a saucepan, warm over medium-low heat, stirring occasionally for 15 minutes. Do not boil or overheat. Remove from the heat, cover with plastic wrap and let stand 20 minutes.

3. Scrape vanilla pulp from the bean and discard the bean husk. Stir the vanilla pulp back into the honey and whisk the honey into the yogurt.

4. Refrigerate at least 4 hours or overnight.

5. Freeze in an ice-cream freezer according to manufacturer's directions.

Note: Non-fat yogurt does not work very well with this recipe.

Peppermint Ice-Cream Sandwiches

ingredients

TO PREPARE THE COOKIE SHEET:

2 teaspoons softened butter
2 teaspoons flour

TO MAKE THE ICE-CREAM SANDWICHES:

3/4 cup all-purpose flour
1/4 cup cocoa powder
1/4 cup (1/2 stick) unsalted butter
1/4 cup vegetable oil
1 cup plus 2 tablespoons confectioners' sugar
1/2 teaspoon vanilla extract
4 large egg whites
3 1/3 cups vanilla low-fat frozen yogurt, slightly softened
10 peppermint candies, crushed with a food processor or rolling pin

nutrition facts
Serving Size 1 ice-cream sandwich

AMOUNT PER SERVING
Calories **203**
Total Fat **8 g**
Saturated Fat **3 g**
Cholesterol **10 mg**
Sodium **57 mg**
Total Carbohydrate **29 g**
Dietary Fiber **1 g**
Protein **5 g**
Percent Calories from Fat **34%**
Percent Calories from Protein **10%**
Percent Calories from Carbohydrate **56%**

Prep Time: **10 minutes**
Cooking Time: **12 minutes**
Serves **10**

cooking instructions

1. Preheat the oven to 350°F and butter and flour a cookie sheet.

2. Sift together the flour and cocoa powder and set aside.

3. In the bowl of an electric mixer, cream the butter, oil, and sugar on high speed until light and fluffy. Stir in the vanilla.

4. Fold in half of the egg whites, then half of the flour-cocoa mixture, the remaining egg whites, and finally, the remaining flour-cocoa mixture.

5. Spread the batter onto the prepared cookie sheet. Bake for 12 minutes or until set and springy to the touch.

6. Using a 3-inch round cookie cutter, quickly cut out 20 cookies before they have a chance to cool. Using a spatula, quickly transfer the hot cookies from the cookie sheet to a wire rack and allow to cool.

7. When the cookies are cool, spoon 1/3 cup of the frozen yogurt between 2 cookies. Repeat with the remaining cookies. Roll the edges of the ice-cream sandwiches in the crushed peppermint candies so that the candies adhere to the ice cream.

8. Wrap each sandwich in plastic wrap and freeze until ready to serve. (These sandwiches may be made in advance and stored in the freezer for several weeks.)

Curried Yogurt Dip

ingredients

2 cups plain low-fat yogurt
1 teaspoon olive oil
1 cup minced onion
2 teaspoons curry powder

Prep Time: **10 minutes**

Cooking Time: **5 minutes**

Serves **8**

cooking instructions

1. Line a strainer with cheesecloth and place it over a deep bowl. Add the yogurt to the strainer, cover and refrigerate overnight. The yogurt will drain and thicken in the refrigerator overnight. Discard the liquid. (This can be done in advance and stored for up to 1 week.)
2. Heat the oil in a skillet over medium heat, add the onions and cook until they become translucent, about 3 minutes. Add the curry powder and cook 1 minute more.
3. Stir the curry mixture into the strained yogurt. Chill for at least 1 hour. (This can be made in advance and stored in the refrigerator for up to 3 days.) Serve with fresh vegetables and pita wedges for dipping.

nutrition facts

Serving Size about 3 tablespoons

AMOUNT PER SERVING

Calories **64**
Total Fat **1 g**
Saturated Fat **1 g**
Cholesterol **5 mg**
Sodium **39 mg**
Total Carbohydrate **10 g**
Dietary Fiber **1 g**
Protein **3 g**
Percent Calories from Fat **19%**
Percent Calories from Protein **21%**
Percent Calories from Carbohydrate **60%**

APPENDIX A
About the FoodFit Chefs

Bonnie Moore
Bonnie Moore has been executive chef of FoodFit.com since it was founded in 1999. During the past five years, she has created more than 2,000 healthy, delicious recipes for FoodFit. Her culinary credentials include an associate's degree in Culinary Arts from Johnson & Wales University and a degree in pastry arts from L'Academie de Cuisine.
www.foodfit.com

Jody Adams
Chef Jody Adams creates carefully researched regional menus that combine New England ingredients with Italian culinary traditions.

RIALTO
Cambridge, MA

RED CLAY
Chestnut Hill, MA

BLU
Boston, MA
www.blurestaurant.com

John Ash
John Ash is a spokesman for Fetzer Vineyards, a columnist, a cookbook author, and a food and wine educator.

FETZER VINEYARDS
Hapland, CA
www.fetzer.com

JOHN ASH AND COMPANY
Santa Rosa, CA
www.vintnersinn.com

Lidia Bastianich
Lidia Matticchio Bastianich is widely regarded as the "first lady" of Italian cuisine in the United States. She is the star of the public television series *Lidia's Italian Table,* and in 1999 was named American Express Best Chef, New York City, by the James Beard Foundation.

FELIDIA
BECCO
New York, NY

LIDIA'S KANSAS CITY
LIDIA'S PITTSBURGH
www.lidiasitaly.com

Jeff Buben
The South and the Chesapeake Bay area inspire the cuisine at Chef Jeffrey Buben's acclaimed restaurant, Vidalia. Through his restaurant Bis, he has introduced New American Cuisine to the nation's capital.

VIDALIA
www.vidaliadc.com

BIS
Washington, D.C.
www.bistrobis.com

Kathy Cary
Kathy Cary is the chef/owner of Lilly's, a four-star restaurant celebrated for its eclectic menu that reflects the chef's French-inspired use of traditional Kentucky ingredients with unexpected, contemporary twists.

LILLY'S
LA PECHE
Louisville, KY
www.lillyslapeche.com

Ann Cashion

Chef Ann Cashion was named Best Mid-Atlantic chef, 2004, by the James Beard Foundation. Her two Washington, D.C., restaurants have attracted celebrities, awards, and all-around popularity.

CASHION'S EAT PLACE

JOHNNY'S HALF SHELL
Washington, D.C.
www.cashionseatplace.com

Ann Cooper

Ann Cooper was one of the first 50 women to be certified as an executive chef by the American Culinary Federation. She is the former Executive Chef of The Ross School in East Hampton, New York.

ANN COOPER CULINARY CONSULTING

Roberto Donna

Roberto Donna is a James Beard Award–winning chef and restaurateur. Patrons of Galileo come from around the world to savor his authentic, sophisticated Italian cuisine, emphasizing the flavor of Northern Italy and the Piedmont region.

GALILEO

LABORATORIO DE GALILEO
Washington, DC
www.robertodonna.com

Tom Douglas

Chef Tom Douglas has helped to define the Northwest, or "Pacific Rim," style of cooking, which borrows from many cultures and uses the best and freshest ingredients of the Pacific Northwest.

DAHLIA LOUNGE

ETTA'S SEAFOOD

PALACE KITCHEN
Seattle, WA
www.tomdouglas.com

Todd English

Chef Todd English developed his unique style and approach to cooking, drawing on his own Italian heritage, as an apprentice in Italy. His Olives restaurants have received international recognition for their interpretive rustic Mediterranean cuisine.

OLIVES
Boston, MA; Washington, D.C., New York City

FIGS
Boston, MA
www.toddenglish.com

Susan Feniger/Mary Sue Milliken

Susan Feniger and partner Mary Sue Milliken, the Food TV Network's "Too Hot Tamales," have had a trailblazing career bringing them many awards. The chefs' sophisticated and lively menus explore the cooking of South America and Spain.

BORDER GRILL
Santa Monica, CA
Las Vegas, NV
www.bordergrill.com

CIUDAD
Los Angeles, CA
www.ciudad-la.com

Gale Gand

Pastry chef/partner Gale Gand is accomplished in many areas of culinary arts. Her desserts have received stellar reviews, and Gale was honored as one of the Top Ten Best Pastry Chefs by *Food and Wine* in 1994.

TRU
Chicago, IL
www.trurestaurant.com

Joyce Goldstein

Joyce Goldstein is an award-winning cookbook author and a consultant to the restaurant and food industries. For 12 years she was chef/owner of the ground-breaking Mediterranean restaurant Square One in San Francisco.

Author/Consultant
San Francisco, CA

Susan Goss

Executive chef Susan Goss opened Zinfandel with her husband, Drew, in 1992. As a chef, she celebrates ethnic American cooking and features an all-American wine and spirits list.

WEST TOWN TAVERN
Chicago, IL
www.westtavern.com

Andy Husbands

Chef/owner Andy Husbands serves boldly flavored American cuisine, with inventive global influences. He has earned a reputation as one of the country's most exciting young chefs.

TREMONT 647
Boston, MA
www.tremont647.com

Kate Jansen

Kate Jansen is pastry chef and founder of Firehook Bakery, which has five locations in the Washington, D.C., area. Her desserts are prepared with the finest European and American ingredients for mouthwatering cakes, tarts, and cookies.

FIREHOOK BAKERY
Washington, D.C., and Alexandria, VA
www.firehook.com

Michael Lomonaco

Former chef/director for the Windows on the World complex in the World Trade Center, Michael Lomonaco is known as one of the country's brightest culinary talents. He avidly supports area greenmarkets.

GUASTAVINO'S
New York City
www.guastavinos.com

Brian McBride

As executive chef at Melrose, Brian McBride creates a menu that celebrates worldwide cuisine. His cooking features the freshest ingredients and emphasizes simple, flavorful combinations.

MELROSE AT THE PARK HYATT
Washington, D.C.

Nora Pouillon

Nora Pouillon is chef/owner of two popular Washington, D.C., restaurants and a pioneer in the use of organic food. In April 1999, her Restaurant Nora became the first certified organic restaurant in the country.

NORA

ASIA NORA
Washington, D.C.
www.noras.com

Anne Quatrano

Anne Quatrano and her partner, Clifford Harrison, are chef/owners of three restaurants in Atlanta. Their food philosophy is "simplicity with subtle complexities."

BACCHANALIA

FLOATAWAY CAFÉ

STAR PROVISIONS
Atlanta, GA
www.starprovisions.com

Steven Raichlen

Steven Raichlen is the author of 21 books, including the IACP/Julia Child Award-winning *Barbecue Bible* and *Barbecue Bible Sauces, Rubs, and Marinades* (Workman).

Author/Consultant
www.barbecuebible.com

Michael Romano

Chef/partner Michael Romano's American-Italian bistro fare has consistently won rave reviews and earned the restaurant many awards. Union Square Cafe was the Number One Most Popular Restaurant from 1997 to 1999 in the *New York City Zagat Survey*.

UNION SQUARE CAFE
New York, NY

Anne Rosenzweig

Anne Rosenzweig is formerly chef/owner of the Lobster Club in New York City and currently co-owner of Inside.

INSIDE
New York, NY

Jimmy Schmidt

Chef/proprietor Jimmy Schmidt's The Rattlesnake Club is a spacious, contemporary restaurant on the river that accents his fresh, seasonal fare.

THE RATTLESNAKE CLUB

DIAMONDBACK CATERING
Detroit, MI

Annie Somerville

Chef Annie Somerville employs an imaginative approach to vegetarian cooking. She emphasizes seasonal dishes that are influenced by the cuisines of the Mediterranean, Mexico, and the American Southwest.

GREENS RESTAURANT
San Francisco, CA
www.greensrest.citysearch.com

Susan Spicer

Bayona executive chef/co-owner Susan Spicer features flavors from the Mediterranean as well as Alsace, Asia, India, and the Southwest in her menu. Spicer and her restaurants have received numerous awards over the past decade.

BAYONA

COBALT

HERBSAINT
New Orleans, LA
www.cobaltrestaurant.com
www.herbsaint.com

Allen Susser

Chef Allen Susser's restaurant showcases his New World Cuisine—a blend of regional and cultural influences along with the flavors of the Caribbean, Latin America, and Europe.

CHEF ALLEN'S
Aventura, FL
www.chefallen.com

Rick Tramonto

In 1995, chef Rick Tramonto and pastry chef Gale Gand opened Brasserie T to stellar reviews. The award-winning culinary team then opened Tru in 1999 to wide acclaim.

TRU
Chicago, IL
www.trurestaurant.com

Norman Van Aken

Norman Van Aken is considered the father of New World Cuisine and has consulted, written, and lectured on it all over the globe. His celebrated restaurant serves as home base for his inspired menus.

NORMAN'S
Coral Gables, FL
www.normans.com

Alice Waters

Chef Alice Waters has been blazing trails in American cuisine since the 1970's by relying on seasonal, local, organic produce for her restaurants, including the renowned Chez Panisse. Her numerous awards include being named one of the ten best chefs in the world by Cuisine et Vins du France.

CHEZ PANISSE

CAFÉ FANNY

Berkeley, CA
www.chezpanisse.com
www.cafefanny.com

Bill Wavrin

The former executive chef at Rancho La Puerta, Chef Bill Wavrin has now taken the reins at Miraval Resort and Spa. Chef Wavrin always starts with the freshest local ingredients to create his famed low-fat, high-flavor cuisine.

MIRAVAL RESORT AND SPA

Catalina, AZ
www.miravalresort.com

APPENDIX B
About FoodFit.com and the FoodFit Plan

Looking for more delicious, healthy recipes and expert nutrition advice?

Visit our website at **www.foodfit.com** where you'll find:

SOLUTIONS FOR HEALTHY LIVING

- Menus for the Week and our Dinner Tonight features make it easy to feed your family healthy, nutritious meals quickly
- More than 2,000 original healthy recipes developed by our Executive Chef Bonnie Moore, as well as hundreds of recipes from the country's best chefs
- Our array of e-mail newsletters deliver exclusive recipes, expert advice and creative ideas directly to your inbox

TOOLS FOR HEALTHIER HABITS

Interactive tools make it easy to manage meal preparation and improve your health:

- Cook It Safe Calculator
- Pantry Stocker
- Recipe Box
- Weight Calculator

INFORMATION FOR SMARTER CHOICES

- Helpful guides to seasonal fruits and vegetables, beans, cheeses, grains, rice, and herbs and spices
- A comprehensive guide to local Farmer's Markets with tips on what to buy and how to use the bounty from your local Farmer's Market
- Recipes and tips for cooking with kids that will help make good food and healthy eating a family affair
- A robust Chef's Area that features our Chef's Network, Chefs @ Home features and our popular Chef's Table

and more!

INDEX

Note: The Fit Foods are listed in **bold**.

A

B

C

D

E

F

G

H

J

K

L

M

Q

R

S

T